Are Africans cursed or do they misunderstand
Adeboye has meticulously discussed the concep
its theological, spiritual, and academic dimensio.
The book seeks to evangelize the African mystical curses worldview and to speak out its understanding in modern African society against the mismanagement, paradox of plenty, corruption, poor interpersonal relationship, laziness, bribery, negative ethnicity, disobedience to God, unhealthy politics, insecurity, banditry, kidnapping, rape, etc. This book is therefore highly recommended to Christians, theologians, and church ministers in the contemporary African context.

George P. Atido, PhD
Professor of Missiology & World Christianity,
Shalom University of Bunia, Democratic Republic of the Congo

The subject of curses is one that troubles individuals and church denominations around the world. Though several other scholars have offered solutions to this problem, this work addresses the reality and presents a unique solution for Africa. Adeboye provides a theological response to this particular set of African Christian experiences in a timely, simple, and readable way. He shines a clear light on curses and how readers can understand and biblically respond to them. This work will enrich the international discussion on curses and help readers to better their understanding. It is essential reading for all and my honor to recommend this book for use in institutions of higher learning, churches, and society as a whole.

Stephen O. Y. Baba, PhD
Professor of Biblical Studies,
ECWA Education Director, Jos, Nigeria

In almost all African ethnic groups, people take curses seriously. Indigenous religions have elaborated at length on how to conduct oneself to avoid or limit the consequences of curses. Although Christians live within a different spiritual framework, it is not rare to observe worries, fear, and even panic when people, especially parents or elders, curse them with or without reason. Adeboye's book provides an in-depth analysis of the phenomenon. It brings comfort through a particular focus on the sovereignty of God, who has the power to overrule any human curse. I highly recommend this book to all African believers, particularly Christian educators.

Moussa Bongoyok, PhD
Professor of Intercultural Studies and Holistic Development, and President,
Institut Universitaire de Développement International (IUDI), Cameroon

This book empowers African Christians to confront their fear of curses with thorough biblical exposition. It provides the theological grounds on which African Christians can solve their dilemma and confusion in relation to curses. The major strength of this book is the practical guidelines provided for Africans to engage their life experiences. I believe this book is a good step in the right direction for the growth and development of African Christianity.

Helen A. Labeodan, PhD
Professor of Philosophy of Religion,
University of Ibadan, Nigeria

This book scores high in its clarity and mode of expression. While the author's interest is to make the book useful to every category of readers, he does not compromise the required academic and technical rigor. It is an invaluable resource, meticulously presented. It touches the heart of major doctrinal issues on curses in Africa. I am convinced that what African Christianity needs is contextually brewed theological responses to the living experiences of its people. Adeboye has seen this need and responded to it. This book is a gift to African Christians.

J. B. Lawal, PhD
Professor of Christian Apologetics and Ethics, and Former Provost,
ECWA Theological Seminary Igbaja, Nigeria

The issue of curses and related problems examined and presented in this publication is serious and critical for the advancement of the gospel in Africa. Evangelical faith which flourished from the 1950s to 1970s in Nigeria has been influenced from the 1980s onwards by the prosperity gospel movement, with a lot of emphasis on dramatic religious experiences over and against correct biblical and Christian living. The author brings a fresh and bold analysis of African reality from the perspective of biblical revelation. The publication is a beautiful juxtaposition of biblical hermeneutics and theological methodology.

This is a book that all church and denominational leaders, other gospel ministers, theological educators, and ministers in training need to read. I am pleased to recommend it.

Rev. Emiola Nihinlola, PhD
President, Nigerian Baptist Theological Seminary, Ogbomoso
Chair, Association for Christian Theological Education in Africa (ACTEA)

Adeboye has offered a fresh and invaluable contribution towards our understanding of biblical Christianity in Africa. The fear of curses is widespread on the African continent. To the best of my knowledge, this book is the first attempt to engage this fear from in-depth theological and cultural perspectives. Although it exhibits solid academic research and novel theoretical grasp, it also possesses a strong degree of empathy. These make the book useful for both professional and lay theologians. I enthusiastically commend this book to all.

Babatomiwa M. Owojaiye, PhD
Senior Pastor, First ECWA Ilorin, Nigeria
Fellow, Research & Innovation Centre, ECWA Theological Seminary Igbaja, Nigeria
CEO, Centre for Biblical Christianity in Africa

Godwin Adeboye's book tackles a difficult subject of huge relevance to the everyday lives of Christians in Africa. For this is a context where the believers struggle against the spiritual forces of evil in the heavenly realms is very clear and intense. The fear of curses, and especially generational curses, runs deep even among Christians. Adeboye explains that this is because not enough effort has been made to interrogate the reality of Africans lived experiences of curses within a biblical theological framework. Adeboye states, "The best antidote to the hermeneutical anomolies and theological syncretism of curse preachers and teachers in Africa is to produce healthy doses of biblical theology based on excellent exposition of texts that are then applied properly to to African lived reality in ways that are both biblical and contextual." (p. 146) This he proceeds to do. Adeboye explains that Christian moral responsibility is vital because curses are a form of moral evil. He discusses how to distinguish which of lifes misfortunes are caused by curses, the importance of true conversion and Christian faith, and how to pray in a New Testament way for deliverance from spiritual principalities who respect only the name of Jesus, rather than in the way of the Old Testament's imprecatory psalms. Combining biblical theology with practical and pastoral help, this careful, detailed, and wide-ranging book will be useful for pastors, preachers, theologians, seminary students, and lecturers, and all Christians in Africa.

Patrick Sookhdeo, PhD
Executive Director, Oxford Centre for Religion and Public Life, UK
International Director, Barnabas Aid, UK

In this well-researched and intentionally easy-to-read book, the author provides an evangelical response to the belief in curses in contemporary African Christianity. Many African Christians live in fear because they believe that they have been cursed. Some have sought the help of traditional healers while some have fallen into the hands of misleading preachers who often take advantage of such desperate people. The book provides a deep description of the problem but doesn't stop there. It provides a carefully crafted prescription of remedies to it. I don't think I have seen a book that addresses this issue with such depth. This is a gem for the African church and the academy. I highly recommend it to every serious African pastor, theologian, and lay Christian. Every African theological library must have a copy of this book.

Rev. David Tarus, PhD
Executive Director,
Association for Christian Theological Education in Africa (ACTEA),
Nairobi, Kenya

Can a Christian Be Cursed?

HIPPOBOOKS

Can a Christian Be Cursed?

*An African Evangelical Response
to the Problem of Curses*

Godwin O. Adeboye

HIPPOBOOKS

© 2023 Godwin Adeboye

Published 2023 by HippoBooks, an imprint of ACTS and Langham Publishing.

Africa Christian Textbooks (ACTS), TCNN, PMB 2020, Bukuru 930008, Plateau State, Nigeria
www.actsnigeria.org
Langham Publishing, PO Box 296, Carlisle, Cumbria CA3 9WZ, UK
www.langham.org

ISBNs:
978-1-83973-826-5 Print
978-1-83973-827-2 ePub
978-1-83973-828-9 Mobi
978-1-83973-829-6 PDF

Godwin Adeboye has asserted his right under the Copyright, Designs and Patents Act, 1988 to be identified as the Author of this work.

All rights reserved. No part of this publication may be reproduced, stored in a retrieval system or transmitted, in any form or by any means, electronic, mechanical, photocopying, recording or otherwise, without the prior written permission of the publisher or the Copyright Licensing Agency.

Requests to reuse content from Langham Publishing are processed through PLSclear. Please visit www.plsclear.com to complete your request.

All Scripture quotations, unless otherwise indicated, are taken from the Holy Bible, New International Version®, NIV®. Copyright ©1973, 1978, 1984, 2011 by Biblica, Inc.™ Used by permission of Zondervan.

British Library Cataloguing-in-Publication Data
A catalogue record for this book is available from the British Library

ISBN: 978-1-83973-826-5

Cover & Book Design: projectluz.com

The publishers of this book actively support theological dialogue and an author's right to publish but do not necessarily endorse the views and opinions set forth here or in works referenced within this publication, nor guarantee technical and grammatical correctness. The publishers do not accept any responsibility or liability to persons or property as a consequence of the reading, use or interpretation of its published content.

Dedicated to Lois Adeboye (CLN), a loyal and committed wife and a soulmate in my commitment to the pursuit of Christian theological scholarship for the development of the African church.

Dedicated to the evergreen memory of Prince Tinuoye Adeboye, my late father who never lived to see me finish even my primary school education due to his sudden death on 25 June 1996, for his life and gift of intellectual creativity while it lasted.

Contents

	Foreword xiii
	Abbreviations xvii
	Acknowledgments xix
1	Is the Experience of African Christians Different? 1
2	The Problem, the Controversy, and the Debate 11
3	Theological Method for a Theology of Curses 23
4	Biblical Theology of Curses and Cursing 31
5	Curses in Traditional African Religio-Cultural Context............ 75
6	The Reality and Fear of Curses in African Christianity 93
7	The Treatment of Curses in Contemporary African Christianity ... 109
8	An Evangelical Solution to the African Dilemma and Fear of Curses... 131
9	Christian Moral Responsibility and the Dilemma of Curses 147
10	A Contextual and Biblical Guideline for Responding to Curses 153
11	The Real African Curses 169
12	God Is Sovereign and Christ Is Lord Over All Curses 175
	Bibliography 179
	Subject Index... 191
	Scripture Index 197

Foreword

Since the introduction of Christianity to the African continent, in the first century, to the continent's encounter with the 1900s modern missionary movement, and the development of technology, science and theological reflections, many aspects of African cultures have been undergoing phenomenal changes and transformation. Yet, although everything else is changing in the African cultural context, African religious beliefs and practices have refused to change. Many African Christians are still afraid of the spirit world and its so-called ability to negatively impact and shape the future of individuals and/or hold a community to ransom through its human agents. This challenge has baffled African Christians who have genuinely accepted Christ as their Savior, and it has led them to wonder why it is still possible to have believers in Christ, to whom Christ has given "power and authority to drive out all demons and to cure diseases" (Luke 9:1–2), still controlled by the world view of their former way of life.

Many African Christians are afraid of the power of curses. As such they fear people who are perceived to have the ability to communicate with the spirit world and use its demonic power to harm those they see as a threat. Africa is in great need of men and women with theologically sound minds who will do creative and innovative thinking. The church needs people like Godwin Adeboye who are capable of engaging in concrete self-reflection and self-criticism. They are able to profoundly and hermeneutically engage with the life experiences of the African people, to the praise of God's glory.

Given the challenge above, the theoretical framework, thesis, and objectives of Adeboye's book are extremely important. The birth of this book brings a new dawn in the development of African Christian theology. While African traditional cultural worldviews are closely similar to the culture of Biblical times, they also have some striking differences to the Bible's teachings. Due to this, many African Christians found out that their cultural beliefs sometimes came into conflict with the teachings of the Scriptures.

In addition, many Africans, even Christians, have some kind of experience related to cursing. Godwin Adeboye shows that if you listen to the yearnings of many African churches, Christians, preachers, and leaders, you will see that African Christianity is largely experiential. Experiences have played a significant role in the content of African Christianity. From church meeting agendas to prayer points, to church liturgy, to official constitutions, to the mode of dressing, to the theology of prayer, African Christians are influenced by their day-to-day experiences. These experiences often seem to conflict with Biblical perspectives. This leads to confusion and theological problems that give birth to syncretism, religious and doctrinal manipulation, unhealthy prophetic ministry, and commercialization of religion in Africa. To make Christ incarnated in the African context, these challenges must be confronted theologically. And this is what Godwin Adeboye has creditably done in this book.

Unfortunately, many African theologians who have attempted to provide answers to the above problem have been largely unconcerned with investigating the "ordinary" experiences of the African Christians theologically. I have not seen any academic, theological book dealing with particular issues such as an African theology of curses. But the fear of curses is real in Africa. Almost all Africans fear curses and interpret their life incidences as curses. In his discussion on the fear of curses in Africa, Adeboye sees some questions that Africans are asking:

- Can a Christian be cursed?
- Are unfortunate incidents in life called curses, truly curses or is this a misinterpretation?
- Is there any conflict between the Bible's teaching on curses and Africans' belief in curses?
- How can we offer relevant theological responses and valid pastoral care to those who have a fear of curses?

In raising these questions, Godwin Adeboye has not merely scratched the surface, he has dealt with deep theological issues.

The genius of *Can a Christian Be Cursed? An African Evangelical Response to the Problem of Curses* is that it adopts appropriate theological and exegetical perspectives to tackle practical African problems from theoretical beginnings to practical conclusions. Godwin Adeboye proves that Christian theology is not only an abstract study of God; it also involves dealing with practical, contextual, anthropological, economic, cultural, political, legal, historical, and ontological issues with theological tools. This is a sample of what I can call "African incarnational theology" – Christian theology seen, built, informed and developed to meet the needs of the specific African context. This is making Christian teachings speak to the concrete experiences of the Africans.

It is refreshing to see how Adeboye reveals African experience of curses with appropriate methodological tools, theological approaches, and biblical rigour. He brings new discoveries to light from his expository engagement of selected cursing texts in the Bible. He challenges the traditional interpretation of those texts, and he places his arguments in an appropriate cultural context by adopting qualitative techniques to bring primary data from several countries in Africa. This book is not mere desktop research but grounded and relevant. The reader will see his or her own belief and experiences on curses restated, challenged, analysed, and reframed on the pages of the book. The problem of curses is real and deep in Africa. The fear is strong to such an extent that the contemporary church in Africa has begun to unknowingly develop the approach of using curses to cure curses in their liturgy. This is pathetic!

The climax of this book is how the author brings to the African fear of curses a clear evangelical ethos. This leads to the formulation of a practical guide to how individual Africans can know if they are under curses or rather another form of life misfortune.

It also leads to the formulation of a biblical model of prayer against curses, relevant biblical interpretation to deal with curses, and relevant pastoral care. The author is both sympathetic and critical. This makes the book relevant to both ordinary African Christians and theologians. The sympathy with African experiences is to serve as an eye-opener to African Christians, pastors and preachers on how to handle the concept of curses from devotional, homiletical, and pastoral perspectives while the technical and critical dimension of African experiences makes the book very relevant for theologians, researchers and seminarians for their theological enterprises in Africa.

The simplicity and rigor with which the author presents his arguments attest to this work's high standard and profound contribution to academic research and ongoing conversations in Christian theological discourse. I strongly recommend this book to all Christians, theologians, seminarians, church leaders, and counsellors.

Rev. Prof. Sunday Bobai Agang,
Professor of Theology, Ethics, & Public Policy, and Provost,
ECWA Theological Seminary, Jos, Nigeria

Abbreviations

AEA	Association of Evangelicals in Africa
AIC	African Indigenous Churches
AIDS	Acquired Immunodeficiency Syndrome
AJBT	*American Journal of Biblical Theology*
AJET	*African Journal of Evangelical Theology*
ANE	ancient Near East
CAC	Christ Apostolic Church
CAN	Christian Association of Nigeria
CCC	Celestial Church of Christ
CITAM	Christ is the Answer Ministries
DLBC	Deeper Life Bible Church
EAEP	East African Educational Publisher
ECWA	Evangelical Church Winning All
EDT	*Evangelical Dictionary of Theology*
EMS	Evangelical Missionary Society
FGCN	Foursquare Gospel Church in Nigeria
FM	Frequency Modulation
HIV	Human Immunodeficiency Virus
HTS	*Historical Theological Studies*
IVP	InterVarsity Press
JBL	*Journal of Biblical Literature*
JTS	*Journal of Theological Society*
KJV	King James Version
MET	Methodists Evangelical Together
MFMM	Mountain of Fire and Miracle Ministries
NABIS	Nigeria Association for Biblical Studies
NAE	National Association of Evangelicals
NBC	Nigerian Baptist Convention
NBTS	Nigerian Baptist Theological Seminary
NIDNT	*New International Dictionary of New Testament Theology*

NIGTC	New International Greek Testament Commentary
NIV	New International Version
OCRPL	Oxford Centre for Religion and Public Life
RCCG	Redeem Christian Church of God
SBL	Society for Biblical Literature
SBJT	*Southern Baptist Journal of Theology*
SIM	Sudan Interior Mission (now Serving in Mission)
TDNT	Theological Dictionary of the New Testament
TSA	The Shepherd Academy
UI	University of Ibadan
UP	University of Pretoria
WCC	World Council of Churches
WEA	World Evangelical Alliance

Acknowledgments

Many great persons have contributed to the success of this book. First of all, I thank God the Father, the Son, and the Holy Spirit, the giver of life and wisdom who called me into the ministry of his word. May his name be praised. I also foremost thank my editor, Professor Elizabeth Mburu, for her support and help in providing editorial insight into this work despite her busy schedule. The staff and leadership of Langham Literature (UK) deserve a huge space of thanks not only for publishing this book but also for their persistent vision and efforts to see African Christians engaging the contextual realities of African society with the word of God through publishing. I express my unreserved appreciation to my academic mentors: Professor Maniraj Sukdaven, Dr Jacques Beukes (UP), Professor Mousa Bongyok, Professor Patrick Sookhdeo, Dr. Chris Sudgen, Dr. Prassad Philip, Ven. Dr. Julius Adekoya, and Dr. Anna Beleke of the Oxford Centre for Religion and Public Life (UK), and to Professors H. A. Labedoan, A. O. Dada, J. K. Ayantayo, O. O. Familusi, Dr. A. O. Adebo, Dr. S. K. Olaelye, Dr. Ike Moody, and Dr. Gbadamosi of the University of Ibadan, Nigeria. I also express my profound gratitude to my mentor and leader Professor H. A. Labeodan who handled my postgraduate research at the University of Ibadan, Nigeria. Her affectionate love and passionate guidance contributed to the reality of this book. In fact, the vision to write this book resulted from a discussion in her office in 2016. Besides, I sincerely appreciate Joshua Nurcombe-Pike, the TSA/OCRPL program leader and the entire TSA team.

I appreciate my mentor, the scholar Professor Sunday Bobai Agang who agreed to write the foreword to this book, and all the people who endorsed the book: Rev. Dr. Babatomiwa Owojaiye, Rev. Professor Stephen Baba, Professor Julius Lawal, Professor Emiola Nihinlola. My thanks also to Professor Labeodan, Dr. David Tarus, Professor Mousa Bongyok, Patrick Sookhdeo, and Professor George Atido for sparing their time to go through the manuscript and endorse it. I am very grateful.

I especially appreciate the leadership and staff of ECWA Theological Seminary, Igbaja, Nigeria for giving me a challenging atmosphere in which critical thinking is possible and where young scholars are trusted. In this Rev. Professor J. B. Lawal (a former provost), Rev. Professor S. Baba (a former provost), Rev. Dr. J. Adetoyese (present provost), Rev. Mathew Ndana (a former deputy provost administration), Rev. Professor A. M. Amodu (a former deputy provost), Rev. Dr. Z. O. Apata (a former dean), and Pastor Dr. J. Adeyanju (a former deputy provost) must be mentioned for their labor with the younger generation for the future of the church in Africa.

Presentable and coherent thought is not possible without an inspiring circle of influence. Therefore, I especially appreciate members of ECWA Good News Ijagbo, ECWA Chapel Igbaja, ECWA Chapel Ibadan, and ECWA Olla, Nigeria for giving me the good mental support and providing a Christian environment in which vision and its fulfilment is possible.

I especially appreciate all my friends, colleagues, mentees, and mentors who supported me in the fieldwork that allowed me to gather firsthand information on the work in Ghana, Benin Republic, Uganda, Angola, Kenya, Nigeria, Cameroon, Malawi, Zambia, Namibia, and other countries. I am very grateful. I equally heartily appreciate the preachers, Christian drama ministers, and writers in Africa who permitted me to use their original content as illustrations and pieces of evidence.

Pastor Sunday Daniel Ajayi, "my twin brother," gave me the good esteem and warm friendship that can birth a book like this. The rumination to publish with Langham started in a discussion with him. He is my "Jonathan," trusted and truthful. I also appreciate my friends Oyebiyi John, Damu Shedrack, Segun Adenigba, Adenigba Olatayo, Emmanuel Ogunjobi, Olasehinde Sesan, Idowu Theophilus, Akogun Richard, Samuel Yoahana, and several others who have inscribed their love and affection on my heart.

I thank God for the support I received from my wife, Lois Adeboye (*Moi*), who lovingly endured my long absences as I concentrated on this work and many times covered my absences with responsibility and love. She rightly captures the description of the ideal Christian woman idealized in Proverbs 31. I also appreciate 'Romade Bayon'le, and 'Romayo Adedibu, my sons and the strength of my youth. My family is indeed a happy one! I appreciate my mother and siblings, my in-laws, the family of Bishop Dr. Richardson Oyeniran, the family of Rev. G. O. Abikoye, the family of Rev. Aiyeobasanmi, the family of Dr. Wale Peters, the family of Elder and Dr. Mrs. Eunice Abogunrin, the family of Rev. and Mrs. S. O. Oshoaro, the family of Rev. Dr. and Mrs. S. K. Awoniyi, the family of Rev. Dr. and Mrs. E. O. Malomo, the family of Pastor and Mrs. Victor Hussain, Rev. Dr. and Mrs. Adebiyi, Lieutenant and Bar. Mrs. Shola Awoniyi, and a host of others for their love and care for my life and ministry.

1

Is the Experience of African Christians Different?

How do African Christians interpret life and life occurrences, and what are the implications of their interpretations? If you visit a church in the West and another church in Africa, you will quickly notice clearly different types of Christianity. These differences are occasioned by many factors. Paul Gifford gives a good example of such wide differences in church experiences. He attended the eighth General Assembly of the World Council of Churches (WCC) in 1998 in Harare as an observer. Major problems of the world were discussed in that meeting: third-world debt, the rights of women, the rights of minorities including sexual minorities, intellectual property rights, global warming, etc. Gifford noticed that this WCC assembly was influenced by some "modern" concerns. However, in the same week, he visited some churches that are Africa-based and noticed that they manifested a different type of Christianity. For example, Gifford visited a Pentecostal church that had lived in Africa for more than two decades. The issues addressed in this church were very different from those addressed by the WCC. These issues were not structural but personal: deliverance, demons, joblessness, homelessness, sickness, childlessness, business failures, failure to find a spouse, issues with spirits, and spiritual powers at play in all areas of life and responsible for every ill and failure.[1] This attitude toward supernatural powers and principalities is one of the things that separates the churches in the global South from those in the West.[2] This view is the reality in African Christianity that emanates from

---

1. P. Gifford, *Christianity, Development and Modernity in Africa* (London: Hurst, 2015), 1.

2. E. E. Acolaste, *Powers, Principalities and the Spirit: Biblical Realism in Africa* (Grand Rapids: Eerdmans, 2018), 10. Acolaste offers brilliant expository insight on distinguishing the differences in spiritualties of the church in the West and that in the South. She also examines

the experiences of African Christians and is distinctly different from other contexts.³ African Christians have different and unique experiences that are worth studying and ruminating over.⁴

The Peculiarity of the African Christian Experience

Many African Christians have some religious or spiritual experiences that are unique and largely unavailable in some other climes. For example in Yoruba culture there is a popular radio-television program called *"Iriri aye"* (mystical experiences of life) which collates and presents strange, mysterious, unbelievable but real-life experiences. As a pastor in an African country, I have heard and seen samples of such strange experiences. Narrating one or two will sufficiently explain the point. In a village where I once lived was the family of a man who had six wives. Out of the six wives, only one of them was privileged to give birth to children. She had nine children, while the other wives in that household had not even one child. The husband of the mother loved her more than his other wives due to her fertility. Suddenly, the woman lost one of her sons. After a brief period of deep mourning, the woman summoned courage. Then, when she was seen to have summoned courage, one of the other wives in the family asked her, "Is it because we killed one of your sons who was not well to do (was not prosperous) that you quickly forgot your tears of mourning? We will kill another one, even the one who is the best educationally, publicly, socially, and financially among your children." The women belong to a group of cults who are known for cursing and their words are judged demonic. After a few months, the woman lost another son who was a professor in a well-known university. It was believed the son was murdered through witchcraft and cursing.

Another example is the story of a pastor in one of the church denominations in Africa, a young man who came to me for prayer and counseling. He narrated to me that he had a dream in which a strange old woman was feeding him a strange, bitter meal. When he woke up from sleep, he found the traces and

---

the social, political, and economic worlds of African peoples and suggests the texture of the pastoral care that can be appropriate.

3. David T. Adamo, "What Is African Biblical Hermeneutics?" *Black Theology* 13, no. 1 (2015): 62.

4. Lucie Sarr, "The Christian Experience in Africa is a very specific Experience," *Religion*, LACROIX International, 2018. Available at: https://international.la-croix.com/news/%20religion/the-christian-experience-in-africa-is-a-very-specific-experience/7613.

remains of the food in his mouth, and since that day he lost his health and wellness. What is amazing is how Africans interpret experiences of this type.

Most of the time when there is a funeral or something terribly painful has just happened, what is in the mind of most Africans is "who could be responsible for this misfortune?" As creditably noted by J. Kwabena Asamoah-Gyadu, if success or prosperity does not happen, Africans usually try to find a reason for the failure, and a supernatural explanation is often sought.[5] Examples of these kinds of experiences are many in Africa, and they are part of the experiences of many Africans, even Christians.

Writing on the current experiences of Christians in Ghana, Daniel Silliman and Griffin Jackson note that while Pentecostals everywhere sing about the power of Jesus's name, in Ghana they sing that his name is powerful against witches. They do so because up to ninety percent of Ghanaian Christians believe witchcraft is a real problem in the country, and more than half of the visits to prayer camps and shrines are to look for deliverance from demons. Women are often accused of witchcraft and are exiled over allegations of having connections with demons. The practice of this type of exile is known as a "scapegoating ritual" because of the belief that when the accused women are exiled, they take the evil attached to their demons away from the community.[6] In one such instance in Ghana, a Pentecostal pastor is reported to have been involved in the process of beating, pouring kerosene on, and setting an accused widow on fire.[7] This behavior is usually contrary to one's expectation that even if African Christians have similar "experiences" with non-Christians, their interpretation and responses to those experiences should be largely different.

Similarly, the African understanding of Christian categories such as "the power of the blood of Christ, the power of Christ, the power of Holy Spirit, the power of God, the power of prayer in the name of Jesus" is widely different to that in other climes.[8] Again the way and manner in which Africans understand spiritual activities such as witchcraft, curses, demon possession, deliverance, and exorcism are largely different to Western notions of these activities. People in many Western societies view witchcraft, demonic possession, and curses

---

5. J. Kwabena Asamoah-Gyadu, "Spiritual Warfare in the African Context, Perspectives on a Global Phenomenon," *Lausanne Global Analysis* 9, no. 1 (January 2020). Available: Spiritual Warfare in the African Context – Lausanne Movement. Accessed August 2021.

6. Daniel Silliman and Griffin Jackson, "Ghana Pentecostals Come to the Defense of Accused Witches," *Christianity Today* (23 November 2020).

7. Silliman and Jackson, "Ghana Pentecostals."

8. Yusuf Turaki, "African Traditional Religious System as Basis of Understanding Christian Warfare," *Lausanne Content Library* (22 August 2000).

as outdated superstitions about mental and physical disorders that can be cured by medical science.[9] But many African Christians would call the name of Jesus several times (repeatedly) for victory over these demonic entities that they believe are actively involved in human affairs and capable of causing painful damage. This perspective may be traced to the African conception of the nature of human beings.

The conception of the personality of human beings is unique in Africa. Africans see humans as spiritual beings whose spirit can easily be attacked by other spirits. To Africans, nearly all parts of the human body have a spiritual replica in the transphysical realm.[10] They also believe that parts of the human body have a spiritual meaning which is beyond the ordinary. The majority of Africans have a tripartite conception of human beings which implies that humans are composed of both physical and spiritual elements. The physical elements constitute only one aspect, while the spiritual aspects have two components. The spiritual force is immaterial and invisible but is the vital force that gives life to the physical body. A third aspect of a human being which is also spiritual is called the "personal ego" or "guardian angel" which controls and guides all the activities of the person.[11] This understanding of human beings provides the ground for Africans to believe that people can easily be affected by spiritual entities as well as physical things. This understanding probably made John Mbiti note that –

> The African society is paradoxically the centre of love and hatred, of friendship, of trust and suspicion, of joy and sorrow, generous tenderness and bitter jealousies. Every form of pain, misfortune, sorrow, or suffering, every illness and sickness, every death whether of an old man or of the infant child, every failure of the crops in the field, every bad omen or dream: these are the other manifestations of evil that man experiences and are blamed on somebody in the society. Natural explanations may indeed be found but mystical explanations must also be given.[12]

---

9. Anastasia Apostolides and Yolanda Dreyer, "The Greek Evil Eye: African Witchcraft and Western Ethnocentrism," *HTS* 64, no. 3 (2008): 1035.

10. Godwin O. Adeboye, "Situating the Yoruba Concept of '*Ori*' within the Soft-Deterministic Frame Work," *International Research on Humanities and Social Sciences* 6, no. 7 (2016): 10.

11. A. Orangu, *Destiny: The Manifested Being* (Ibadan: African Odyssey, 1998), 43.

12. John S. Mbiti, *African Religion and Philosophy* (Nairobi: East African Educational Publishers; London: Heinemann Educational Books, 1969), 209.

How has the church responded to these experiences and unique understandings of Africans?

Creating a Unique Brand of Christianity

To a large extent, the characteristic features of the experiences of Africans have influenced the theology, practice, liturgy, and content of the church in Africa. Spacious emphasis is laid on spirits, demons, Satan, power, and deliverance from spiritual forces in contemporary African Christianity. This focus shows that these entities are more active in the real life and religious encounters of African Christians. The themes of oppression from witches, wizards, and sickness, and deliverance from forms of spiritual oppression, hunger, and poverty resonate louder than any other themes in African Christianity. The proclivity and proliferation of healing prayer, fore-telling prophecy, visions, dreams, preaching on faith in prayer and the renunciation of the devil and all his works, the fear of the power of witches, and exorcisms are pertinent features of the African Christianity. Belief in spiritual agency that incorporates both worldly and other worldly activities are rife in the African setting. A feature germane to the life of African Christians is the acquisition, retention, and manipulation of spiritual power to conquer the myriad of evil forces that populate the world around them. African Christians believe that they need prayers and deliverance to be safe from the evil forces that parade the cosmos.[13] For example, the liturgical and ritual activities of Roho churches in East Africa, the Zionist churches in South Africa, and the Aladura Churches in West Africa show a distinctive attention on the existential questions of life with a uniqueness that is rare elsewhere.[14]

This attention is even louder in African Pentecostal churches. Babatomiwa Owojaiye provides a catalog of belief and praxis in African Pentecostalism that can be used to show the uniqueness of the African Christian experience. According to Owojaiye, African Pentecostals emphasize miraculous intervention in people's lives and the power of the devil and evil spirits to harm human beings, and on ritual deliverance as a remedy for evil attacks.[15] These Pentecostal practices are foregrounded on their experiences. One of

---

13. Afe Adogame and Lizo Jafte, "Zionists, Aladura and Roho: African Instituted Churches," in *African Christianity: An African Story, Perspective in Christianity* (Pretoria, SA: University of Pretoria, 2005), 322.

14. Adogame and Jafte, "Zionists, Aladura and Roho," 322.

15. B. M. Owojaiye, *Evangelical Response to the Coronavirus Lockdown: Insights from the Evangelical Church Winning All* (Nashville: West Bow, 2020), 87.

the reasons Christianity is growing in Africa is the "practical" expectation of Christ to confront daily spiritual and personal warfare.

In the year 2012, I visited my parents in one of the local churches in Ondo State, Nigeria. My visit was during an ongoing prayer revival program in their church, so I had the privilege to attend the program. The invited revivalist, who had instructed everyone on the previous day to come with new brooms, asked the teeming congregants to bring out their brooms and fling them to beat every spirit of the devil that was working against their destiny. I watched with great amazement as people old and young, male and female "beat" the devil with their newly purchased, different sized brooms, and I noticed that the concept of practical spiritual warfare is looming large in African Christianity. I have also observed that while this warfare has been noticed by many scholars and theologians, the experiences behind it and its increasing tendencies into syncretism have not been adequately discussed. However, it will be objective and correct to think that all of these experiences show that African Christians have a unique psyche that should not be overlooked if biblical spirituality will thrive. Asamoah-Gyadu notes that this psyche of spiritual warfare has given birth to the notion of mystical causality and warfare ministry. Asamoah-Gyadu concludes that –

> This ministry of warfare is usually justified based on readings of specific incidences in the Bible and also on the fact that indigenous cultural beliefs, experiences, and worldviews demonstrate affinities or continuities with the biblical material on supernatural evil and how to deal with it. Problems related to education, marriage, international travel, promotion at work, and much else are seen to be due to supernatural activity.[16]

Looking at this entire situation, one is tempted to ask some questions: Is the God of Africans different from the God of the Western world? Are there more demons in Africa than in the West or other places? Is the devil more powerful in the African context than in other places?

Experience is a powerful phenomenon and an integral aspect of human living that influences and affects other aspects of life. It is common and easy to despise the veracity of religious experience due to its nature that it cannot be scientifically verified. However, what is certain is that religious experiences create epistemic, spiritual, and behavioral effects. Although, human spiritual experiences may not be verified empirically, they also cannot be disproved

---

16. Asamoah-Gyadu, "Spiritual Warfare."

totally. For example, while someone else's experience may not be appealing to me, I am not correct in saying that the experience is untrue. Therefore as we are about to deal with the experiences of African Christians related to curses in the light of the Bible, we must remember not to critically and exclusively reject African experiences of curses as un-genuine and superstition. Instead we must examine the phenomenon with empathy and at the same time with theological objectivity that will enable us to formulate biblical guidelines on how African Christians can be helped in their fear of curses.

My purpose in showing this uniqueness of the African Christian experience is not to campaign for African Christianity like others have done. I am also not entering into the reactionary debates on the superiority and inferiority of Christianity in different contexts of the world. My purpose is to show that the African Christian experience is unique, and that with an understanding of this uniqueness, Christian spirituality, Christian practice, and Christian ministry can be understood and engaged in the African context.

Specifically, within this scope of understanding the concept of curses can be discussed appropriately, theologically, and objectively.[17] The topic of curses is even better looked at from one's own unique experience than to live in the shadow of another person.[18] Instead of merely condemning and criticizing the Africans who undergo some of these strange experiences, we will see that the best approach is to be empathetic and to seek to understand their challenges so as to provide relevant pastoral and theological solutions to their dilemma.[19]

What Could be Responsible?

The peculiarity of the African experience is caused by multifaceted factors. These include sociological, psychological, historical, and spiritual factors which have strong influences on how African Christians interpret life issues. For example, it is not uncommon for many Ghanaians and Nigerians to see alcoholism as a behavioral pattern caused by the wickedness of family witches. Some Africans believe that if a person is prone to alcoholism, the cause is the

---

17. A lack of such understanding was one of the factors that caused the separation of some African independent churches from mission and mainline churches. In fact, misunderstanding has caused a lot of rivalry. Many Christian historians and writers in Africa think that the lack of understanding of the African context makes only African independent churches places for Africans to feel at home, unlike the mission churches.

18. J. A. Sofola, *African Culture and the Personality, What Makes an African Person African* (Ibadan: African Resources, 1978), ix.

19. Asamoah-Gyadu, "Spiritual Warfare."

witches in that person's family who want to bring the person's life to ruin.[20] In addition, the uniqueness of African Christianity is caused by the influence of African traditional cosmology in which the spiritual is not separated from the non-spiritual. As a result, Africans have multiple interpretations for events and situations in the economic, medical, social, and cultural spheres.[21] Finally, the religiosity of Africans also contributes to the uniqueness of African spirituality. Naturally, Africans seem to have a strong affinity for religiosity and this affinity causes them to usually seek religious interpretations for every life situation.

Thus we can easily see that the peculiarity of African Christian experience is not only human but also divine and sociological. Nearly all of these factors work together to form the African experience, and their experiences are interpreted from spiritual, sociological, and psychological dimensions of life. As noted above, these experiences must not cause us to look down on Africans as primitive and hopeless. Instead these experiences should inform the route for theological discussion and pastoral care in the African context. Indeed, Africans are unique. The African context and other climes may share some level of similarities and common factors, but the case is as Murray and Kluchohn put it, "Every man is in certain respects like all other men, like some other men, and like no other man."[22] Africans are like no other people in some major aspects of life, especially issues such as belief in the potency of curses.

As a pastor in one of the largest Christian denominations in Africa, I have seen that this uniqueness of African experiences has brewed both good and bad scenes. As related above, this uniqueness has created ingenuity and creativity in some church leaders, but it has also caused fear, anxiety, low self-esteem, hopelessness, and even syncretism. Painfully enough, this uniqueness has not been taken into serious consideration in the training of ministers, in the development and practice of pastoral care, and in theological discussion especially among the mainline churches. Most of the theological enterprises, especially theological discourse and theological institutions in Africa, have been largely centered on issues that have Western patterns.

It is with this general understanding that I welcome you on a journey, a journey of illumination, theological reflection, understanding, and care. The purpose of this journey is to equip us with an adequate understanding and the

---

20. Asamoah-Gyadu, "Spiritual Warfare."

21. B. M. Owojaiye, "The Problem of False Prophets in Africa: Strengthening the Church in the Light of a Troublesome Trend," *Lausanne Global Analysis* 8, no. 6 (November 2019).

22. C. Murray and H. Kluchohn, "Personality." In C. Murray and H. Kluckhohn (eds.), *Nature, Society and Culture* (New York: Alfred A. Knopf, Inc. 1948), 563–565, quoted in Sofola, *African Culture and the Personality*, 3.

deep wealth of knowledge we need to resolve any fear and confusion we may have concerning the dangers of curses and to equip us to help others around us, be they our students, church members, or family members.

This book shall lay the ax at the root of the concept of curses in the African context, which is one of the current defining themes in African Christianity. The concept of curses as perceived and treated in the contemporary African church is surrounded with many themes, issues, questions, concerns, and ruminations. Let us start by opening up the problems, controversies, dilemmas, and debates involved in the concept and also familiarize ourselves with the format of the book. To do so, we turn to the next chapter.

2

The Problem, the Controversy, and the Debate

The fear of curses, especially generational curses, is huge among contemporary Christians in Africa. While many have put their faith in Christ, they still nurse fear and anxiety about the operations of forces in which their traditional belief systems taught them to believe. Should not the transformational power of the gospel have made a greater impact? What went wrong?[1] Many things have gone wrong, and still many are going wrong in African Christianity. Major reasons why African Christianity has not made the expected impact are the lack of proper attention on doctrinal and contextual questions that arise from the people's experiences and the apparent "clash" between biblical teachings and African sociocultural realities. The present and increasing level of occurrences of curses as a theme in African Christianity shows that many African Christians are confused in their Christian life. Therefore, curses as a concept have become one of the contextual themes that forms a cog in the wheel of the growth of true biblical spirituality in Africa. Missionaries came to Africa with their pure interest in evangelizing the continent, but on many fronts, their missionary efforts were not divorced from their foreign cultural structures that in many cases prevented the gospel from becoming truly incarnated and indigenous to the people of Africa.[2] For the gospel to have the full impact in transforming a people and their culture, there must be deliberate efforts toward evangelizing and transforming the people's worldview and orientation on curses. The Bible must be allowed to confront and engage African traditional thought and philosophy of curses.

---

1. Rick Wood, "Africa: Hope in the Midst of Darkness," *Mission Frontiers* 33, no. 6 (November-December 2011): 4.

2. Wood, "Africa: Hope in the Midst of Darkness," 4.

The worldview of African Christians has not been adequately transformed, because so many themes in their worldview have not been properly evaluated in the light of the Bible. One thorough thinker, Evert van der Poll, summarizes this scenario:

> Because the gospel was not brought to the people as a new totally encompassing life view, which would take the place of an equally comprehensive traditional life view, the deepest core of the African culture remains untouched. . . . The convert in Africa did not see the gospel as sufficient for his whole life and especially for the deepest issues of life. For that reason, we find the phenomenon across Africa today that Christians in time of existential needs and crises (such as danger, illness, and death) fall back on their traditional beliefs and life views. It is an area where the gospel should have most relevance, yet the gospel does not mean much in practical terms for the African.[3]

This worldview issue accounts for why the concept of curses shows up as a cog in the wheel of the growth of African biblical spirituality. African Christians struggle with some dilemmas and questions that emerge from cultural beliefs related to curses and with problems for which they have not found solutions. Does this situation mean that the Bible does not have the needed answers and suitable responses for the African dilemma and fear of curses? No! The truth of the matter lies in the fact that not enough effort has been made to interrogate the reality of African lived experiences of curses within a specific theological framework that would help African Christians to adequately receive answers to the questions that arise from their contextual lived experiences.

Traditionally, Africans believe that spoken words are potent and powerful, and that these potent spoken words can control strongly negative metaphysical and spiritual powers which can be transmitted from generation to generation in a particular family, community, village, and country for several years. These spoken words are seen to be very dangerous and to be a source of great trouble for the affected people.

However in the African context, the belief in curses is more complex than the realm of spoken words. Curses are also seen as a form of misfortune or an evil force cast on someone that manifests in that person's life or in that of

---

3. Evert van der Poll quoted by Ken Turnbull, "Discipling Africa through Higher Education: A Proposal for African Christian University," *Mission Frontiers* 33, no. 6 (November-December 2011): 17.

related people which may not have been spoken out but can become a reality if the person offends a deity or contravenes certain traditional stipulations. In contemporary African societies, this belief is still popular and has been a major cause of fear, confusion, and dilemma. Many spiritual and religious programs such as deliverance ministrations, prayer and fasting sessions, and ritual actions such as head washing and bathing are often organized in many African churches. These activities are done with the aim of removing and destroying the potency of curses, most especially ancestral and generational curses. In fact, some Christians have been found using non-Christian coping strategies to solve the problems of curses they believe are in operation in their lives. Many life difficulties and negative incidences are interpreted as symptoms of curses in operation in people's lives, even the Christians.[4] At present, the confusion on the subject of curses can be likened to wildfire in Africa, and it is threatening to distort the authenticity of biblical spirituality. A majority of African Christians believe in the power of curses in one way or the other. As a result, many Christians are confused about whether the power of curses can inflict their lives even after they have given their lives to Christ.

Stories, shared experiences, narratives, myths, and interpretations on the reality, potency, and fear of curses are prevalent in African churches, sermons, and prayers, as well as Christian films, narratives, stories, movies, program posters, media, songs, prayers, and publications. I have personally witnessed some incidences, two of which are noteworthy in relation to the contemporary notion of the power of curses in Africa. First, in a tertiary institution in Nigeria, a young minister in his final year died on the verge of concluding his theological education. Early in the morning, the news of his sudden death broke out, and many people, particularly the local Christians and ministers, gathered in small group discussions. Some of these groups argued that there must have been a particular curse on the deceased's family that when people are on the verge of success, they die. They related this minister's sudden death with that of his immediate elder brother, who also died on the verge of a major success a few years before. Should theological students think this way?

Second, I went to visit family members in southwestern Nigeria and attended church prayer sessions with them in which the minister asked the people to queue serially so that he could wash their heads from their inherited family curses. He gave them symptoms that indicated they were under curses such as barrenness, infection with HIV/AIDS, a delay in getting married, experiencing hatred from family and friends, working hard but with little

---

4. S. F. Adeniyi, *Moving from Curses to Blessings* (San Francisco: CCC, 2000).

results or rewards, and coming close to success but never succeeding, among others. With great enthusiasm and high expectations, the congregants arranged themselves in a straight line before the minister, and he washed their heads while reciting portions of the book of Psalms.

From these examples, it is clear that the fear of curses, especially generational curses, is huge among contemporary Christians in Africa. In fact, the number of times many Christians in Africa pray for breaking curses is more than the times they pray for God's blessing. In many instances, prayers are offered during church wedding ceremonies that any family curses on the couple will not follow them to their new home, and such prayers are taken very serious by the couple and the people attending the ceremony. Such prayers are usually said with the couple kneeling and the ministers surrounding them for prayer, sometimes laying hands on them, sometimes washing their heads with "anointed" water or oil. This prayer for the couple is usually said just before they are joined together. The purpose of such prayer is that the curses believed to be in operation in the lives and families of the couple would not be transmitted into the marriage that is to be consummated. The belief is that one or both of the people to be joined together may be carrying some curses that operate in their originating family, and that such must be confronted with fervent prayers. In addition, we hear stories that even some pastors are under inherited transgenerational curses, and that if they do not go for deliverance, their ministry cannot enjoy success no matter how hard they struggle. Sometimes it is reported that when such pastors go for the prescribed deliverance, their ministry begins to blossom. We give detailed discussion on this topic in later chapters.

But can a Christian be cursed? Can those who have confessed Christ be affected by inherited curses in their families, villages, or clans? Does the African experience of the power of curses go in tandem with biblical positions? Personal experience, culture, and the Bible – which should African Christians take as the priority and preeminent? Do the majority of African Christians know and are they sure that the Christ they profess is more powerful than any curses operating in their families, villages, or cities? Are the popular experiences of curses shared by Africans real, or are they merely the results of ignorance or psychological factors? Can we just simplistically disprove African experiences related to curses? These questions need to be handled objectively, empathetically, and theologically.

Two lenses can be used to view these questions. One lens is that once people give their life to Jesus, they cannot be affected by curses any longer. The second is that even Christians must be ready to wage war against the power of their generational curses because these curses can still affect them. This controversy has deep theological implications, particularly for African Christianity. For instance, if one holds the view that curses such as generational curses cannot affect Christians, what about the practical experience and testimonies of some Christians in Africa of what they call inexplicable life difficulties that seem to follow negative patterns in their family and village? What about some Africans who have given their lives to Christ but still have some personal experiences of negative trends in their lives that upon spiritual diagnosis and revelations are believed to be caused by their inherited curses? Again if one holds the view that a Christian can be affected by curses, then what are the theological implications in light of the biblical teaching of total freedom for believers and the potency of the power of Jesus and his cross?

An attempt to examine these issues from an evangelical perspective and in the African context gives the impetus for this work. The development of African Christian theology has taken three stages.[5] The first stage, which started in the first half of the twentieth century, was mostly apologetic and reactionary in responding to what I call the "condemnation pattern" of Western theologians of African belief systems. The second stage, which started in the latter half of the twentieth century, was the attempt of African theologians to develop theological frameworks and suitable methods for doing African Christian theology, during which African theological thinkers concentrated on which relevant methods to adopt in establishing African Christian theology. In the third and present stage, which began at the end of the twentieth century and is still evolving, African theologians have become more assertive and proactive. During the second and third stages, African theologians dealt majorly with contextual issues in the light of the Bible.[6] Their attempt to dissect the African concept of curses from the evangelical framework is a representation of their ongoing efforts in the present stage of the development of African Christian theology. Looking at the current state of the church in Africa, it is easy to see that this stage is the most critical, needed, and purposeful. It is time to examine African contextual themes and life realities in the light of the Bible.[7]

This book addresses the questions that arise from traditional beliefs in curses and the reality of the lived experiences, struggles, perplexities, puzzles,

---

5. Ernest van Eck, "The Word is Life: African Theology as Biblical and Contextual Theology," *HTS* 62, no. 2 (2009): 680.

6. Ezekiel E. Nihinlola, "Human Being, Being Human: Theological Anthropology in the African Context," First Inaugural Lecture, Nigerian Baptist Theological Seminary, NBTS, Ogbomosho, Nigeria published by the NBTS Publishing Unit 2008, 13.

7. G. Muzorewa, "A Definition of a Future African Theology," *African Theological Journal* 2 (1990): 168–79.

complexities, and fears of Africans. It seeks to answer the questions in the light of the word of God. It provides practical guidelines that can be followed in dealing with fear and the dilemmas of curses in Africa.

It is beyond our reach to fully investigate the psychological dimensions of individual personal experiences; therefore, our purpose is to reflect theologically with the keen aim of providing Bible-based solutions to the controversy, dilemmas, and fear that emanate from curses in the present African church. "A study of how curses impact people is one of the most important responsibilities Christian leaders must undertake."[8]

Theology and Experiences of African Christians

The majority of previous attempts to explore theological issues and themes from African perspectives have fallen into the error of addressing a catalog of themes in single volumes. Besides, scholars who have examined some African contextual themes theologically have not usually done so using a specific theological angle or a perspective with a rigorous engagement of Scripture. These errors have not given these efforts enough space for the in-depth handling that such themes demand. In most instances, those efforts are only introductory discussions of the basic truths of Christianity as they relate to the context of traditional African life but do not engage specific themes in deeper length. These efforts have only been able to produce African Christian theology that is "introductory," and Christians are wide in ritual expressions but inches in depth and understanding. For instance, Wilbur O'Donovan states that while he has attempted to survey Christian theology from African perspectives, "some issues raised in my book will require a more thorough treatment by other theologians."[9] This work is an answered prayer to such a commendable yearning on the topic of curses.

The few scholars who have worked on the concept of curses from African cultural perspectives seem to have presumed that African notions of curses are inextricably or exclusively related to witchcraft, giving an impression that the African concept of curses is limited to witchcraft. Again, even when the lived experiences of Africans are examined biblically, they are often not examined from a specific theological spectrum and understanding. As a

---

8. Passmore Hachalinga, "How Curses Impact People and Biblical Responses," *Journal of Adventist Mission Studies* 13, no. 7 (2017): 55.

9. Wilbur O'Donovan, *Biblical Christianity in African Perspective* (Chicago: Oasis International, 1997), 2.

result, such previous efforts by African theologians have created ambiguous recommendations which confuse African Christians even more. The situation in which clear, unambiguous answers are not given for perplexities in the lived experiences of African Christians has resulted in syncretism, heretical doctrines, emotional dissonance, and fear, and has given way to many quasi-magical and self-made messianic deliverance ministers and prophets. Due to these issues, the state of African Christian spirituality has not been thorough, biblical, and distinct in relation to non-Christian spiritualties in the African continent.

Arrangement and Pattern of Discussion Clarified

In this book we engage the beliefs about the concept of curses in contemporary African Christianity and provide African Christians with guidelines on how to tackle this phenomenon with biblical integrity. To make this discussion salient and lucid, a simple structure is followed. First is a brief discussion of the theological method adopted. Biblical understandings of curses are examined followed by the African religio-cultural conception of curses. At first, the presentation and discussion of the African concept of curses is purely neutral and empirical. We survey the beliefs of African Christians in the power of curses as seen and depicted in African church programs, sermons, writings, liturgy, media, deliverance and prayer sessions, program posters from the contemporary church, and the practices of contemporary African Christianity. These two views are compared: the biblical theology of curses and the African religious-cultural understanding of curses, using the evangelical understanding of the biblical concept of curses and blessings. From this interrogation, practical, simplified biblical guidelines and steps for proper Christian responses to the concept of curses are recommended to help African Christians who are confused about the concept of curses in view of their lived experience. A viable evangelical theological approach on how the concept of curses can be handled in the contemporary African church is framed and simplified. Providing and discussing this information makes this book useful to lay Christians, church pastors, and Christians in academia in Africa and beyond.

To change lives, theology must be made to speak to the lived experiences of Christians. Therefore, we engage the reality of curses and the degree and expression of fear of curses in view of the responses in African Pentecostalism. A major source of confusion about the concept of curses among many African Christians is the biblical interpretation model used by the majority of African preachers. Therefore, we hermeneutically engage popular biblical texts that are commonly used in African discussions of curses to clarify the confusion.

A Quick Note on "Evangelicalism"

The term "evangelicalism" is used in this work primarily to refer to evangelical teachings rather than denominational or institutional movements. Evangelicalism is not viewed uniformly in every context. For example, in British Anglicanism, it can be seen as a style of Sunday service, while in the United States, the term is used as a "polite substitute for fundamentalism which is sometimes considered to be militant, unreasonable, backward and uneducated Protestantism."[10] In fact, there is also what can be referred to as a problem of identity in the present discourse on evangelicalism. In this book, evangelicalism is used in relation to biblical teachings rather than political identity, to the teaching of Christians who believe in the Bible's verbal, plenary inspiration and in the primacy of Scripture, the centrality of the saving cross of Christ, the necessity for personal conversional experiences and needfulness of active mission, and the discipleship and care for the growth of believers. This definition implies that evangelicals can be found in virtually any Christian denomination, either in those which are not traditionally and institutionally identified as evangelical and in denominations which are institutionally established on the evangelical ethos. Bebbington's quadrilateral dimensions of evangelicalism which stress personal conversional, activism, biblicism, and the centrality of the cross as the defining marks of true evangelicalism is adopted.[11] Bebbington's position can be summarized as follows: evangelicals are those who believe that having a conversion experience, actively sharing the gospel, and good works are needed; that the Bible is inspired and authoritative above experience, reason, and culture; and that salvation is only possible through the work of Christ on the cross. As noted by Timothy Larsen, Bebbington's definition is "routinely employed to identify evangelicals, and no other view on evangelicalism comes close to rivaling its level of general acceptance."[12]

Although evangelicalism has been seen, and can indeed be seen, as a dynamic force that started in Great Britain in the 1730s and later in the United

---

10. Owojaiye, *Evangelical Response*, 57.

11. David Bebbington, *Evangelicalism in Modern Britain: A History from the 1730s to the 1980s* (Oxfordshire: Rutledge, 1989), 20.

12. Timothy Larsen, "Defining and Locating Evangelicalism," in *Cambridge Companion to Evangelical Theology*, ed. T. Larsen and D. Trier (Cambridge: Cambridge University Press, 2007), 1.

States in the nineteenth century, it is now a global phenomenon. Evangelical bodies that emerged from this force include the Lausanne Movement, the World Evangelical Alliance (WEA), and Association of Evangelicals in Africa (AEA).[13] In this book, the primary use of evangelicalism is not foregrounded on these politically distinct movements but on the content of teachings that can be tagged "evangelical teaching." This use is in line with Owojaiye's argument that if evangelicalism is de-denominationalized and de-politicized in the African context, churches such as Redeemed Christian Church of God (RCCG), Deeper Life Bible Church, Four Square Gospel Church, Christ is the Answer Ministries, and The Assemblies of God which have been categorized as non-evangelicals will be seen as purely "evangelical" due to their teachings and doctrines on the Bible, the conversion experience, the atoning work of Christ on the cross, and sharing the gospel message.[14] While all the members of these denominations may not have a uniform doctrinal emphasis, they include individual Christians who believe in the place of the Bible above cultural beliefs, Christ's atoning death as the exclusive way to reconciliation with God, and the importance of an individual, personal conversional encounter with Christ. Individual Christians scattered across denominations strongly believe in these four points irrespective of the institutional classification of their churches. In fact a majority of Christians either in charismatic, Pentecostal, neo-Pentecostal, African indigenous churches (AIC), and historic mission churches believe these points. The ruminations in this book cover all these points and are not limited only to Christians who are in denominations that are historically tagged "evangelical." This transdenominational definition of evangelicalism is adopted in this work because the basic evangelical themes of the primacy of the Scripture, the centrality of the cross and Jesus's atonement, the necessity of personal conversion, and the usefulness of active mission have serious bearings on the fear of African Christians of the power of curses, and these themes help to answer and clarify the questions and confusion in the minds of these African Christians.

In addition, Bebbington's quadrilateral is used with a lens of approach from the Wesleyan quadrilateral. The term "Wesleyan quadrilateral," credited to John Wesley,[15] was coined by the twentieth-century theologian Albert C. Outler. It is a distinctive theological method with Scripture as the preeminent norm but interfaced with Christian experience, tradition, and reason as dynamic and

---

13. Owojaiye, *Evangelical Response*, 51.
14. Owojaiye, 52.
15. John Wesley, *John Wesley's Forty-Four Sermons* (Peterborough: Epworth, 1944).

interactive aids in interpreting the word of God in Scripture.[16] This theological method involves the argument that while the Bible should be the primary source of Christian theology and practice, it should not be exclusive. Christian theology should also interrogate experience, tradition, and reason. Christian theology and teachings are based on the divinely inspired biblical text, but they cannot affect the life of real people until they are contextual. Therefore this work adopts the Wesleyan quadrilateral as an additional theoretical framework. While many evangelicals are careful in applying the Wesleyan quadrilateral, the quadrilateral gives us a good approach to interpreting Scripture firmly and concretely within a context of human lived experience. It also affords us a way to interrogate contextual themes such as curses in the African context in the light of the Bible.[17] Some contemporary discussions in Africa have taken this kind of contextual approach. For instance, Emiola Nihinlola in his inaugural lecture adopted a similar position to argue for the need to engage Christian theology in the African context. Samuel Waje Kunhiyop did outstanding introductory spade work on African Christian theology and has subsequently interrogated some contextual issues such as witchcraft in the light of the Bible.[18] Also, Wilbur O'Donovan did a study of Christianity in the African context. In the light of these works, this book understands "Christian theology" as an analysis and interpretation of the revelation of God involving church tradition and human experience from a particular worldview.[19]

As Martin Luther contended, every human tradition and belief should be brought under the word of God. With a cautious empathetic mindset, this work brings the African belief in the power of curses under the light of the word of God. The Bible is the highest authority in any theological discussion of the practice of Christian faith and spirituality. The experience of African Christians on curses is not blindly criticized but examined in the light of the Bible with the view to helping equip confused, marooned, and frightened African Christians and guiding African pastors and church leaders on how to guide their church members. I strongly believe that whenever the Bible conflicts with any cultural belief, the Bible takes the primacy and preeminence. Meanwhile, to have a personal and contextual understanding of biblical

---

16. Albert Outler, "The Wesleyan Quadrilateral – in John Wesley," in *Doctrine and Theology in the United Methodist Church*, ed. Thomas Langford (Nashville: Abingdon, 1991), 86.

17. G. H. Mellor, "The Wesleyan Quadrilateral," *MET – Methodists Evangelical Together* (2003).

18. S. W. Kunhiyop, *African Christian Theology* (Grand Rapids: Zondervan Academic, 2012).

19. Nihinlola, "Human Being, Being Human," 15.

teachings, biblical primacy should not be taken as synonymous to biblical exclusivity in theological discussion.

Now to foreground the debate in the ongoing theological conversation and introduce the critical issues involved on curses as presented in this work. In chapter three, I intentionally include a brief discussion on a relevant theological method, Elizabeth Mburu's intercultural hermeneutics, that I adopted and the rationale for the method. Thereafter, the biblical theology of curses and blessings is presented with thorough exposition of cursing texts and historical contexts both in the Old and New Testaments. I tried to understand any text used in this book in its historical, literary, and cultural context before applying it to contemporary Africans.

I am fascinated by O'Donovan's approach to doing Christian theology in Africa.[20] He presents three simple steps and approaches to guide the formulation of biblical Christianity in Africa. First, I ask what does the Bible teach on the subject of curses? Second, what are the actual African beliefs and practices on the subject of curses? This question also includes the lived experience of the Africans. Third, I deal with how we can express the truth of the Bible on the subject of curses in ways that will be very clear and useful for Africans in solving the dilemmas and fears that emerge from their lived experiences.

To analyze the concept of curses in the contemporary African society, the empirical approach is adopted to engage the lived experiences of the people, and qualitative research data is gathered from primary sources for discussion and evaluation. I employed both participatory observation and oral interviews to interact with some African Christian practices and some key church leaders across the major ethnic groups in Africa. I am well aware of the diversity in African Christianity, but it would be wearisome to take into consideration the different brands and groups that have emerged in African Christianity one by one. As revealed in the findings, there is an overarching trajectory within African Christianity which is sufficient to support my discussions on the issues surrounding the concept of curses in the African context. I do not presume that all of the illustrations from the respondents represent all of the opinions of Africans in a hard sense, but they are representative enough to argue my point. I deal with those experiential issues that underlie similar, hard, confusing, and common lived experiences of Africans related to curses. I predominantly deal with African Christian experiences with a very cautious effort to avoid overgeneralization.

---

20. O'Donovan, *Biblical Christianity in African Perspective*, 6.

I invite you to follow the discussion with this background in mind. There are surprising stories and illustrations herein. But the discussion is simplified for lay readers, and the expected end is that you will examine your own life experiences in the light of the Bible as guided by this work. This type of examination will definitely enhance true spiritual formation and the growth of biblical spirituality in Africa.

One final note. At this juncture, especially informal theologians may see that I am tempted to go theologically technical at some points. Please have it in mind that while some aspects of the discussion may look technical, adequate and simplified explanations are given to clarify the points. To frame out a holistic and relevant practical guideline that confronts the fears, dilemmas, and confusion of curses, the discussion has to pass through some flames of technical grounding and rigor. But to make it accessible to non-technical theologians, the work also employs adequate simplicity.

3

Theological Method for a Theology of Curses

The theological method adopted for this work must be well stated to adequately create a proper context for the arguments made. Many methods have been used in the contemporary discourse on African Christian theology. The period from the 1980s to this time has seen an institutional as well as hermeneutical breakthrough of Africanized theological scholarship and the contextual responsibilities of discipline required.[1] This breakthrough has resulted in a methodological conglomerate of interests and perspectives of theologians and thinkers such as Samuel Abogunrin, John Mbiti, Charles Nyamiti, J. W. Zvomunodinta, Kwesi Dickson, Peter Kanyandago, Dapo Asaju, Itumelenge Mosala, Musa Dube, Jesse Mugambi, Elizabeth Mburu, Samuel Waje Kunhiyop, and a host of others. A brief analysis of these contemporary theological methods is made here before attention is given to the intercultural hermeneutic method as a valid approach to developing African theology and hermeneutic of curses. This chapter is an attempt to help us prepare for the journey ahead in this book and to easily assimilate the flow of thought which will eventually be used to formulate practical theological and hermeneutical guidelines for African Christians to deal with the dilemmas and fears of curses and with the theological controversies involved.

Current Theological Methods and Approaches

The debate on which method is most appropriate to formulate relevant African Christian theology is huge. Some African theologians such as David

---

1. Knut Holter, "The 'Poor' in Ancient Israel – and in Contemporary African Biblical Studies," *Mission Studies* 33 (2016): 209–21.

Tuesday Adamo devised an aggressive Afrocentric reading of Scripture which is a reversal of the Euro-cultural perspective. Adamo commits his research to a reappraisal of ancient biblical tradition and African worldviews with the purpose of correcting the effects of the European cultural ideological orientation to which Africans have been subjected. Adamo and others argue that Eurocentric approaches to biblical interpretation do not meet the needs of Africans on issues such as acute poverty, deliverance from witches and wizards, and internalized colonized consciousness. The decolonization efforts have been made to break the Western hermeneutical hegemony and ideological stranglehold that Eurocentric biblical scholarship has long had. This theological method rejects the superintending tendencies of Western intellectual tradition.[2] While this African method shows a level of openness for cross fertilization of ideas with other interpretive approaches, it seems to be overreactionary to European interpretation which makes it look hyperbolically suspicious. In addition, the method does not clarify the role of transcontextual biblical truths in the application of biblical texts to the African reality. Only a few proponents of this method use the Bible to interpret African reality; the majority use African reality to interpret the Bible. This practice is similar to the approach of West and Dube who say that the trend of studying the Bible to see what it says to Africans should be reversed to what Africans have to say to the Bible.[3] These methods ignore some paramount biblical truths that are valid in any cultural context which faults the method of asking what Africans have to say to the Bible. I believe that the study cannot be one way. While Africans have many things to say to the Bible, the Bible also has many things to say to Africans because some biblical truths are valid and must been seen as the same in any context, even though the application may be differently contextual.

These issues and many others have made the appropriateness of theological methods for African Christian theology to be matters that are fiercely debated. The result has been an extensive search for which method is most appropriate. For example, Dapo Asaju calls for a new direction in African Christian theology that will create a form of biblical studies that can provide answers to the many emergent issues that confront the present and coming generations in Africa.[4]

---

2. Adamo, "What Is African Biblical Hermeneutics," 62.

3. Gerald O. West and Musa S. Dube, (eds.), *The Bible in Africa: Transactions, Trajectories and Trends* (The Netherlands: Brill, 2001), 1–11.

4. Dapo Asaju, "Afro-centric Biblical Studies: Another Colonization?" in *Decolonization of Biblical Interpretation in Africa*, vol. 4: *National Association of Biblical Studies*, ed. S. O. Abogunrin (Nigeria: Alofe Enterprises, 2005), 121–29.

Similarly, Justin Ukpong and Teresa Okure argued for inculturation hermeneutics as a viable method for African Christian theology.[5] Together with others, they devised a new contextual methodological paradigm for contextual study of the Bible. Ukpong seeks to make the common reader and their social-cultural context to be the subject of biblical interpretation, which awards a level of epistemological privilege to ordinary readers of the Bible. According to this argument, the primary reading of the text lies not in isolated scholarly readings but in common, ordinary communal reading. While this method is contextual in approach, it creates questions about preparation and the rigorous capacity needed to adequately interpret biblical texts. If the epistemological privilege given to common readers is not laced with some extent of training on hermeneutical technicalities, ordinary readers can inadvertently creep into syncretism because they may be left without any practical guidance on how to read the text. This lack of training may be a reason why many pastors in Africa are syncretic. For example some pastors order their followers to eat grass, rats, and snakes and drink petrol in the name of displaying their special anointing.[6] To what extent can we accord epistemological privilege to ordinary readers who are not exposed to any rigor of disciplined biblical interpretation and application?

In addition, adherents to the liberation method as a response to social injustice and unjust situations see Jesus as the greatest liberator. They see the biblical exodus and the book of Amos as revealing Yahweh as a defender of the poor and the oppressed. The liberation method emphasizes political liberation as part of the teaching of Jesus Christ. Adherents to this theological method believe that theology must be prophetic in declaring justice for the oppressed and liberating people from the oppressive political and economic tyranny of the minority who make up the ruling class.[7] While this method is valid for helping African churches in their prophetic calling and in liberating the poor

---

5. J. S. Ukpong, "Reading the Bible with African Eyes: Inculturation and Hermeneutics," *Journal of Theology for Southern Africa* 91 (1995): 3–14. T. Okure, "First was the life not the book," in T. Okure (ed.), *To cast fire upon the Earth: Bible and Mission collaborating in today's Multicultural Global Context* (Pietermaritzburg: Cluster, 2000), 194–227. See also J. S. Ukpong, "Natural Hermeneutics: An African Approach to Biblical Interpretation," in *The Bible in a World Context: An Experiment in Contextual Hermeneutics*, ed. D. Walter and L. Urich (Grand Rapids: Eerdmans, 2002), 17–32.

6. Madiopane Masenya, "Ruminating on Justin S. Ukpong's Inculturation Hermeneutic and Its Implication for the Study of African Biblical Hermeneutics Today," *HTS* 72, no. 2 (2016): 1–6.

7. I. J. Mosala, *Biblical Hermeneutic and Black Theology in South Africa* (Grand Rapids: Eerdmans, 1989).

and oppressed, its political outlook opens it up for diverse methodological criticisms bordering on the genuineness of its biblical spirituality.

Another popular theological method in African Christian theology is the African feminist approach. Mercy Modupe Oduyoye, Teresa Okure, Musa Dube, Ronke Olajubu, Helen Labeodan, and many others have written to argue against the male domination and patriarchal organization of African society. These scholars have brought to the fore the various problems confronting women and children in African society and argue that the Bible must be interpreted to liberate the plight and domination of women. This method is just mentioned so that you may have a glimpse of what is going on among African theologians and to situate your understanding in the right context.

Jesse Mugambi of Kenya takes a different theological approach. He advances reconstruction theology as a viable method for African Christian theology.[8] The theological metaphor of reconstruction implies that African scholars should discuss new insights to inspire a new way of making theological conclusions that can help Africans regain their self-esteem and integrity for societal transformation. He believes that such transformation should start with the individual and move to the societal level.

Similarly, Afe Adogame brings a new dimension to methodological development for African Christian theology.[9] He argues that theological research can profit from an interdisciplinary approach to develop-grounded theology from ordinary grounded theory. He believes that empirical research should be adopted to develop a bottom-up approach that will inform new theories and rubrics of integration between lived experience and theological theories to form new perspective and fresh theological reflection. Adogame argues for theological research that is grounded in the living experiences of the people.[10] This theological method is very useful for this work, and it informs my opinions on how theology can employ a transdisciplinary method that can be used to study the experiences of ordinary people.

---

8. J. N. K. Mugambi, *Religion and Social Construction of Reality* (Nairobi: EAEP, 1995) and J. N. K. Mugambi, *From Liberation to Reconstruction* (Nairobi: EAEP, 1995).

9. Afe Adogame, "African Christianity in Diaspora," in Diane B. Stinton (ed), *African Theology on the way: Current Conversations* (Minneapolis: Fortress Press, 2015). Adogame also presented these thoughts to me and other students in VID Specialized University's course on "African Biblical hermeneutics," in May 2021 during his lecture titled "Making Sense of Theology via Ethnography: Decolonizing theology through the prism of 'Bottom-up' methodologies," to the class.

10. See Diane B. Stinton, ed., *African Theology on the Way: Current Conversation* (London: SPCK, 2010).

Intercultural Hermeneutics as a Viable Theological Method

Primarily, this work adopts intercultural dialogue as a theological method to interrogate the African experience of curses in the light of evangelical biblical spirituality. This method was chosen because many efforts of the African Christian theologians enumerated above are overreactionary against ecclesiastical colonialism and others are only introductory. While those moves toward the decolonization of African biblical hermeneutics are genuine and represent a valid and relevant effort to make Christianity speak to the life realities of Africans, Elizabeth Mburu's model of intercultural hermeneutic is adopted here because it has clear processes that can be practically followed to engage the African theology of curses. Besides, Mburu's model considers not just biblical interpretation of the text; it also deals with the theological nature of the text and viable application.

There are many expositions of intercultural hermeneutics,[11] but this work sticks to Elizabeth Mburu's model of intercultural dialogue.[12] Mburu opines that lack of dialogue between contextual reality and biblical cultural reality has created double hermeneutical gaps in the current European methods of biblical interpretation. This situation has also not allowed a theological engagement of practical issues in African contexts. She argues that readers come to the Bible with lived experiences, and their contextual situations affect their interpretation and application. This form of biblical hermeneutics is complementary rather than a total rejection of Western approaches. The intercultural hermeneutics approach is a dialogue between the African context and the biblical context, a dialogue between the world of the biblical text and the world of contemporary African experience. It is a hermeneutics of trust rather than of suspicion.

Specifically, what fascinates me in Mburu's theological model is her four-legged interpretive hypothesis. Mburu develops a four-legged stool model to concretize practical steps to creating a dialogue between the biblical text and the African context. The first leg is to access the parallels between African traditional experience and the culture of the Bible. This step involves interrogating and comparing the African worldview with the worldview of the Bible and seeks to determine what is negotiable and non-negotiable. It develops a truly biblical worldview while retaining what is uniquely African. The second leg deals with the theological context and content of biblical texts.

---

11. See U. C. Manus, "Decolonizing New Testament Interpretation in Nigeria," in *Decolonization of Biblical Interpretation in Africa*, vol. 4: *National Association of Biblical Studies*, ed. S. O. Abogunrin (Lagos, Nigeria: Alofe Enterprises, 2005), 288.

12. Elizabeth Mburu, *African Hermeneutics* (Carlisle: HippoBooks, 2019).

This step involves examining the main emphasis of the text. The third leg deals with the literary context and identifying the literary features of the biblical text. These literary features include genre, technique, language and flows of the text. This step is a painstaking process of thorough biblical interpretation. The fourth leg deals with the historical and cultural contexts of the texts. It is believed that biblical texts come from particular historical-cultural contexts. This step involves the attempt to identify what the biblical text meant in its original context to its original audience, entering into the world of the biblical authors. The last part of Mburu's model of intercultural dialogue is the "seat" of the stool which deals with the rightful application of the text. The application must be done to ensure transformation of Africans, but transcontextual truth must be sustained without mixing with culture-bound truths.[13]

A major strength of this approach is that it easily detects and avoids syncretism because it sees biblical primacy as non-negotiable and differentiates between culture-bound values that can be negotiated and transcultural values that cannot be negotiated and must apply in all cultural contexts. This approach guides this work to interrogate African practical life reality and experiences in such a way that they will be true to Scripture and true to the African context. It is a dialogical approach that creates interrogation between the African culture and the biblical culture. What will make African Christian theology embrace the practical living experiences of Africans is the ability of African theologians to evaluate African interpretations of life occurrences which influence their religious worldview.[14] This method allows the interpreters to move from known to unknown. Even though the interpreters are influenced by their experience and cultural context, this theory of interpretation of the Bible is not entirely subjective because the text is allowed to guide them to its true meaning. This approach allows internalizing biblical truth and transformation of experience. Using this method will allow us to transform some undesirable elements of African culture and correct the error of substituting culture for the gospel concerning African beliefs in curses. African culture is an invaluable tool, but it is not inspired and should not be taken as equal to the Bible.

Gaining from these patterns of theological ruminations, this work creates a dialogue between the African concept of curses and the biblical concept of

---

13. Andrew Mbuvi, "African Biblical Stories: An Introduction to an Emerging Discipline," *Currents in Biblical Research* 15, no. 2 (2017): 147.

14. Gerald West, "Interpreting the Comparative Paradigm in African Biblical Scholarship," in *African and European Reading of the Bible in Dialogue: In Quest for Meaning*, ed. Gerald West and Hans de Wet (Leiden: Brill Academic, 2008), 40.

curses. The four legs of Mburu's interpretive model are adopted practically to create biblical guidelines on how cursing texts should rightly be interpreted by African biblical interpreters.

To be true to our commitment to the evangelical framework mentioned earlier, we will first deal with a biblical theology of curses and exegete some principal biblical texts. Starting from the Bible and ending with the Bible allows a thorough engagement with and adequate interrogation of an African theology of curses in the light of the Scripture.

4

Biblical Theology of Curses and Cursing

Since the purpose of this book is to examine African beliefs in curses in the light of the Scriptures, it is good to start with the biblical concept of curses and some texts that are central to the biblical understanding of curses. Attention is given to some basic relevant biblical texts intertextually. The concept of curses is also examined in the prevalent sociocultural contexts of the biblical times so as to bring to the fore the understanding of curses in the ancient Near Eastern and Greco-Roman societies. An adequate understanding of the biblical stance on the concept of curses will help Africans and other readers of this book to properly engage and respond to the controversy, dilemmas, and fears surrounding beliefs in curses in contemporary contexts. Please take note that the dialogue between the African theology of curses and the biblical theology of curses is not the aim of this chapter. Full attention is given to that dialogue later. What is here is a pure exposition of the biblical theology of curses gathered from both Old and New Testament texts situated in their historical and cultural contexts. Therefore, you are counseled to enter this chapter with patience because it is the lengthiest part of this work as it includes both Old and New Testament analysis of biblical cursing texts.

Biblical and Theological Definitions

Biblically, a curse is defined as the opposite or reversal of a blessing.[1] Many themes are used for curses in the Bible. The Hebrew word translated "curse" comes from the root *rr* which means to curse or to cover with misfortune.

---

1. Merrill C. Tenney, *The Zondervan Pictorial Bible Dictionary* (Grand Rapids: Zondervan, 1970), 191.

A similar Hebrew word is *alah* which means "curse." Three Hebrew verbs – *alah*, *arar*, and *qalal* – can be translated "curse," though they cover a variety of meanings including oaths, imprecations, and maledictions.[2] The New Testament uses the Greek words *akatapa*, *anathema*, and *kataraomai* that define a curse as an imprecation or an expressed wish for evil.[3] Biblically, a curse may be a desire uttered in words against God or against a fellow human being. If a curse is uttered against God, it is referred to as blasphemy.[4] On the human level, these words are used to wish harm or catastrophe, while on the divine level they are used to "impose judgments."[5] Biblically speaking, a curse can be defined as using "powerful words to invoke supernatural harm," be it human, divine, oral, written, personal, or collective.[6] However, curses are more complicated than mere spoken words, for sometimes negative words may not have to be pronounced for curses to become effective if the person concerned has contravened a stipulated standard of God.

Blessings and curses are powerful pronouncements in the Bible, especially in the Old Testament, and are part of important acts of Yahweh after the creation. To grasp the biblical definition of curses, curses and blessings must be contrasted. While blessings are connected with obedience, curses are connected with disobedience (Gen 3; Deut 28; Mal 2:2).[7] Curses are seen in the Bible as punishment and an effective deterrent to antisocial behavior (Gen 4:9–12; Ps 1; 41; Matt 25:41–46). Curses, blessings, and covenants are interrelated in most of the biblical instances of curses, especially in the Old Testament. Sometimes a curse is seen to be powerful in itself to carry itself into effect. A good example of this kind of curse is found in Zechariah 5:1–3 which recounts where the prophet saw a flying scroll referred to as the curse looking for its victims: thieves and those who swear falsely. In another instance in Numbers 22–24 related to heathenism, Balaam's curse is depicted to possess the power of self-realization. In addition, curses are depicted in the Bible as part of dedicating something to God in such a way that the thing cannot be used again for personal or for private purposes.[8] A good example of this is found in

---

2. Brian M. Britt, "Curses in the Hebrew Bible," Bible Odyssey (16 August 2022).

3. Walter A. Elwell, ed., *Evangelical Dictionary of Theology*, 2nd ed. (Grand Rapids: Baker, 2001), 313.

4. Elwell, ed., *Evangelical Dictionary of Theology*, 313.

5. Tenney, *Zondervan Pictorial Bible Dictionary*, 191.

6. Brian M. Britt, "Curses in the Hebrew Bible," Bible Odyssey (16 August 2022).

7. Claus Westermann, *Elements of Old Testament Theology*, trans. Douglas W. Stott (Atlanta: John Knox, 1982), 102.

8. Elwell, ed., *Evangelical Dictionary of Theology*, 314.

Leviticus 27:28–29, which states that "No person devoted to destruction may be ransomed, they are to be put to death" (Lev 27:29). Achan's theft of devoted things and resulting destruction of his family in Joshua 7:1–26 can also be seen as a good example. The people of Canaan were similarly doomed to destruction for their immoral behavior (see Gen 15:16; Josh 2:10; 6:17). In other instances in the Old Testament, the term "curse" is related to a vow, and failure to keep vows results in curses (Mal 1:14; Deut 23:21–23; Jas 5:11–12).

Although many biblical scholars such as Hermann Gunkel define "curse" as merely a wish of harm,[9] many other biblical scholars agree that the wish must be expressed, whether written, spoken, or implied. What is more certain, however, is that the purpose of a curse is to negatively affect the object which may be human or non-human.

The definition of curse given in the *Evangelical Dictionary of Theology* is more relevant to our discussion because it situates "curses" in different, various possible biblical contexts.[10] Accordingly, sometimes, curses are used in the Bible in a general sense as an imprecation or expressed wish for evil. It is a blasphemy when such a wish is directed against God (Job 2:5, 9). It may be uttered to God by a person against another person. It may be seen as what has innate power to effect itself (Zech 5:1–3). When the Bible makes reference to "curse" it is supposed to be possessed of the power of self-realization (Num 22–24). On many occasions, it was related to sin (Gen 3) and disobedience (Deut 11:28; Isa 24:3–6). Sometimes, it is related to an oath (Judg 17:2; Isa 65:15). In a New Testament context, "curses" are christologically presented (Gal 3:13). These show that biblical definitions of curses are not to be discussed in isolation from biblical contexts: both textual contexts and historical contexts. Thus, the New Testament definition of curses is inextricably linked to the christological context unique to New Testament theology. In sum, what we can deduce from biblical definitions of curses is the fact that when cursing expressions are made, they do not necessarily have sacred associations; they are more related to breaking a covenant of the Lord and contravening a social standard.[11] References to divine curses and satanic connections to curses are rare in the New Testament and when used, they have Christological or soteriological associations. These deductions should have a bearing on any

---

9. Hermann Gunkel, *Psalm: A Form-Critical Introduction*, Biblical Series 9 (Philadelphia: Fortress, 1967), 20.

10. C. Blaising, "Curse" in Elwell, ed., *Evangelical Dictionary of Theology*, 313–14.

11. A good example of curses related to a covenant are the curses pronounced on Mount Ebal (Deut 27:13–26), contrasted with the blessing pronounced on Mount Gerizim.

discussion of curses. Later we see how Africans traditionally define curses and compare those definitions with the biblical definitions highlighted here.

Biblical Theology of Curse

The ongoing discussion shows that the depiction of curses in the Old Testament and New Testament is different and that each has unique purposes and presentations. It is, therefore, good to briefly examine the concept of curses in each of the testaments to show their uniqueness and the implications of such uniqueness to contemporary Africa. This side-by-side presentation of curses in the Old Testament and New Testament will help us to later make a clear theological judgment on the African theology of curses.

The Old Testament notion of curse

The belief in the power of curses held by the people in the Old Testament is related to the Hebrew belief that spoken words are potent and powerful. Spoken words were seen as active agents who have the capacity to endanger recipients. But more than this, curses are used in the Old Testament to reveal the theme that some of God's promises are conditional and the Deuteronomic theology of retribution.[12] The theology of curses in the Old Testament shows that obedience to God's precepts will result in blessing, but that disobedience will result in sickness, pain, loss, disasters, and death. The Israelites sometimes used the term "curse" as closely similar to the term "blasphemy" (see 1 Kgs 21:10, 13; Job 1:5; 2:5, 9). To some extent, the Israelites may have originated their concept of curses from their nomadic context in which curses were used for self-acting social expulsion of those who did what was forbidden in communal life (Gen 4:9–16).

Scholar J. Scharbert did a semantic analysis of the term "curse" in the Old Testament.[13] He scrutinized the Semitic roots surrounding Old Testament words that are usually translated "curse" and discovered that the Hebrews had different terms that are meant to convey the ideas of conditional and unconditional curses in the Old Testament. This discovery brings the

---

12. Raymond B. Dillard and T. Longman III, *An Introduction to the Old Testament* (Grand Rapids: Zondervan, 1994), 105.

13. J. Scharbert, "'Fluchen' und 'Segnen' im Alten Testament," *Biblical* 39 (1958): 1–29; see also H. C. Brichto, "The Problem of Curse in the Hebrew Bible," *Journal of Biblical Literature Monograph Series* 13 (Philadelphia: SBL, 1963), 70.

importance of context into our understanding of Old Testament curses. They must be understood in their particular context and in the larger context of the Bible. Understanding the contexts of the Old Testament curses will inform our understanding of their varied purposes. A curse may be pronounced by God to enforce obedience like in Deuteronomy 27–29. Some curses express discouragement (Job 2:9), and some serve political or theological aims (Jer 24:9). Some curses are ethnically oriented (Josh 9:22–23), and some are changed to blessings due to God's intervention (Num 23). Some are insults on a leader (2 Sam 16:5–14), and some are sent like a flying scroll looking for erring victims in the community (Zech 5:1–4). Some curses are spoken by individuals on themselves (Job 3:1–10), and some use figures of speech (Gen 3:14–20). The curses in Genesis 3:14–20 use figures of speech. For example, one of the punishments pronounced on the serpent and Eve is that their offspring will live in enmity and eventually Eve's offspring will crush the serpent's head. But the serpent will also strike the heel of Eve's offspring. The use of "offspring" here is figurative and transliteral. Also, the punishment on Adam in sweating before eating is far more than literal. This particular scenario is important because the negative pronouncements here go beyond the disobeying parties. It also extends to their offspring. This has become a major text used for preaching on generational curses in Africa. We will do an exposition study on this text later in this chapter.

There are several categories of curses in the Old Testament. For example, curses can be spoken, written, personal, collective, or conditionally binding like the covenant curses in Deuteronomy 27–29. In the Semitic context, a curse was understood in relation to the power of the word in a similar way to the Old Testament conceptualization of curses.[14]

Unlike the contemporary understanding of curses, cursing in the Old Testament world was not just a pronouncement and invocation of negative words. Rather curses were usually used to pronounce the judgment that would result from disobeying God. However the incidences in Genesis 3:13–18 and Proverbs 3:33 show that the divine curses pronounced in the Old Testament were more than pronouncements of devastating judgment; they also involved the stipulations related to the holiness of God and the punishment of sins.[15] We can see that the majority of curses in the Old Testament are conditional,

---

14. George A. Buttrick, ed., *The Interpreter's Dictionary of the Bible: An Illustrated Encyclopedia*, vol. 1 (Nashville: Abingdon, 1983), 750. See also Cyrus Gordon, *Ugaritic Literature* (Rome: Pontificium Institutum Bistirum, 1949), 84.

15. Don Fleming, *Bridgeway Bible Dictionary* (Brisbane, Australia: Bridgeway, 2009), 83.

meaning they only came into effective when certain divine prohibitions or stipulations are violated. What does this information imply? It implies that Old Testament curses are to be studied and understood in relation to God's holiness, faithfulness, and covenantal relationship with the people of Israel. Therefore, curses are not just wicked pronouncements from God but punishments which only come to pass when there is intentional contravention of God's orders. Is this Old Testament notion equal to the New Testament notion of curses? What are the differences between Old Testament and New Testament notions of curses? The next section brings us to these questions.

The New Testament notion of curse

With a few commonalities, the understanding of curses in the New Testament is generally different than that of the Old Testament. Like many other New Testament concepts, the concept of curses is presented in special relationship to the atoning death of Christ, which is especially seen in Pauline arguments. Under the central word "curse" are included all the terms which carry the sense of verbal, as opposed to physical, hurt and cursing as a contrast to blessing. Paul discusses curses in relation to the law and blessings which come from the redemptive work of Christ (Gal 3:10–13). Aust and Muller contend that the expression of cursing in New Testament theology is similar to the meaning of the Greek words *kakologeo* (evil slander and deliberate disparagement), *blasphemeo* (abuse), and *katalaleo* (invective).[16] However, the Greek word used for the term "curse" in the New Testament is *kataraomai* which is a verbal adjective and related to the term *anathematizo*.[17] The words *katara* and *ana katathematizo* mean curse, enchant, or bewitch which is accompanied by a corresponding gesture.[18] The Greek word *anathema* is related to what is banned and separated either for destruction or for punishment. People who take what is under anathema are themselves placed under anathema. This sense is borrowed from the Old Testament, and its use in Luke 21:5 reflects this old connotation. The New Testament books present curses as judicial actions of God or the consequences of human sin against God, not necessarily against fellow human beings. For example, the emphasis on curses in Galatians 3:10–13; Hebrews 6:8;

---

16. H. Aust and D. Muller, "Curse, Insult, Fool," in the *New International Dictionary of New Testament Theology*, ed. Colin Brown, vol. 1 (Grand Rapids: Zondervan, 1975), 413–15.

17. Gerhard Kittel, ed., *Theological Dictionary of the New Testament* (Grand Rapids: Eerdmans, 1972), 448.

18. Aust and Muller, "Curse, Insult, Fool," 414.

and 2 Peter 2:14 lays more on the consequences of sin against God. The curses of God in the New Testament pronounced through those he has authorized such as the prophets and apostles are designed to reveal the divine judgment that is already initiated by the disobedience of human beings, especially when they deny the work of the Holy Spirit or reject the gospel.[19]

In addition, in the New Testament, Jesus discouraged his followers from cursing. He did not authorize them to curse as an act of revenge but to bring good news to people (Matt 12:36; 15:10–11; Luke 6:45). As will be seen from the exposition of Galatians 3 below, the notion of curse – *anathema* in the New Testament – is related to the concept of law and the substitutionary atonement of Christ, which shows that curses in the New Testament have specific Christological and soteriological references.[20] Jesus himself is said to have become a curse on the cross so as to redeem the world to God. He became a curse to remove the curse of the law (Gal 3:10–13).[21] Even when Paul used the word *anathema* to describe those who blaspheme under demonic ecstasy, who partake in the holy communion unworthily, and who preach false gospels, the theological expression is not a disciplinary order of some human court to prosecute the offending people; rather it deals with handling those who are connected to God.[22] What is central to New Testament understanding of curses is the individualized relationship with God and the redemptive work of Christ. Now that we have seen some differences between Old Testament and New Testament curses, one question that we must raise is among the Old Testament and New Testament, which influences African Christian understanding of curses more? Is the African Christian conception of and response to curses tending toward the Old Testament or tending more toward the New Testament? We answer these questions in later chapters with full attention.

In sum, the concept of curses is related to the themes of salvation and sin in the New Testament more than it is in the Old Testament. Before we look at the main biblical cursing texts, let us examine the theology of curses in the world of the Bible.

---

19. Kittel, ed., *Theological Dictionary of the New Testament*, 449.
20. C. L. Feinberg, "Curses," in Elwell, ed., *Evangelical Dictionary of Theology*, 314.
21. Donald Guthrie, *New Testament Introduction* (London: Tyndale, 1970), 469.
22. Aust and Muller, "Curse, Insult, Fool," 413–15.

Curses in Biblical Social and Cultural Contexts

Although curses functioned in ancient times in ways that are different from our own,[23] some commonalities and features in the ancient understandings of curses can help us adequately understand the biblical concept of curses. As seen from ancient texts and sources such as the Mari text, Tell Harmal, Terqa, and others, curses were believed by ancient civilizations to be very powerful. The ancients were very familiar with the concept of curses and blessings. In fact, the concept of curses has been common in the important periods of religious history. While most of the theological concepts in ancient Israelite contexts originated from the revelation God gave them, the ancient Israelites may have understood those theological concepts in relation to their knowledge of familiar contextual themes. Therefore, their interpretation of "divine reality" is not totally void of their understanding of concepts from contemporary societies. Curses are found in Ugaritic mythology and Akkadian and Semitic contexts as seeking divine approval through imprecation.[24] In the judicial systems of ancient people, curses played important roles in the execution and enforcement of laws. Curses were also used sometimes to concretize oaths and vows. In these contexts, curses were closely related to vows and oaths. It is good for us to discuss one of these contexts so that the biblical exegesis that follows will be easy to flow.

Curses in the ancient Near East

In ancient Near Eastern (ANE) societies, beliefs in and the reality of curses were expressed in every aspect of life. For example, in Mesopotamia, Akkadian areas, and Israel, many people from young to old, males and females, kings and slaves knew and feared the power of curses. Understanding the concept of curses in the ANE will help us understand (1) both similarities and differences between the ancient concept of curses and that in in our own time; (2) the evolution and development of curses across different cultures and civilizations; and (3) the proper historical and cultural contexts of Old Testament curses.

The Akkadian term for curses is *mamitu*, or *ararum* which means imprecation, malediction, and imposition of evil and its operations which are contagious, transferrable, and predatory and can destroy a person, place,

---

23. Anne M. Kitz, *Are You Cursed?: The Phenomenology of Cursing in Cuneiform and Hebrew Texts* (Pretoria, SA: University of Pretoria, 2013), 43.
24. Kittel, ed., *Theological Dictionary of the New Testament*, 449.

or object.[25] This term is also related to the Sumerian word *namerim* and the Aramaic term *momata* which can both be translated "curse" or "oath."[26] These terms imply the oral character of curses in the understanding of ancient people. They understood curses as oral expressions of prayer or invocations for harm or injury to come upon someone. There was a special relationship between curses, words, and actions in the ancient Near East. Sometimes curses were not restricted to oral expressions, they also involved acts like cutting an animal into pieces, or the act of invoking some gods and goddesses. This understanding is partly the context for the Yahweh-Abram covenant in Genesis 15:7–21.

In the ANE, curses expressed the desire of the speaker. They were wishes and future-oriented, or harmful statements to affect the future. Grammatically, the tense of verbs used in cursing was modal future, and the mode used was optative, while the voice could be active or passive. For example some curses from a treaty with the Assyrian King Esarhaddon read, "May you be smashed by the gods"[27] and "May Girra, who gives food to small and great, burn up your name and your seed."[28] These examples of curses from the ANE context show that curses were usually pronounced in future tenses, which is similar to a curse in Nehemiah 5:13: "I also shook out the folds of my robe and said, 'In this way may God shake out of their house and possessions anyone who does not keep this promise. So may such a person be shaken out and emptied!'"

In Sumerian, Akkadian, Hebrew, and Hittite texts are two distinct types of curses which can illuminate our understanding of biblical curses: conditional and unconditional curses.[29] Conditional curses deal with specific actions that if performed would be considered sin and provoke divine wrath, while unconditional curses deal with current events without qualifications or conditions. According to Pedersen, conditional curses are hypothetical curses, threats, defenses, and latent violence, while unconditional curses are active

---

25. S. A. Mercer, *The Oath in Babylonian and Assyrian Literature* (Paris: Geuthener, 1912), 38.

26. E. Reiner, *Surpu: A Collection of Sumerian and Akkadian Incantations* (Osnabruck: Biblio Verlag, 1970), 4.

27. M. J. Geller, *Forerunners to Udug-Ḫul: Sumerian Exorcistic Incantations*, Freiburger altorientalische Studien 12 (Stuttgart: Steiner, 1985), 172. See also A. R. George, "Forerunnners to Udug-Hul: Sumerian Exorcistic Incantations," DM 56, *Journal of the Royal Asiatic Society of Great Britain & Ireland* 118, no. 2 (1986): 260–63.

28. S. Parpola and K. Watanabe, *Neo-Assyrian Treaties and Loyalty Oaths* (Helsinki: Helsinki University Press, 1988), 23.

29. Kitz, *Are You Cursed*, 93.

condemnations and maledictions.[30] In these ANE contexts, curses could be spoken or written, but they were usually accompanied with actions that were believed to strengthen the curses. In all, death, sickness, and pain were believed to be end results of curses.

In the ANE, curses were sometimes inscribed on the lintels of houses and tombs, on tomb stele, and on sarcophagi. Curse pronouncements were used in political documents, treaties, international relations and bonds, business agreements, sale contracts, inheritance texts, hymns extolling deities, and marital covenants. The ancients saw curses and blessings as one of the multiple dimensions of their spiritual and social life. In the ANE, curses were seen as petitions to the divine world to render judgments and execute harm on identified hostile forces. Curses then were seen as part of the involvement of divine beings in the affairs of human beings related to social justice and retribution.

Curses were used to manage situations.[31] Proactively curses were used to protect because cursing one's enemies was considered to be equal to blessing oneself. Reactively curses were used to respond to curses. The prayers, epics, rituals, and texts of the ancients show us their expectations regarding the effectiveness of curses. Both humans and gods made curses. The curses made by the gods were believed to be very powerful because these deities were believed to have full power to execute their curses. In fact, the curses by the deities were seen as decrees and orders.

In the ANE, the use of curses was not just a game for the amateurs but also a recognized professional practice. For example in the cults of Akkadian societies, professional cursers were consulted to help curse enemies, foreign nations, and foreign rulers.[32] These professional cursers lived in the cult centers where they could use cult singers singing temple hymns to stimulate their cursing practices. These professionals were hired and paid and were cultic functionaries associated with the deities. Professional cursers used special locations to make curses including temples, springs or rivers, wilderness areas, or shrines because they believed that these locations would add special strength to the curses. The most fearful group of professional cursers were

---

30. Johannes Pedersen, *Israel: its Life and Culture* (London: Oxford University Press, 1973), viii.

31. Kitz, 93.

32. Mercer, *Oath in Babylonian*, 34.

called *kassapu*. They were hidden, difficult to know, and elusive, but their curses were feared more than any other curses.[33]

In addition to these professionals were curse healing specialists who exorcised curses from the bodies of the cursed. These specialists were referred to as *asipu*, and they earned their living from the practice of removing curses. They used curses to remove curses through a ritual practice known as *surpu*.[34] In addition, these specialists were supported by a group referred to as *asu* who were like medical doctors. The *asu* used magic and medicine to heal people who suffered from curses. Understanding this context of cursing specialists helps us better understand the curses associated with some prophets, priests, and poets in the Bible who pronounced curses in the name of Yahweh.

Curses were strongly feared, especially the curses seen as manifestations of divine judicial power to which no one is immune. The ancients believed that demons known as executioner deities were assigned to bring curses to effect. They employed methods and strategies to remove these curses including hiring curse-cure professionals who used curses to counter curses or who prescribed certain ritual washing to remove curses.[35] Due to their expert skill in removing curses, these people became significant in society. Can we relate these professionals to some deliverance ministers and prophets in Africa who have become significant because of their ministry of curing curses-related misfortunes? Sometimes to have an adequate understanding of present phenomenon, the historical past may have to be studied, which is illustrated by the similarities between curse-curing professionals in the ANE and curse deliverance ministers in the present African church. We come back to this topic in later chapters.

In the ANE literature, West Semitic and East Semitic curses are different based on different formulations in the Akkadian and Hebrew languages. In Akkadian, curses appeal to God or a divine being directly, while in the Hebrew context, curses not only appeal to God but are also social and personal pronouncements. People can even curse themselves in the Hebrew context. On extreme occasions, some can attempt to curse God. An example is the advice of Job's wife, but such an act would lead to death as we can see from her admonition (Job 2:9). Old Testament scholars referred to this type as "self-cursing," which is often represented in the ANE treaties. For example Korošec and Mendehall both examined the concept of curses in the common Hittite

---

33. Kitz, *Are You Cursed*, 93.
34. Mercer, *Oath in Babylonian*, 34.
35. Kitz, *Are You Cursed*, 93.

vassal treaty formula: preamble, historical prologue, stipulations, provision for public recitation, presence of divine witnesses, and a concluding register of blessings and curses, expressions of rewards for obedience and punishment for disobedience. In particular the divine witnesses and the register of blessings and curses showcase the divine nature of an ANE treaty, which provides adequate justification for punishment of treaty defaulters.[36] Examples of such treaty curses can be found in the treaty of the Assyrian King Ashur-nirari V (754–745 BC) with the king of Arpad, Mati-illu, and the vassal treaty of King Esarhaddon (680–669 BC).[37]

Some ancient curses involved using an animal part or blood to reinforce the process of cursing. For example, the ancients included the concepts of "eat the curse" and "cut the curse" as features in some sophisticated curses.[38] In the process of making these sophisticated curses, especially treaty or covenant curses, an animal was cut into pieces, and a meal was made from the animal. This animal was referred to as the curse, and so when the animal was cut up in the process of establishing a treaty curse, the curse was said to have been cut. So when the parties and witnesses of the treaty curses are made to eat the animal meal, it was referred to as "eating the curse." This practice of cutting up an animal helps clarify our understanding of 1 Samuel 11:6–7:

> When Saul heard their words, the Spirit of God came powerfully upon him, and he burned with anger. He took a pair of oxen, cut them into pieces, and sent the pieces by messengers throughout Israel, proclaiming, "This is what will be done to the oxen of anyone who does not follow Saul and Samuel." Then the terror of the LORD fell on the people, and they came out together as one.

This ANE practice also informs the background of some other biblical curses and sacrifices. For example, Jesus became a curse for us in the process of making the new covenant. The lamb of God carried sins and became a curse for us (John 1:29).

In ancient cultures, people believed that gods could curse a human being and that a god could curse another god. For example, in a Sumerian myth

---

36. G. Mendenhall, "Covenant Forms in Israelite Tradition," *BA* 17 (1954): 50–76; Viktor Korošec, *Hethitische Staatsverträge: Ein Beitrag zu ihrer juristischen Wertung* (Leipziger rechtswissenschaftliche Studien 60; Leipzig: Weicher, 1931), 118.

37. Parpola and Watanabe, *Neo-Assyrian Treaties*, 30.

38. I. J. Gelb, P. Steinkeller, and R. M. Whiting, Jr., *Earliest Land Tenure Systems in the Near East*, vol 2, *Ancient Kudurrus* (Chicago: Oriental Institute of the University of Chicago, 1989), 2.

of Enki and Ninhursaga, the god Enki is cursed by an offended goddess for eating her plant. The Babylonian Code of Hammurabi also records a situation in which the god Enil is invoked to curse a man. More than any other types of curses, the curses from gods and goddesses were the most feared. Anne Kitz notes that the fear and power of divine curses put the ANE people on guard and made them extraordinarily aware of their environment. They were ever watchful for any change, any transformation in their surroundings that could indicate that the effects of divine curses may have been invading their homes, cities, lands, properties, and children.[39]

Not only did the people of ANE believe that gods and goddesses could curse, they also believed that mortal humans could also curse. They believed the only difference was the fact that curses pronounced by mortals had to be approved by the gods before they would come to pass effectively. For example in the Babylonian Gilgamesh epic, Enkidu appeals to the god Samas to approve his curse so that it can be effective, for without the approval of Samas, the curse would be void.[40] It is in the light of this context that some biblical curses such as Balak's curses for which he was hired to put on Israel, Goliath's curses on David, and Shimei's curses on David must be understood (see Num 23; 1 Sam 17:42–44; 2 Sam 16:5–12).

There is however, a great caution related to the act of cursing deities. A tablet recovered from the library of the Assyrian King Assurbanipal relates a situation in which a person can only curse an attribute of a deity but must not curse the deity directly. Such an act is prohibited in the handbook of the Asipu professional ritual experts, according to which people would lose their sight if they curse deities. This prohibition against cursing God is replete in the Bible. In Leviticus 24:10–16, cursing God is greatly disallowed. The admonition of Job's wife that he curse God and die shows how severe was the punishment for cursing God (Job 2:9). In ANE thinking there is a close relationship between the deities and curses. The Akkadians even believed that some curses were deified, becoming gods so as to strengthen their effectiveness. This belief could have been held by the original audience of Deuteronomy 28: that these curses on their own could run and overtake the offenders of Yahweh's laws.

What was the purpose of curses in the ANE context? Painful, premature, and sudden death was the main end of these curses. This end may have been achieved through many events such as sickness; making the land infertile for productive farming and an easy life (see Gen 3:17); banishment due to skin

---

39. Kitz, *Are You Cursed*, 152.
40. Kitz, 154.

infections like in the Akkadian curses of *saharsubbu* or Miriam sister of Moses (Num 12:10–15); destruction of livestock and other means of livelihood; or removal of one's name and destruction of one's seed (see Ps 109). Both in Hebrew and Akkadian contexts, curses can lead to banishment into places called "the wilderness" where the accursed is sent.

In his work, Fensham argues that the universal nature of ancient vassal treaties foreground the commonalities in the curses made in the contexts in which the Old Testament was written.[41] However, there are significant differences between ANE curses and biblical curses. The major difference that is noteworthy for our observation is the fact that curses in the Bible are more often the conditional type, more often related to covenants, and more often use the punishment approach – or the curses that come to pass only if the "accursed" offends the stipulations of a covenant and the laws of God. Also, to God alone are appeals to bring curses to pass. Contrarily, curses in ancient Mesopotamia and Babylon were more magical and ritualistic and used ritual pronouncements. In Assyria, the curses, oaths, magic, and acts were intrinsically interwoven, but in the biblical literature, curses and oaths are understood in the light of the covenants and the laws of Yahweh and his revelation to the people of Israel.

Curses and covenant in the Bible

Many instances of curses in the Bible clearly show that these curses are closely related to covenants and vows. Curses play a vital role in covenantal relationships, especially in the Old Testament where to disobey the stipulations of a covenant is to merit certain consequences which are curses. For instance, when God made the covenant with Abraham described in Genesis 15, the cutting of animals represented a conditional curse that indicated what would happen to Abraham if he broke the stipulations of the covenant.

In addition, curses are used in relation to faithfulness to marital covenants, which is seen in Numbers 5:11–31. If a man suspected that his wife was involved in adultery, the wife was made to drink water with a portion of dust and written curses mixed in. Then if the woman was truly guilty of the suspicion, she became accursed.

---

41. F. Charles Fensham, "Common Trends in Curses of the Near Eastern Treaties and *Kudurru*-Inscriptions Compared with Maledictions of Amos and Isaiah," *ZAW* 75 (1963): 155–75.

From these examples, we can see that biblical curses represent a shattered relationship with God and the community and a shattered relationship between human beings. In fact, some scholars such as Brian Britt referred to these as *karet* curses – the curses that emanate from the breaking of a covenant in the Bible.[42] J. L. Aitken also identifies certain types of curses in the Old Testament that can be referred to as "covenant-agreement" curses that are activated in breaking a covenant.[43] The curses in the Bible, especially Old Testament curses, are not just mechanical pronouncements of woes but are made to show the formula for relationship between Yahweh and the people that he loves and chose.

Curses in Greco-Roman context

In the context of Greco-Roman socioreligious culture, curses were connected to a variety of speech-acts, many of which were malicious and involved using rituals and invoking supernatural powers. As in the ANE context, curses were not just pronouncements; they also involved magic, cult, and ritual. The Greek terms for "curse" are *agos*, *ara*, and *euche*, while the Latin terms include *devotio*, *dira*, *exsercratio* and *imprecatio*.

The large numbers of Greco-Roman documents including cursing tablets and papyri show that the fear of curses was very strong in these societies, as do the cursing sanctuaries and recorded rites through which curses were made or reversed. In the Greco-Roman context, curses were both emotive and emotional because curses were pronounced out of emotional feelings such as hatred, jealousy, anger, bitterness, or sorrow. When the curses were pronounced, they also caused certain emotions.

Similar to ANE curses, references were made to certain gods who were invoked to energize the fulfillment of the curses. A sampling of a few curses from three shrines can give us a good understanding of this type: from Demeter in Corinth (AD 1–2), "I bind down Secunda Postumia before Herakleides and before all men, her mind, her wits, her hands, her sinews, her knees"; from Isis and Magna Mater in Mainz (AD 1–2), "(Whatever) Aemilia Prima, (the lover?) of Narcissus may do, whatever she attempts, whatever she does, let it all turn into its opposite"; and from Kore in Corinth (AD 1–2), "I bind Protophanes (?) down – him and his hands and feet and tongue and mind before Hermes

---

42. Britt, "Curses in the Hebrew Bible."
43. J. L. Aitken, *The Semantics of Blessings and Curses in Ancient Hebrew*, Ancient Near Eastern Studies 23 (Leuven: Peters, 2007), 63.

Eriounios."[44] In these quotations, we can see that these curses emerged from certain emotions and that often gods and goddesses were invoked to energize the curses, such as calling on Hermes and Herakleides. Another thing we can see from these curses is the use of fearful, dangerous, and strongly malicious words. Curses can be frightening! When such dangerous words like these were pronounced, they were believed to become part of malevolent magic.

Also as in the ANE, the Greeks had strong beliefs in the effectiveness of wearing apotropaic amulets and written phylacteries to protect themselves against curses.[45] The popularity of cursing tablets (*katadmus*) and Greek magical papyri indicate that the practice of cursing was pervasive in Greco-Roman contexts. People in these cultures also had a notion of binding spells that could bind a victim as a punishment for certain disobedience.

Structurally, some Greco-Roman curses follow certain forms which include invoking gods, dedicating the victims to gods, and inscribing the curses on tablets. In addition, some people became syncretistic by including necromancy in the cursing processes. Usually a small, dark room, ritual experts performed cursing rituals at night. This cursing room had smoky incense and lamps, and to empower the cursing process, chanting spells and things the curser would lick were used.[46] Humans have used religious means for personal interest since time immemorial.

Unlike in the ANE, curses served more public and civic roles in Greco-Roman societies. Some curses were used to strengthen justice, enhance civic stability, and maintain public order. The violators of social order were turned over to the gods. These uses are similar to how curses are used in some African cities to enforce laws and social order. For example, while I was doing research for my masters in the University of Ibadan, Nigeria, I lived in Ibadan for two years. Ibadan is the largest city in West Africa. Like in many other cities in Africa, I discovered that to motivate people to obey some public orders such as "Do not dump refuse here," some cursing elements are often introduced. For example, curses such as "You will lose all your children and all your fortune if you urinate here" are very common in major streets of the city. The amazing part is that in some places where such cursing words were not added, people

---

44. Irene Salvo, "Experiencing Curses: Neurobehavioral Traits of Ritual in Spatiality in Roman Empire," *De Gruyter* (2020): 161–67.

45. J. G. Gager, *Curse Tablets and Binding Spells from the Ancient World* (Oxford: Oxford University Press, 1992), 83.

46. Gager, *Curse Tablets*, 93.

seem to easily disobey the public order, but they strictly complied in places where dangerous cursing words were used.

There are types and categories of curses in Greco-Roman contexts including conditional and unconditional. Conditional curses involve the condition which would cause curses to come to pass.[47] Conditional curses were used to enforce oaths, promote civic order, and protect the oaths and allegiance of those in office. They were also used in protecting properties. Conditional curses were more pronounced and popular than unconditional curses in the Greco-Roman world, which supports the argument that in almost every culture, curses are mostly conditional. Unconditional curses are few because most are usually expressions of human wickedness.

In Greco-Roman societies in which the prevailing trend was downward to indulgence and lawlessness which resulted in corruption in politics, debauchery in pleasure, fraud in business, and deceit and superstition in religion, which happen in Rome, life was depressing for many and unendurable for the few.[48] Thus the uses of curses, vows, and spells as social control mechanisms can be well and easily understood. This was the dominant culture at the time of the New Testament.

The concept of inherited curses was not uncommon in Greco-Roman culture. People believed that curses could be inherited, especially curses pronounced by the gods or that were divinely incurred.[49] The Greece notion that the *miasma* (pollution) on cursed people could be spread to their family and community. It was in this context that the people who were involved in the crucifixion of Jesus said, "His blood is on us and on our children!" (Matt 27:25).

From these details on the concepts of curses in the ANE and Greco-Roman contexts, we can see that the notions of curses and fear of them among the ancients was similar to the notions and fears of Africans. We can also see many similar themes related to curses in the Bible and in the ANE and Greco-Roman contexts. However, we also see a wide margin of differences between the curses in the Bible and those in ancient milieus. For example, curses in the Bible are more conditional than unconditional, and they are closely related to covenant and the punishment of breaking a covenant. Biblical curses are not wicked, blind curses. Rather they were pronounced by God as expressions of his faithfulness to his covenants and his readiness to punish anyone who breaks

---

47. Gager, 102.
48. Merrill C. Tenney, *New Testament Survey* (Grand Rapids: Eerdmans, 1961), 59.
49. Esther Eidinow, "Curses, Greece and Rome," in *The Encyclopedia of Ancient History*, ed. R. S. Bagnall, et. al. (Oxford: Wiley-Blackwell, 2012).

a covenant with him. The clear differences between ANE and Greco-Roman curses and those of the Bible are evidence of the inspiration of the Scripture. While biblical concepts are to be studied in their historical contexts, it does not necessarily follow those biblical concepts emanated from context absolutely. They are inspired concepts!

Theological Themes in Biblical Curses

Studying biblical concepts in their historical contexts sheds light on the larger world of the Bible. In this case, we can only adequately exegete biblical curses if we place them in their historio-cultural contexts, as we have done in the section above. But before we exegete selected curse texts in the Bible, a few comments are needed on the theological themes in biblical curses to provide theological justification for the presence of curses in the inspired Bible. For critics may want to argue that curses should not be found in the Scripture.

No causeless curses in the Bible

As Britt points out, "biblical curses sometimes fail to work (1 Sam 14; Judg 19–21)."[50] For example, Balaam could not curse the people of Israel because God did not allow it, even though Balak wanted the curses to be pronounced (see Num 22–23). Basically, the biblical curses resulted from disobedience to God's statutes. In many instances God placed curses for disobedience in one form or the other, for example on the snake (Gen 3:14–15) and the ground in Eden (Gen 5:29; 3:17), on property (Mal 4:6; 2:2), and on communities or houses (Prov 22:14). For instance, Deuteronomy 27 lists human behaviors that can warrant divine curses. These include idolatry, dishonoring parents, injustice, incest, homosexuality, bribery, perjury, and others. But these curses do not operate unconditionally. God is sovereign, and it is human responses to God that determine whether they will be cursed or blessed. Cursing words that we see in the Bible are, therefore, not expressions of carnality but of the holiness of God. And unless people have sufficiently done what warrants the curses, they do not become victims.

---

50. Brian M. Britt, "Curses in the Hebrew Bible," Bible Odyssey (16 August 2022).

Authority to pronounce curses

The biblical curses have certain restrictions. One such restriction concerns the personality of the person who can pronounce curses. In the Bible, the authority to make curses valid rests with God alone. Applying the speech-act theory of Austine and Searle to biblical curses, Anthony Thiselton shows that the major peculiarity of biblical curses lies in the fact that only priests and other authorized individuals had the authority to curse in "God's name because the power to effect this sort of outcome only comes from God."[51] Placed in the context of speech-act theory, biblical curses are only executed by Yahweh. The other orally declared curses are solicitations of a deity in which the name of Yahweh is not mentioned nor an appeal made to him and are only self-fulfilling curses.[52] However, individuals utter cursing words on themselves to prove their truthfulness (see Num 5:19–22; Job 31:7–10, 16–22; Ps 137:5–6). However, the Torah clearly prohibits using the name of God in pronouncing curses (Exod 20:7). Apart from this prohibition, the Bible forbids cursing one's parents (Exod 21:17; Prov 20:20; Matt 15:4); cursing the deaf (Lev 19:14); and cursing God (Lev 24:10–16; Job 2:9; Isa 8:21–22). The use of curses is strictly restricted among the people with whom God has made a covenant.

These prohibitions indicate that cursing is a cultic matter and not just a personal issue in the Bible. One of the clearest formulas for curses and cursing in the Bible is in Deuteronomy 27:15–26 which shows that the right and power to curse reside with God.[53] The divine curses recorded in the Bible – like those that God pronounced on Adam, Eve, the serpent, Cain, and those who would curse Abraham and his descents, as well as those who would put their trust in humans – are to denunciate sin and to pronounce his judgment as a result of disobedience.[54] In fact, while the curses and blessings related in Deuteronomy 27–28 are materialistic, a thorough study of the text shows that the "focus is not the mechanistic application of rewards and blessings; rather it is a blessing to be in a relationship with God while otherwise is a curse."[55] Many African preachers have used Deuteronomy 27–28 out of its literary, theological, and

---

51. A. C. Thiselton, "The Supposed Power of Words in the Biblical Writings," *JTS* 25 (1974), 284.

52. Kitz, *Are You Cursed*, 25.

53. Watson E. Mills, ed., *Mercer Dictionary of the Bible* (Macon: Mercer University Press, 1990), 188.

54. J. A. Motyer, "Curse," in *New Bible Dictionary*, ed. I. Howard Marshall, et. al., 3rd ed. (Downers Grove: InterVarsity Press, 1996), 248–49.

55. Hachalinga, "How Curses Impact People," 58.

historical context. We will engage in a detailed exposition of these texts in a short while.

Not only is the authority to pronounce curses restricted, who and what can be cursed is restricted. For example it is a great sin to curse a deaf person (Lev 19:14); anyone who curses God will die (Lev 24:10–16); rulers are not to be cursed (Exod 22:28); and no children should curse their parents (Exod 21:17).

Biblical curses as the opposite of blessings

There is a very close relationship between curses and blessings in the Bible, which maintains clear distinctions between the two opposites and contraries. Biblical curses and blessings are forms of distinction between what is beneficent and what is maleficent.[56] In fact, the Bible reveals that one's blessings can be cursed, which shows that blessings and curses are opposites, and to have one is not to have the other. If people are blessed by God, they cannot be cursed at the same time. For example, Yahweh told the priests who abused his name that he had cursed their blessings:

> "And now, you priests, this warning is for you. If you do not listen, and if you do not resolve to honor my name," says the LORD Almighty, "I will send a curse on you, and I will curse your blessings. Yes, I have already cursed them, because you have not resolved to honor me." (Mal 2:1–2)

The relationship between biblical curses and blessings is expressly seen in Israel's exodus story. From many of the plagues that Yahweh used to attack Pharaoh and the Egyptians, the children of Israel were clearly spared. The Lord separated the Israelites from the Egyptians as Exodus 9:4 makes it clear: "But the LORD will make a distinction between the livestock of Israel and that of Egypt, so that no animal belonging to the Israelites will die." The same words and phrase are used in Exodus 8:23 and 11:7 to indicate that the Israelites would not be affected by the divine maledictions on the Egyptians, which shows that the malediction was counteracted by the benedictions. Curses and blessings can thus be seen as boundaries between where there is the love of God and where there is the wrath of God. When people are not cursed, they enjoy blessings, but when they are cursed, they do not have blessings. The distinction between the Israelites and Egyptians is a distinction between blessings and curses. The same trend is seen in the Balak and Balaam narratives in Numbers 22–24.

---

56. Kitz, *Are You Cursed*.

The Moabite king knew that for him to be blessed, the people of Israel had to be cursed. So when his hired professional curser, Balaam, could not curse the people of Israel but had to bless them instead, Balak knew that the blessing of Israel was equal to the cursing of Moab.

The Israelites' reading both curses and blessings on Mounts Gerizim and Ebal shows the dual dynamic of curses in the context of the Old Testament. If the people of Israel obeyed, they would receive God's blessings; if they disobeyed, they would receive his curses. At the entrance to the land of Canaan, Moses set before the people both curses and blessings. The blessings would overtake the obedient while curses would overtake the disobedient (Deut 28:2, 15).

The Yahweh curses in the Bible

As commonly believed in the milieu of the Bible, a divine being could be involved in a cursing process, and Yahweh is sometimes seen in the Bible pronouncing curses. For example, Yahweh uses the phrase "I will curse" in Malachi 2:1–2 when confronting the lack of faithfulness of the priests who abused his name. He cursed the ground and the serpent (Gen 3:13). He cursed Cain (Gen 4:9–12) and the land (Isa 24:6). Deuteronomy 28 gives a catalog of dangerous pronouncements by Yahweh, and through the prophet Jeremiah he cursed those who trust in mortals (Jer 17:5–6). More profound examples are in the Scriptures. But what were the main goals and objectives of these Yahweh curses, and what implications do they have for us as contemporary Christians? How do we interpret and understand these Yahweh curses? How can Yahweh, from whom all the blessings proceed, utter curses?

First, the Yahweh curses should be understood in the social and cultural milieu of the Bible, especially the Old Testament context, part of which we highlighted above. Second, the Yahweh curses are to be understood in light of the nature of curses. And third, the curses are to be understood in the larger context of the Bible. Starting from the cultural milieu of the Bible lands, cuneiform and Hebrew texts show that deities were believed to utter curses when their followers disobeyed certain warnings and stipulations of suzerain and vassal treaties. The curses of Yahweh may have been understood by the people of Israel in the light of this context. When Yahweh pronounces curses, he does so to denounce sin (Num 5:23; Deut 29:19–20) or to judge sin (Deut 28:15), and people under the curse of Yahweh are referred to as "a curse" (Jer 29:18).[57] Yahweh curses falling on his people are not an abrogation of his

---

57. Motyer, 248.

blessed character but the implementation of his faithful covenant with his people.

Additionally, the nature and emphasis of Yahweh curses are unique and different from other curses in the Bible. Almost all of the curses traceable to him are conditional curses. They are not just a set of negative utterances coming from a callous mind. They are punishments stated as the results of a lack of faithfulness to a covenant and precepts of Yahweh. In many instances, Yahweh curses are given in response to a solicitation by a human being to execute punishment for injustice or human stubbornness. Instances like this can be found in Judges 9–10 and in the curse of Elisha on the abusive children (2 Kgs 2:23–24).

The background presented in this chapter is needed to create a proper context for us to adequately understand biblical curses. If we are going to examine the controversy and dilemmas involved in the belief in curses in the contemporary African church, we first have to understand the biblical stance on the subject matter. Now our attention is turned to studying a few selected Bible texts that are important to understanding the biblical theology of curses. Although we have discussed many biblical texts above, now we look at these texts more specifically so as to create a deep, complete theological understanding. You should be ready to unlearn and relearn in the following sections of exposition of these curse texts because the traditional interpretations of some are shaken.

Expository Engagement of Selected Texts

A Christian discussion on curses must be biblically grounded. There are many curses in the Bible that call for discussion, but here we focus on five selected curses that are central to our understanding of curses from biblical perspectives. For the purpose of our discussion, we will go through simple expository activities on the texts. For the benefit of non-technical readers, we carefully limit the technicality. However, to affirm the authorial intention and proper contexts of these texts, I use the historical-grammatical method. For simple interpretation and understanding, we follow Wayne McDill's seven steps of biblical interpretation: (1) identify the kind of literature the text is; (2) consider the context of the passage; (3) read the text to determine its plan and obvious meaning; (4) try to discern the writers' intention; (5) look carefully at the language of the text for what it reveals; (6) notice the theological themes in the text; and (7) interpret the text from a God-centered perspective.[58]

Biblical texts were not written in a vacuum. They were written for certain purposes: some to commend the audience, others to correct or instruct on certain teachings, and others as biography. It is therefore an exegetical fallacy to interpret any biblical text without considering the textual context in which it was written.[59] Three contexts need to be examined for proper understanding of any biblical text: the immediate context, the more remote context, and the context of the entire Bible.[60]

We start with Old Testament texts.

Did God curse Adam and Eve? Genesis 3:14–19

Let us first consider Genesis 3:14–19 which contains very strong cursing words:

> So the LORD God said to the serpent, "Because you have done this,
>
> Cursed are you above all livestock
> and all wild animals!
> You will crawl on your belly
> and you will eat dust
> all the days of your life.
> And I will put enmity
> between you and the woman,
> and between your offspring and hers;
> he will crush your head,
> and you will strike his heel."
>
> To the woman he said,
>
> "I will make your pains in childbearing very severe;
> with painful labor you will give birth to children.
> Your desire will be for your husband,
> and he will rule over you."

---

58. Wayne McDill, *12 Essential Skills for Great Preaching* (Nashville: B&H, 2018). See also 7 Principles of Biblical Interpretation – Lifeway Research (Accessed July 2021).

59. Godwin Adeboye, "The Relevance of Pauline Theology of *Charismata* and *Sumpheron* in 1 Corinthians 12:1–7 to Christian Ecumenism in Nigeria," *AJBT* 16, no. 18 (2015): 7.

60. Paul Enns, *The Moody Handbook of Theology* (Chicago: Moody, 1989), 176.

To Adam he said,

"Because you listened to your wife and ate fruit from the tree
   about which I commanded you,
'You must not eat from it,'
Cursed is the ground because of you;
     through painful toil you will eat food from it
     all the days of your life.
It will produce thorns and thistles for you,
   and you will eat the plants of the field.
By the sweat of your brow
   you will eat your food
until you return to the ground,
   since from it you were taken;
for dust you are
   and to dust you will return."

The contexts of the text

The biblical context of this text is the punishment pronouncement of God on the erring Adam and on evil. The first two chapters of Genesis reccount how God created the universe and made human beings as the supreme creatures. The remote context is the inauguration of the marriage institution by God from when he began to relate with Adam not as individual but as a man in a marriage. He gave the man Adam a garden, a wife he named Eve, and regulations. Verses 1-13 of this chapter reccount how the devil came in the form of a serpent and deceived Eve, and Eve influenced her husband. The immediate context is the primeval narratives (Gen 1:1-11:26) that deal with human transgression, divine punishment, and God's mercy.[61] The Lord came to the garden of Eden as usual to visit his creatures and found out that they had disobeyed his laws. He asked them questions to motivate them to confess their sins, not that he did not know their sins without asking.[62] Then as seen in our highlighted text, he pronounced judgments on their sins. Several strong curses are included in the pronouncement. Let us look closely into this text by dividing it into three parts: the curse on the serpent, the punishment on Eve, and the punishment on Adam. Note that I avoid the use of the word "curse"

---

61. John E. Hartley, *Understanding the Bible Commentary Series: Genesis* (Grand Rapids : Baker, 2000), 4.

62. Gordon Wenham, "Genesis" in *New Bible Commentary,* D. A. Carson, et. al., eds. (Downers Grove: InterVarsity Press 1994), 63.

for what God pronounced on Adam and Eve because I do not see that God cursed them. Did God curse Adam and Eve? We shall see.

Structurally, this text follows a judicial formula of the ancient time. It starts with interrogation (vv. 8–13) and moves to declarations of judgment and punishments on the various parties involved in the sin (vv. 14–19).[63] However, the pronouncements of curses and punishments are surprisingly and unexpectedly laced with mercy and the promise of redemption.

The curse on the serpent (Gen 3:14–15)

The serpent was cursed for the moment, and for the future. From that moment, it would start crawling and eating dust which would continue for the rest of its life. Futuristically, the serpent was cursed in that its offspring would be an enemy of the offspring of the woman, and the head of its offspring would be crushed. The serpent was directly cursed. That the serpent would eat dust does not necessarily mean that dust would be its only food, but this punishment shows how humiliating and shameful the curse was, for the snakes automatically eat dust in their crawling position. Looking carefully and intertextually at the serpent eating the dust reveals that a literal meaning is intended, not a figurative meaning as some interpreters opine. Comparing this text with the similar figurative expressions in Psalm 72:9, Isaiah 49:23 and Lamentations 3:29 may lead one to think that it is figurative, but that can be misleading. The comparison made in the context of the whole Bible is Micah 7:17:

> They will lick dust like a snake,
>   like creatures that crawl on the ground.
> They will come trembling out of their dens;
>   they will turn in fear to the LORD our God
> and will be afraid of you.

This text supports the idea that the curse of the serpent was not figurative but literal. And it was this curse that changed the serpent's locomotion. Much may not have changed in other aspects of the snake, but its structure for mobility did change.[64]

The use of the Hebrew word *zera* in Genesis 3:15 has been understood as a maternal promise pointing to the proto-evangelion, which Christ's redemption

---

63. D. Guthrie, et. al., eds. *The New Bible Commentary*, rev. ed. (Grand Rapids: Eerdmans, 1970), 85.

64. G. Aalders, *The Students' Bible Commentary*, vol. 1 (Grand Rapids: Zondervan, 1981), 105.

work fulfils. The word can also be understood as pointing to Jesus as the head of the human race.[65] In the content of the curse on the serpent is embedded a promise for mankind. This is the promise that Eve would give birth to a son who would save mankind, which is seen as the first messianic promise. Here we see how the very first pronouncement of a divine curse is laced with hope and mercy. The way in which the words "heel" of the seed of the woman and "head" of the serpent are used is noteworthy and has theological importance. Both words are used in singular form which mean that while the conflict between the woman's seed and the serpent shall affect the entire human race, the ultimate understanding can be traced to Christ as the singular seed of the woman who will emerge to crush the head of the serpent (see Gen 3:15; Rom 16:20). Here the serpent is usually interpreted to mean the devil and the enmity is understood as the enmity between Christ and Satan who comes to save mankind.

The punishment of Eve (Gen 3:16)

The serpent, the experience of child bearing, and the ground were cursed in this text, but the woman and her husband were not cursed directly. God punished her with very painful childbirth, and her relationship with her husband changed from sinless friendliness, mutual love, reciprocated fellowship, and equality to a rulership-followership complex. The Hebrew word לִמְשֹׁל (*meshal*), which means to govern or rule, is used to refer to what her husband would become to her. The word *meshal* has the meaning of a high-ranking official or military officer of the highest rank. The original relationship in which the woman stood as an equal to the man was replaced with domination and authority, and the woman would always have her desire for her husband. The punishment on the woman's child bearing and her relationship with her husband is interrelated. But her main punishment concerns her childbirth pain. In this way, the relationship between woman and her husband contributes to the fulfilment of her own punishment.[66] This is because while the desire for her husband is not restricted to their sexual relationship, this sexual relationship leads to more childbirth and therefore more pain of childbirth.

A point on gender and the sexual debate is needed here. The marshal-follower relationship between a woman and her husband was not the original plan of God; it was after the fall that the relationship became spoiled and ended

---

65. R. A. Harrisville and W. Sundberg, *The Bible in the Modern Culture: Theology and Historical-Critical Method from Spinoza to Kasemann* (Grand Rapids: Eerdmans, 1995), 20.

66. Aalders, *Students' Bible Commentary*, 108.

in this situation. Christian couples are expected to live with the understanding that the purpose of Christ's redemption of the world is to undo the effects of the fall (including on Christian marriage). Therefore, modern readers must be cautious not to use the punishment on Eve as a means of advancing gender domination in Christian marriages. The best marital relationship that we must crave having should be the "pre-fall" ideal, not the post-fall shattered relationship. Specifically, Christian marriage must be characterized by the values of Christ's redemption and ethics of oneness and equal service (Mark 10:42–45). A fuller discussion on this is beyond our scope here and giving it wider space may become an interruption on the flow of our argument. Scholars and theologians may take this up for fuller conversations.

One final fact on the punishment on Eve we have seen is that God did not curse Eve directly; he only punished her with painful childbirth and a broken marital relationship. This argument becomes clearer if we consider the fact that with this punishment pronouncement, God revealed that Eve would have a son who would destroy the serpent. Therefore, the mercy that the world receives from God through Jesus was part of the pronouncement of punishment in Genesis 3. It is not a blind, total punishment but a pronouncement of the great future blessing that we now have in Jesus. This focus toward blessing is not to play down the painfulness of Eve's punishments including painful child birth and eventual death, but to show that the blessing of the coming of Jesus is greater than the pain of those punishments.

The punishment of Adam (Gen 3:17–19)

Note that Adam was not cursed directly either, but that the ground was cursed because of him. The curse on the ground is the origin of hard labor and frustration for humanity.[67] This curse on the ground is related to the heaviness and pain that Adam and his descendants would have in cultivating the ground. The work of human beings that had been naturally easy and peaceful became tiresome labor and sweat. Related to the cursing of the ground is the pronouncement of impairing weeds, thorns, and thistles.[68] Another punishment of Adam was that he would not cease from this hard labor till the day of his death. It was not the working that God cursed but the element with which Adam would work – the ground. The greater consequence for Adam was that he would die, and he would be in difficult labor till his death. The

---

67. Robert B. Hughes and J. Carl Laney, *Tyndale Concise Bible Commentary* (Carol Stream: Tyndale, 1990), 11.

68. Aalders, *Students' Bible Commentary*, 109.

fact that the curse on the ground relates only to agricultural businesses may confuse us into thinking that this curse only affects people who do farming. But the curse said here applies to all kinds of work in human culture.[69] Divine curses can be very powerful; we can notice that the punishment of sin on each of the three parties has collective negative effects on all of them. For example, when God said the ground is cursed for Adam, the consequence of this curse did not exclude the woman and even the serpent.

In verse 19, inverted parallelism is used to make a very clear point:[70]

> "By the sweat of your brow
> > you will eat your food
> until you return to the ground,
> > since from it you were taken;
> for dust you are
> > and to dust you will return."

These phrases are used to bring the punishment of Adam to a climax. The Lord had told him earlier that he would die if he ate the forbidden fruit in the garden given to him (Gen 2:17). The punishment of death is related to this original command.

The biblical theology of curse inferred from this text is that the Lord cursed the serpent and the ground but did not curse his children: Adam and Eve. The curses pronounced have great spiritual, physical, cosmological, and cosmic effects. The sentences the Lord gave Adam and Eve and their descendants were not curses that destroy but punishments that are meant to foster repentance. Here God's wrath is mixed with his mercy. The Lord had a specific purpose in these pronouncements of curses and punishments: to give the hope of messianic redemption through the seed of the woman, even the disobedient woman. No sooner was the wound given than the remedy was provided and revealed.[71] In the very curses lay the promise of the Redeemer who by his own suffering destroyed the power of the devil.

---

69. Aalders, 109.

70. E. W. Bullinger, *Figures of Speech Used in the Bible Expanded and Illustrated* (1898; reprint Grand Rapids: Baker, 2011), 356.

71. Mathew Henry, *Commentary on the Whole Bible*, ed. Leslie Church (Grand Rapids: Zondervan, 1960), 11.

The Balaam curses: Numbers 22–24

The people of Israel had journeyed in the wilderness for almost forty years. They were now approaching the promised land. They had conquered many nations on the way, and now they were approaching Moab. The story related here is crucial because it has to do with when the people of Israel reached a very sensitive stage in their journey; in only four months the journey of forty years would reach completion.[72] Their battles against the people of Canaan had been largely physical, but the battle strategy used by Moab was strange: curses. Three chapters describe the events that took place when Balaam was invited by the king of Moab, Balak, to curse the people of Israel. For the sake of space and to avoid redundancy, a few verses are selected from Numbers 22–24 to present the idea of what happened in the entire episode.

> [2] Now Balak son of Zippor saw all that Israel had done to the Amorites, [3] and Moab was terrified because there were so many people. Indeed, Moab was filled with dread because of the Israelites.
>
> [4] The Moabites said to the elders of Midian, "This horde is going to lick up everything around us, as an ox licks up the grass of the field."
>
> So Balak son of Zippor, who was king of Moab at that time, [5] sent messengers to summon Balaam son of Beor, who was at Pethor, near the Euphrates River, in his native land. Balak said:
>
> "A people has come out of Egypt; they cover the face of the land and have settled next to me. [6] Now come and put a curse on these people, because they are too powerful for me. Perhaps then I will be able to defeat them and drive them out of the land. For I know that whoever you bless is blessed, and whoever you curse is cursed."
>
> [7] The elders of Moab and Midian left, taking with them the fee for divination. When they came to Balaam, they told him what Balak had said.
>
> [8] "Spend the night here," Balaam said to them, "and I will report back to you with the answer the LORD gives me." So the Moabite officials stayed with him.
>
> [9] God came to Balaam and asked, "Who are these men with you?"

---

72. Peter Naylor, "Numbers" in *New Bible Commentary*, eds. Carson, et. al., 189.

¹⁰ Balaam said to God, "Balak son of Zippor, king of Moab, sent me this message: ¹¹ 'A people that has come out of Egypt covers the face of the land. Now come and put a curse on them for me. Perhaps then I will be able to fight them and drive them away.'"

¹² But God said to Balaam, "Do not go with them. You must not put a curse on those people, because they are blessed."

¹³ The next morning Balaam got up and said to Balak's officials, "Go back to your own country, for the LORD has refused to let me go with you."

¹⁴ So the Moabite officials returned to Balak and said, "Balaam refused to come with us."

¹⁵ Then Balak sent other officials, more numerous and more distinguished than the first. ¹⁶ They came to Balaam and said:

> "This is what Balak son of Zippor says: Do not let anything keep you from coming to me, ¹⁷ because I will reward you handsomely and do whatever you say. Come and put a curse on these people for me."

¹⁸ But Balaam answered them, "Even if Balak gave me all the silver and gold in his palace, I could not do anything great or small to go beyond the command of the LORD my God. ¹⁹ Now spend the night here so that I can find out what else the LORD will tell me."

²⁰ That night God came to Balaam and said, "Since these men have come to summon you, go with them, but do only what I tell you." (Num 22:2–20)

³⁷ Balak said to Balaam, "Did I not send you an urgent summons? Why didn't you come to me? Am I really not able to reward you?"

³⁸ "Well, I have come to you now," Balaam replied. "But I can't say whatever I please. I must speak only what God puts in my mouth." (Num 22:37–38)

⁵ The LORD put a word in Balaam's mouth and said, "Go back to Balak and give him this word."

⁶ So he went back to him and found him standing beside his offering, with all the Moabite officials. ⁷ Then Balaam spoke his message:

"Balak brought me from Aram,
>the king of Moab from the eastern mountains.
'Come,' he said, 'curse Jacob for me;
>come, denounce Israel.'
⁸ How can I curse
>those whom God has not cursed?
How can I denounce
>those whom the LORD has not denounced?
⁹ From the rocky peaks I see them,
>from the heights I view them.
I see a people who live apart
>and do not consider themselves one of the nations.
¹⁰ Who can count the dust of Jacob
>or number even a fourth of Israel?
Let me die the death of the righteous,
>and may my final end be like theirs!"

¹¹ Balak said to Balaam, "What have you done to me? I brought you to curse my enemies, but you have done nothing but bless them!"

¹² He answered, "Must I not speak what the LORD puts in my mouth?"

¹³ Then Balak said to him, "Come with me to another place where you can see them; you will not see them all but only the outskirts of their camp. And from there, curse them for me." (Num 23:5–13)

The contexts and the structure of the text

Numbers 23:7–10 is the first oracle; the second (23:18–24), third (24:3–9), and fourth (24:15–19) follow the same pattern. Balaam could not curse Israel but blessed them. These texts contain some of the oldest poetry in the Bible. Balak, the king of Moab, was afraid of the population size and military capacity of the people of Israel due to the news he had heard that they had conquered many other nations, especially about their victory against the powerful Amorites. Balak then formed a confederate alliance with the elders of the tribes of Midian. Still deeply frightened by the large number of Israelites, Balak resorted to attempting to use curses to destroy them.

For adequate understanding, we shall look at this narrative in two simplified parts. The first is the invitation to Balaam, a professional curser, and the divine restraining on him (Num 22:1–35). Balak believed that he could not overpower the Israelites without first cursing them. That is he believed that curses could be used to weaken people. He then sent a special invitation to a renowned professional curser and diviner, Balaam. Balak describes the ability of Balaam in 22:6: "For I know that whoever you bless is blessed, and whoever you curse is cursed." Although Balaam was not an Israelite, he is depicted as one who received information from Yahweh.[73] Balaam's character has been judged to be the strangest in the Bible. However when referencing Balaam, Peter shows that he is not to be regarded as a true prophet of Yahweh (2 Pet 2:15–16).

When Balaam received the first invitation, the Lord told him not to go, and he gave the reason: "You must not put a curse on those people, because they are blessed" (Num 22:12). However when Balaam received the second more impressive invitation offering a greater reward, the Lord permitted Balaam to go but instructed him to only say whatever the Lord told him to say (22:20). Meanwhile, God was angry with Balaam for going, and through the agency of an angel blocked the way of Balaam's donkey (22:22–23). What could have caused God to permit Balaam to go and later show him displeasure for going? Perhaps to show Balaam that his going was under a special divine resistance and instruction, and to show Balak the peculiar character of the people of Israel he feared.[74]

The supremacy of God's blessing over all human curses (Num 22:36–24:25)

Instead of curses, Balaam pronounced four oracles of blessings on the people of Israel. These oracles are poetic in form. Before each of the oracles was given, Balaam was taken to special mountain heights from which he could see the people he was employed to curse, and special altars and sacrifices were made. On each occasion, Balaam inquired of the Lord, and the Lord put words of blessings into his mouth instead of curses. The pronouncement of blessings in place of curses offended Balak, but Balaam replied that he could only say what God permitted him to say. The security of God's blessings was displayed in the blessings Balaam gave instead of curses. The first, second, and third oracles are connected to the Abrahamic covenant. For example, the first oracle emphasizes the fact that Yahweh will curse anyone who curses Abraham descendants (Num

---

73. S. R. Driver, A. Plumber, and C. A. Briggs, *A Critical and Exegetical Commentary on Numbers* (Edinburgh: T&T Clark, 1986), 315.

74. Peter Naylor, "Numbers" in *New Bible Commentary*, eds. Carson, et. al., 190.

23:8; see Gen 12:3; Num 24:9). Another element of the oracles is that they point to the future victory of Israel against nations and their occupation of Canaan and the ultimate enthronement of the Davidic dynasty culminating in Jesus (Num 24:8, 17–19). Part of the fourth oracle states, "A star will come out of Jacob; a scepter will rise out of Israel. He will crush the foreheads of Moab, the skulls of all the people of Sheth" (24:17). Even though Balak did not solicit this fourth oracle, it is definitely a messianic prophecy referring to Christ. We can then notice that instead of cursing, Balaam celebrated the prosperity and present and future glory of Israel.[75]

A theological inference is this: even when the children of Israel did not know that curses were planned to be put upon them, without any prayer or intercession, the Lord fought for them. The intended curses became blessings due to the divine blessings of Yahweh whose blessings supersede any human curse. This theological point has significant import for African Christianity where currently only prayer, deliverance, and anointing oil are often prescribed as solutions and preventions of curses.

The covenant conditional curses: Deuteronomy 28:15–68

Deuteronomy 28 is frequently used to enumerate the results of obedience to God's commandments and the punishments for the disobedience. Interestingly, the amount of text that describes the blessings for obedience is smaller than text that describes the curses for disobedience. Verses 1–14 are dedicated to blessings while verses 15–68 are used to discuss the curses for disobeying the laws of God.

The contexts and the structure of the text

Deuteronomy 28 can be situated in three contexts. First the general context of the Bible. In particular we need to consider the biblical concept of divine holiness and justice. Throughout the Bible, the theology of God's holiness and justice is uncompromised. God does not change. It is the nature of a person's response to divine commandments that determines what he or she gets from God. However, the demands of God's justice are always made clear to people and a person is given freedom to choose whichever path they want. Not only are the demands of God's justice made clear to people, the consequences of the person's choice are also made clear. There were two generations connected to Israel's journey from Egypt to Canaan: the Exodus generation which all

---

75. Driver, Plumber, and Briggs, *Critical and Exegetical Commentary on Numbers*, 315.

perished in the wilderness due to disobedience, and the new generation which entered the promised land.

The second context is the remote context, the positioning of this text in the context of the book of Deuteronomy. The text of Deuteronomy 28:15–68 is situated in the context of the Mosaic reiteration of divine laws. This took place when the Israelites were camping at Moab's plain about to cross the Jordan river. At this point, Moses needed to reiterate the laws to this new generation before they enter the promised land. What is unique in these specific statements of laws is the inclusion of several curses and blessing to establish the clear consequences of possible obedience and disobedience. This is what I can call inclusion of "moral responsibility formula" Disobedience equals curses while obedience equals blessings. The texts represent a reintroduction or reawakening of covenant between God and the Israelites that had been broken by the Exodus generation.

Finally, the immediate context relates how Moses was preparing the new generation to enter into the promised land. The text of Deuteronomy is close to what we can call a "covenant renewal ceremony."[76] The Israelites were about to move from a nomadic life to a settled lifestyle. For them, Moses presented the renewal, ratification and sanctions of the covenant (Deut 26:10–30:20). Specifically, Deuteronomy 28 includes a declaration of renewed covenant sanctions which include curses and blessings.

Structurally, the cursing verses in this text can be divided into two parts: part one describes extreme vexation (Deut 28:15–44), and part two describes final and total destruction (vv. 45–68).[77] The formula followed is similar to that of ANE treaties in which blessings are listed as the rewards for keeping a treaty and curses are listed to discourage disobedience. In this text, the Lord used blessings and curses as tools to motivate loyalty and obedience to his covenant.[78]

Representative excerpts are taken from the passage because it is lengthy. The introductory verses are quoted so as to allow our discussion to be put in the right context.

> If you fully obey the LORD your God and carefully follow all his commands I give you today, the LORD your God will set you high

---

76. P.J. Gentry, "The Relationship of Deuteronomy to the Covenant at Sinai," *SBJT* 18, no. 3 (2014): 37–38.

77. Henry, *Commentary on the Whole Bible*, 197.

78. J. Gordon McConville, "Deuteronomy" in *New Bible Commentary*, eds. Carson, et. al., 224.

above all the nations on earth. All these blessings will come on you and accompany you if you obey the LORD your God:
You will be blessed in the city and blessed in the country.
The fruit of your womb will be blessed, and the crops of your land and the young of your livestock – the calves of your herds and the lambs of your flocks. (Deut 28:1–4)

However, if you do not obey the LORD your God and do not carefully follow all his commands and decrees I am giving you today, all these curses will come on you and overtake you:
You will be cursed in the city and cursed in the country.
Your basket and your kneading trough will be cursed.
The fruit of your womb will be cursed, and the crops of your land, and the calves of your herds and the lambs of your flocks.
You will be cursed when you come in and cursed when you go out.
The LORD will send on you curses, confusion and rebuke in everything you put your hand to, until you are destroyed and come to sudden ruin because of the evil you have done in forsaking him. (Deut 28:15–20)

Let us discuss the curses section of this text in two simplified sections.

The equity of these curses
These curses are not mere callous pronouncements from an unjust God but are well merited curses that occur when people act in disobedience. These conditional curses are referred to as "if curses." That is, the curses only come into effect if certain sins are committed. The introductory phrase for the verses describing blessings states, "If you fully obey the LORD your God and carefully follow all his commands" (Deut 28:1), and the introductory phrase for the verses describing the curses states, "However, if you do not obey the LORD your God and do not carefully follow all his commands and decrees" (Deut 28:15). From these phrases we can see that the blessings and curses related here are conditional.

The extent and the purposes of these curses
Acts of disobedience automatically make all the curses here active: "all these curses will come on you and overtake you" (Deut 28:15). The comprehensiveness of the curses shows that Yahweh is the Lord over all aspects of human life: political, economic, national, agricultural, marital, and so forth. Once the

Israelites disobeyed Yahweh, no other god could save them. In sum, these curses can rightly be understood in the context of God showing his supremacy over other gods, especially the Canaanite gods such as Baal that the Israelites were forbidden to worship. Thus these curses are signposts of the dangers of apostasy. When understood according to the context and plot, we can see that these curses are not blind punishments or heavy negative pronouncements. They were pronounced as the continuation of the curses declared on Mount Ebal (Deut 28:15–68) and the blessings declared on Mount Gerizim (Deut 28:1–14). These curses and blessings were proclaimed to the Israelites when they were close to entering the promised land. The curses and blessings are purposeful. They are to show that only the God of Israel can control the affairs of human beings and that only he is worthy of obedience. These curses and blessings also present the people of Israel with the opportunity to know the divine rule that guides the universe, which may be unknown to other people who do not know Yahweh. The Israelites were protected by knowing who can cause blessings, progress, joy, and victory in battle fronts and who can cause curses, loss, poverty, and defeat in battle, and death.

We can draw some theological inferences from this text. The curses in Deuteronomy 28 are not unconditional curses. They are not blind, dangerous curses from God but expressions of the identity of Yahweh as the God who controls the affairs of human beings and as the God who wants his people to obey him, thereby communicating to people what they can do to please him and what displeases him. In other words, the curses and blessings as listed here are a revelation of what pleases God and what irritates him, not a condemnation or a set of blind destructive pronouncements on the people.

Imprecatory curses: Psalm 109

Psalm 109 is perhaps the most outspoken of all the imprecatory Psalms, and it has been a psalm of interest for many preachers especially in the African context. Some scholars think that this psalm lacks the Christian ideal, and they see it as contradicting the values of the Gospels especially the Beatitudes and the New Testament values of love and forgiveness. Some suggest that Christians are not to follow the example of the psalmist to imprecate.[79] In the African context, this psalm has been used by many prayer ministers because of content that is relevant to African experiences.

---

79. J. L. McKenzie, "A Note on Psalm."

For the director of music. Of David. A psalm.
¹ My God, whom I praise,
    do not remain silent,
² for people who are wicked and deceitful
    have opened their mouths against me;
they have spoken against me with lying tongues.
³ With words of hatred they surround me;
    they attack me without cause.
⁴ In return for my friendship they accuse me,
    but I am a man of prayer.
⁵ They repay me evil for good,
    and hatred for my friendship.
⁶ Appoint someone evil to oppose my enemy;
    let an accuser stand at his right hand.
⁷ When he is tried, let him be found guilty,
    and may his prayers condemn him.
⁸ May his days be few;
    may another take his place of leadership.
⁹ May his children be fatherless
    and his wife a widow.
¹⁰ May his children be wandering beggars;
    may they be driven from their ruined homes.
¹¹ May a creditor seize all he has;
    may strangers plunder the fruits of his labor.
¹² May no one extend kindness to him
    or take pity on his fatherless children.
¹³ May his descendants be cut off,
    their names blotted out from the next generation.
¹⁴ May the iniquity of his fathers be remembered before the LORD;
    may the sin of his mother never be blotted out.
¹⁵ May their sins always remain before the LORD,
    that he may blot out their name from the earth.
¹⁶ For he never thought of doing a kindness,
    but hounded to death the poor
    and the needy and the brokenhearted.
¹⁷ He loved to pronounce a curse –
    may it come back on him.

> He found no pleasure in blessing –
>> may it be far from him.
> ⁱ⁸ He wore cursing as his garment;
>> it entered into his body like water,
>> into his bones like oil.
> ¹⁹ May it be like a cloak wrapped about him,
>> like a belt tied forever around him.
> ²⁰ May this be the LORD's payment to my accusers,
>> to those who speak evil of me.
> ²¹ But you, Sovereign LORD,
>> help me for your name's sake;
>> out of the goodness of your love, deliver me.
> ²² For I am poor and needy,
>> and my heart is wounded within me.
> ²³ I fade away like an evening shadow;
>> I am shaken off like a locust.
> ²⁴ My knees give way from fasting;
>> my body is thin and gaunt.
> ²⁵ I am an object of scorn to my accusers;
>> when they see me, they shake their heads.
> ²⁶ Help me, LORD my God;
>> save me according to your unfailing love.
> ²⁷ Let them know that it is your hand,
>> that you, LORD, have done it.
> ²⁸ While they curse, may you bless;
>> may those who attack me be put to shame,
>> but may your servant rejoice.
> ²⁹ May my accusers be clothed with disgrace
>> and wrapped in shame as in a cloak.
> ³⁰ With my mouth I will greatly extol the LORD;
>> in the great throng of worshipers I will praise him.
> ³¹ For he stands at the right hand of the needy,
>> to save their lives from those who would condemn them.
>> (Ps 109)

The context and structure of the text

Matthew Henry thought that this psalm was written by David and perhaps when David was running from Saul or when his son Absalom rebelled against him.[80] While the authorship is not certain, we have ample evidence from the content of the psalm to think that it was written from a deeply aggrieved heart. The following themes can be used to understand the psalm in its rightful biblical context.

The view of God expressed by the psalmist

It is evident from Psalm 109:21–27 that the psalmist was weak and helpless and expected God to save him, as no other hope was in sight. In verses 21 and 26, the psalmist portrays God as sovereign, loving, and good. Contrary to the enemies who loved cursing and hated blessing, the psalmist trusted that God will bless, and in verse 31 describes how God "stands at the right hand of the needy, to save their lives from those who would condemn them."

The characterization of the enemy and enemies of the psalmist

The personality of the psalmist's enemy described in the psalm is a direct contradiction to the attributes of God depicted in the psalm. The psalmist gives enough vivid description of his enemy that we can see that the imprecation is justified. There are two senses in which the psalmist refers to his enemies: as a group (Ps 109:1–5) and as a particular person (vv. 6–19). The psalmist describes his group of enemies as wicked, deceitful, backbiters, slanderers, liars, and unfriendly (vv. 2–3). They have repaid his kindness with evil and attacked him without a cause (vv. 3, 5). In verse 17 the psalmist describes his particular enemy as a person who loved cursing people and found no pleasure in blessing. Hyperbolically, the psalmist states that this enemy "wore cursing as his garment" (v. 18a). Not only is his cursing external, but cursing had "entered into his body like water, into his bones like oil (v. 18b). This person sounds like a professional curser or that cursing was the regular and pleasurable habit.

As if this behavior was not enough, the psalmist continues this list in verse 16, where he states that his enemy did not have any concern for the poor and the needy but "hounded to death the poor," the needy, and the broken hearted. This lack of pity for the downtrodden is discouraged in the Bible in other places (Pss 41:1–2; 35:10; Prov 19:17). The enemy of the psalmist described here was also an enemy of God. His offenses were not only toward the psalmist but also toward God, for he had sinned against God and broke the covenant with God by disobeying what God teaches on how the poor are to be loved and that evil should not be used to pay good (Prov 17:13; 22:16, 22–23; 19:17; 28:7; Ps 41:1–2; 37:14–15). While the psalmist prays, this enemy curses and provides

---

80. Henry, *Commentary on the Whole Bible*, 696–97.

the ground for the imprecation. These imprecations are not just human cursing on a fellow human; the imprecations in this psalm are appeals to God to bring justice to an unrepentant enemy of God.

The content of the imprecatory prayer
The prayer in this psalm that the enemies will not fail to see the word of God fulfilled is an appeal to God based on his promises in Genesis 12:1–3 that anyone who curses Abraham's descendants would be cursed, and anyone who blesses them will be blessed.[81] The prayer also reveals that the psalmist had a good relationship with God (Ps 109:1). The prayer is a special appeal to God to let the enemy receive divine justice according to the will of God, not according to human vengeance. Verses 17–19 imply that the enemy may have cursed the psalmist, and the psalmist thereby made an appeal to God to return those curses to him. While his enemies have cursed, he has prayed as he says in verse 4, "but I am a man of prayer." Based on the personality of the enemy and the content of the imprecation, the prayer is pointing to God's attributes as a savior and helper; the psalm is a call to God.

Assuming that David was the author, "David's experience foreshadows that of Jesus, the ultimate, true and holy speaker of words of cursing."[82] Many of the psalmists express their wish that God would deal with their enemies in accordance with his revealed word. Here the psalmist's wish that the punishment of his enemy would also be on his descendants is likely based on Exodus 34:7, "Yet he does not leave the guilty unpunished; he punishes the children and their children for the sin of the parents to the third and fourth generation," and on Deuteronomy 5:9, "I, the LORD your God, am a jealous God, punishing the children for the sin of the parents to the third and fourth generation of those who hate me." Psalm 109 shows that the psalmist loved his enemies wholeheartedly. In verse 5, the Hebrew word used for his love is יתְבָהֲאַ ('ahabati), which the KJV translates, "And they have rewarded me evil for good, and hatred for my love." The same word used for love here is used for the love of God for Israel (Jer 31:3), between Jonathan and David (1 Sam 20:17), and of Jacob for Rachel that caused him to work for an extra seven years so he could marry her (Gen 29:20). While the NIV translates 'ahabati as friendship, the KJV translation "love" is more proper and sounds more correct.

We can draw theological inferences from this psalm. The imprecations here are appeals to God to establish his justice according to his word against his

---

81. Hughes and Laney, *Tyndale Concise Bible Dictionary*, 223.
82. J. A. Motyer, "The Psalms" in Carson, et. al., eds., *New Bible Commentary*, 559.

enemies, who are also the enemies of the psalmist, because of their violations of the fundamentals of the word of God. The offenses of the enemies that are worth the imprecations are largely offenses against God, and though the psalmist has prayed for them, they refused to repent and turn to God. Biblical imprecations are not just pronouncements of curses on an enemy but an appeal to God in the light of the integrity of his words and covenant.

Jesus becoming a curse for us for redemption: Galatians 3:10–14

As I have shown previously, the New Testament curses are to be understood in relation to the works and ministry of Christ. In fact, not only on the subject of curses, the whole of New Testament theology is expected to be understood in relation to Christ. It is in the context of law, sin, and salvation that the New Testament discusses the concept of curses. Specifically, the New Testament shows how human sin carried to the cross by Jesus made him "a curse," and how Jesus thereby rescued people from the curses of the law. This is a unique spiritual attribute of the New Testament conceptualization of curses. Also, some soteriological themes such as grace, propitiation, faith, and redemption are now associated with curses. To see this clearly, let us choose Galatians 3:10–14 to see how Paul explains the concept of curses in relation to the work and ministry of Christ.

> For all who rely on the works of the law are under a curse, as it is written: "Cursed is everyone who does not continue to do everything written in the Book of the Law." Clearly no one who relies on the law is justified before God, because "the righteous will live by faith." The law is not based on faith; on the contrary, it says, "The person who does these things will live by them." Christ redeemed us from the curse of the law by becoming a curse for us, for it is written: "Cursed is everyone who is hung on a pole." He redeemed us in order that the blessing given to Abraham might come to the Gentiles through Christ Jesus, so that by faith we might receive the promise of the Spirit. (Gal 3:10–14)

The context and the structure of the text

The main aim of Paul in writing the letter to the Galatians was to correct the heresy of legalism by emphasizing that faith in Christ is primary and essential, rather than the works of the law. Paul expounds his teachings on the concept of justification by faith in the preceding verses (Gal 3:1–9), and in verses 10–14, he compares the impossibility of justification by the law to the possibility of justification by faith.[83] Paul quotes several Old Testament passages from Deuteronomy, Leviticus, and Habakkuk to support his arguments.

The causes of our curse (Gal 3:10–12)

When a comparison is made in these verses between a life lived by faith in Christ and a life lived by human effort to obey the law, the result is that a life lived under the law is cursed due to the human inability to keep the law, the fact the law cannot save, and the fact that humans cannot fulfill the righteousness of the law. If people break one part of the law, they are as condemned as if they had broken the entire law, which shows the impossibility of the law to save. This passage is in reference to Deuteronomy 27:26 which states, "Cursed is anyone who does not uphold the words of this law by carrying them out." Martin Luther argued that what Paul means here is that the people to whom the law was given were not obedient to the law, and some may have been obedient only by hypocrisy.[84]

Let us adopt the logic of Merrill Tenney to explain this text clearly.[85] The law pronounces a curse on all those who do not observe every commandment. The implication according to Romans 3:23 is that none have kept the law perfectly; therefore, all are under the curse of the law.

Our redemption from the curse of the law (Gal 3:13–14)

Christ fulfilled all the laws and took upon himself our sins of disobedience by going to the cross, thereby becoming accursed due to our sins. While hanging a living person on a tree was not the Jewish traditional mode of execution,[86] a person who was eventually hung on a tree for a capital offense was accursed as discussed in Deuteronomy 21:22–23. The curse of the law is the punishment for individuals who break the law of God. Christ, through his perfect holiness, is not under any curse of the law, but on our behalf he became cursed so as to redeem us from the curse. Is the redemption work of Christ meant for only the Israelites who were given the laws to obey? No. Galatians 3:14 shows that the

---

83. Hughes and Laney, *Tyndale Concise Bible Commentary*, 583.

84. Martin Luther, *A Commentary on St Paul's Epistle to the Galatians*, rev. Erasmus Middleton (London: I. J. Chidley, 1844), 197–99.

85. Merrill C. Tenney, *Galatians: The Charter of Christian Liberty*, rev. ed. (Grand Rapids: Eerdmans, 1950), 124.

86. F. F. Bruce, *The New International Greek Testament Commentary: The Epistle to the Galatians* (Grand Rapids: Eerdmans, 1982), 165.

redemption work of Christ has brought the non-Jewish to the hope of salvation, and they are also redeemed by faith from the curse of the law.

In addition, when this text is understood in the general context of Paul's theology, we can see from Romans 2:14–16 that non-Jews were also given their own version of the law of God, which all have broken. From the curses emanating from the various disobedience of the laws of God, Jesus has redeemed us. The use of the Greek word πᾶς (*pas*), which means "every" or "all," implies that all are involved, not only the Jews. Finally, Paul shows that blessings and curses are opposite, and that once the curse is removed, blessings result. He argues that since Jesus has removed the curse of the law, we all, Jews and Gentiles, can enjoy and benefit from the blessings of God.

Theological inferences from the texts examined

In the Bible when curses become effective, they are punishments on the people for disobedience. Biblical curses show us the hatred that God has for sin and that no one can commit sin with impunity. However, God does not curse his children, even when they disobey him. He merely punishes them by cursing some entities that are related to them, and in the very act of cursing, he provides the means of redemption and salvation. In many instances, curses in the Bible did not go into effect. In fact, sometimes the curses became blessings when the blessings were authorized by God, which shows that biblical curses are not mere verbal wickedness but point to the sovereignty of God. In the Bible contexts, curses are closely followed with redemption when people repent. In the New Testament, the concept of curses is spiritually related to the redemption work of Christ.

What implications do these facts mined from the Bible have for understanding curses in the present African church? Is there conflict or correlation, similarity or contrast? What are the implications of the biblical theology of curses for African Christians who fear curses? These questions are answered in later chapters. And for appropriate answers to be provided, we need to look at the beliefs in curses in traditional African society. We have arrived at some conclusions and findings on biblical curses which we will keep in mind as we examine African traditional theology of curses. To this topic we now turn.

5

Curses in Traditional African Religio-Cultural Context

This chapter deals with the concept of curses purely as believed by traditional Africans, because bringing to the fore some salient issues that surround and make up the African concept of curses is important. To arrive at this understanding, both primary and secondary sources were consulted. The discussion here was also informed by interactions I had with some Africans through interviews and participatory observation. However, the details explained here represent the opinions of the major ethnic groups in Africa. First, I surveyed different local contexts in several African nations: Kenya, Zambia, Angola, Uganda, Cameroun, the Benin Republic, South Sudan, Ghana, Zimbabwe, Malawi, and the Republic of Congo. Second, I examined relevant literature by African authors and collated an in-depth and concise African traditional theology of curses and cursing. The great scarcity of literature on African cultural beliefs on curses must be mentioned, and I had to augment the meager literature available with rigorous field work. The discussion here is a simplified presentation of the themes and concepts that surround African cultural perspectives on curses.

Definitions of Curses

How do Africans define curses from their cultural perspectives? In the African context, the concept of curses is complex. A curse is called different names in different local contexts. For example, a curse is called *iguno* in the Lambya tribe of northern Malawi, *egun* in Yoruba tribe of southwest Nigeria, *hunaire* in Fufide tribe of the Benin Republic, *kirumi* in Kikuyu tribe of Kenya, *kutukwa* in Karanga tribe of Zimbabwe, *nthembo* in the Tumbuka tribe of Zambia, and so forth. Although each tribe has a special and unique name for a curse, it almost always means the same thing. A curse is seen as a malevolent appeal to a supernatural being for harm to come to somebody or something as a result of that person's misdeeds.[1] In addition, Africans see a curse as negative, verbal aggression influenced by the offensive attitude of an offender which may include the activities of a spiritual power. A curse is the evil intention of the offended on the offender. In this sense, a curse is seen as an irrevocable spell or imprecation that is charged with forceful compulsion.[2] A curse is also seen as a form of negative prayer or invocation to harm or to invoke serious injury on someone. It is believed that when some negative words are pronounced or uttered in the correct places and at the correct time, such words are potent and effective.[3] While some believe that curses are what result from spoken negative words based on offenses committed, others believe that curses may not be spoken words but are the repercussions of breaking covenant or having an unfaithful disposition to statues.

Moreover, the African concept of curses can also be defined as the cause of evil occurrences and repeated negative patterns that happen to members of the same family, bloodline, and community. For instance, if some evil happenings occur in the life of a man that also happen in the lives of his children, Africans see these events as the result of a curse. In the African concept, this type of curse is known as a generational curse.

Apart from these definitions, Africans have sociological conceptions of curses. Many Africans see curses as forms of social justice and of retributive justice that those who are offended but do not have physical means of revenge administer through the use of negative words as a punishment. These words are believed to invoke misfortunes which can affect all the areas of life of the cursed: social, spiritual, physical.[4] The belief is that if a person is indeed offended, a curse can be placed on the offender by the offended. Curses are used in events of such extreme offense that the person whose interests or whose group's interests are directly and seriously threatened or denied call on a deity

---

1. Deji Ayegboyin, "*Epe* (Oath of Cursing), *Egun* (generational Curse) *ati* (And) *Itusile* (deliverance) *Ni Oruko Re* (in His name)," in *Under the Shelter of Olodunmare*, ed. S. O. Abogunrin (Ibadan: John Archers, 2014), 195.

2. Modupe Oduyoye, "Potent Speech," in *Traditional Religion in West Africa*, ed. E. A. Adegbola (Ibadan: Sefer, 1998), 221.

3. David T. Adamo, "Decolonizing African Biblical Studies," 7th Inaugural Lecture, Delta State University, Abraka, Nigeria (Abraka: Delta State University, 2004): 10.

4. Kasomo Daniel, "An Investigation of Sin and Evil in African Cosmology," *International Journal of Sociology and Anthropology* 1, no. 8 (2009): 152.

to avenge them.[5] This practice shows that the African notion of curses is related to the concept of social morality and moral responsibility.

In addition, to some extent, the African understanding of curses is connected to the use of magic. For example, Bolaji Idowu affirms that curses and magical words (*ase*) are almost synonymous.[6] A curse can be described as a personality force by which people impress their authority or will effectively upon another person, or upon a certain situation for their own interest using some spiritually aided mechanism. Associated with the African concept of curses is the power of the word backed up by the personality of the one who utters it. Africans believe that curses can be very powerful particularly when they are backed up with supernatural or magical force.[7] From this perspective, curses are one of the ways magical powers can be expressed from a superior to a subordinate in age, social status, or spirituality. For example, the words of a parent to children carry a lot of power, either for causing sorrow or peace, misfortune or success. John Mbiti notes that in Africa, curses and blessings uttered by the aged are believed to be extremely potent.[8]

Apart from these ideas, some Africans define curses in their connection with witchcraft. This argument implies that curses are one of the activities of witchcraft in African communities.[9] However, not all curses are believed to be occasioned by witchcraft. Parents, grandparents, family members, and other close relatives can also curse people even within their families who may have done or said hurtful things against them, their family, or the community in general.[10] This practice is not to undermine the possibility that witches use curses as a tool of destruction on their victims.

One important dimension of African traditional belief in curses is that curses are associated with the African concept of metaphysical causality and symbiotic interaction between the spiritual and physical realms. Africans believe that causes for all life occurrences must be identifiable, and that most of these causes may not be physical. In other words, everything that happens must have a cause because nothing happens naturally without a spiritual force

---

5. J. O. Kayode, *Understanding African Traditional Religion* (Ile Ife: University Press, 1984), 60.

6. Bolaji Idowu, *Olodumare: God in Yoruba Belief* (Lagos: Longman, 1996), 117.

7. Idowu, *Olodumare*, 117.

8. Mbiti, *African Religion and Philosophy*, 32.

9. G. N. Bernard and N. K. Dickson, "The Impact of Magic and Witchcraft in the Social, Economic, Political and Spiritual Life of African Communities," *IJHSSE* 1, no. 5 (2014): 9–18.

10. Kisilu Kombo, "Witchcraft: A Living Vice in Africa," *Africa Journal of Evangelical Theology* 22, no. 1 (2013): 71.

behind it. Usually, Africans attribute evil to unseen causes such as curses.[11] The African belief in curses and their effects resonates with African philosophy of causality, which is itemized by G. O. Ozumba:

> Africans are not troubled about the Hume's gnoseological intricacies of necessary condition for causality, priority in time, constant conjunction, contiguity in time and space and necessary connection. Neither do the Africans bother themselves on Cartesian problem of interactionism. It is simply believed in Africa that the two worlds: spiritual and physical interact. *And that these two worlds affect each other.* African metaphysical understanding transcends the western indices.[12]

The African notion of curses is also a representative of the African cosmological thought that physical and spiritual life coexist. While people in other cultures may limit their cosmological inquiries to immediate sense experiences and reason, Africans largely go beyond these to employ means that are not empirical or based on human reason because they believe that curses have nonphysical power that can affect the physical life.

Various Types and Forms of Curses

In the African worldview are different types, forms, and hierarchies of curses which are interesting and fascinating. Although Africans believe that all curses are notoriously dangerous, some are believed to be more dangerous than others. The following are the popular types and forms of curses.

Communal curses

Africans believe that not only can a person be cursed, but types of curses can be placed on a group of people, a village, an ethnic group, an association, or a community. Many Africans believe that when a curse is placed on the head of a clan or family or village, the curse may affect the entire population of the village and their children. In addition is a particular type of curse that is placed not on a person but on a group or community of people. When a curse of this nature is made, the symptoms are seen not only in the life of a person.

---

11. P. A. Dopamu, *Esu: The Invisible Foe of Man* (Ijebu-Ode: Sebiotimo Publications, 2000), 26.

12. G. O. Ozumba, "African Traditional Metaphysics," *Quodilbert: Journal of Christian Theology and Philosophy* 6, no. 1 (January-March, 2004): 12, emphasis added.

The dictates of the curse are uniformly seen in the lives of every member of the community. Olufemi Adebo gives startling examples of instances when curses were placed on whole African communities that resulted in several misfortunes such as sudden death:

> There are some families in which nobody lives beyond forty-five years old. In some, their males do not live long or they just die violently. I know of a village in Nigeria where prominent people do not live long. This village was blessed to have some young men and women who had promising careers in the military, banking sector, and civil service about twenty years ago, but this has gone into history today. All these people died either through motor accidents or some forms of mysterious diseases in a short time.[13]

When events like these happen repeatedly in a family, Africans assume that a communal curse is in operation on that family. Curses on communities or families such as these might have been pronounced by a god, by sorcerers or witches, or by any chief priest, sometimes because of a violation of taboo. Moreover, the curse automatically affects all of the members of that family or the community, even the unborn children.

Curses inflicted by metaphysical beings

Some types of curses in the African worldview are beyond the human realm. This category of curses are made by the gods, divinities, spirits, and ancestors. In African cosmology there is a very strong connection between the physical and nonphysical, between the now and the hereafter, and between human affairs and spiritual affairs. Africans believe that if a family deity or a community god is annoyed, it can inflict a curse on the people that has great potency. For example, the Fulani tribe of the Republic of Benin has a tribal god called "Baaboro" who is seriously feared and respected and believed to have the power to inflict curses on the people if they fail to obey or give according to his dictates. Similarly, the Shona and Ndebele tribes of Zimbabwe believe that "Musikava," a supreme god who is cruel, jealous, unscrupulous, and unapproachable except through ancestors and intermediaries, can inflict dangerous and irrevocable curses on the people. In addition, if members of a family or a community undermine the spiritual rank of the family or community gods, or fail to

---

13. A. O. Adebo, *Freedom from Bondage: Expository Sermons on Romans Chapter 8* (Lagos: ADMED Nigeria, 2015), 4–5.

remember departed parents, they could provoke anger and a curse from the departed founders of the extended families and clans.[14] Also the Tumbuka tribe of Zambia believes that spirits living in the world can inflict curses on people, and these spirits can also make any negative words uttered by people concerning themselves to come to pass even more than the people intended.[15]

Curses from parents or the elderly

Another category is curses that are usually believed to come from parents to their children which Africans believe to be very powerful and dangerous, especially when the parents have died. The most dreadful curses are those pronounced by parents, uncles, aunts, or other close relatives against children. The worst is a curse uttered at the death bed. In the African context, a mother can place a curse on her child or children which is seen as one of the most dangerous curses.[16] In some instances, a mother can place a curse on a child by uttering negative words or by placing her hands on her "private parts" or parts of her body that have to do with her femininity such as breasts, womb, knees, and back where she nourished and nurtured the child. Speaking from a Kenyan context, Donald Kisilu resonates well with this practice:

> Some curses involve the use of words and actions. Certain actions are needed to combine with the negative utterances, for instance, a mother exposing her nakedness or private parts to her son while placing a curse on him constitutes a curse which negatively affects the person cursed very dangerously.[17]

Many Africans believe that some parts of the body of a woman constitute power. For instance, a woman's pubic hair, breasts, hair, knees, thighs, and other parts are regarded as symbols of feminine power. If a mother is grossly offended and she places her hands on her pubic hair to curse her children, her curse is believed to be very powerful and almost irrevocable. Generally, the curses of parents are seen as overwhelming and extremely dangerous. This type of dreadful curse is one of the reasons why many Africans respect and obey

---

14. H. A. Mwakana, *Crises of Life in African Religion and Christianity* (Geneva: Lutheran World Federation, 2002), 20.

15. Information gathered through qualitative interview, March 2020.

16. P. N. Wachege, "Curses and Cursing among the Agikuyu: Social-Cultural Benefits," *Journal of Philosophy and Religious Studies*, University of Nairobi, Kenya 12, no. 6 (2014): 1–11.

17. Donald Kisilu, "Witchcraft: A Living Vice in Africa," *A Journal of Evangelical Theology* 22, no. 1 (2003): 76.

their elderly parents. They also believe that if a parent places a curse on his or her child, the curse may not end with the child, but children of the child will also be affected by the same curse, and so on.

Not only do Africans fear a mother's curse, they also fear a curse coming from a father. If a father is offended by his child, he can also expose his manhood as a sign of annoyance and place a curse on his erring child. This type of curse usually results from grievous and serious disrespect of the father. For instance, if a son sleeps with his father's wife or if a grown-up daughter deliberately holds the penis of her father during a confrontation to assault her father, the father may place a curse.[18]

Inherited or generational curses

Generational curses are among the most feared and most common curses in African societies. This category of curses is believed to run from generation to generation, transmitted from the fore parents. Families in which a generational curse is perpetuated experience a uniform negative trend. Members of such families are said to experience recurring misfortunes and challenges such as certain types of sickness and diseases, financial difficulties, marital instability, sudden and untimely deaths occurring at a particular age and a particular season, barrenness, delays, unemployment, and other problems. In most situations in Africa, these problems are considered to be the result of an inherited curse that runs across the family lineage. Many Africans see an inherited curse as a spiritual bondage that is passed down from one generation to another. Their belief in inherited curses is illustrated by the opinion of Tolulope Monisola who through research found out that ancestral curses are considered to be one of the factors responsible for the problem of childlessness and infertility among many men and women in southwest Nigeria.[19] Ejikeme Jombo Nwagwu opines that mental, social, intellectual, moral, spiritual, material, and psychological poverty in Africa is caused by inherited curses.[20]

Omosade Awolalu and Adelumo Dopamu narrate a story that best illustrates the African understanding of these types of curses. Once upon a time, a well to do man who had many wives and slaves impregnated one of

---

18. Information from field work.
19. Tolulope Monisola, "The Socio-Cultural Perception and Implication of Childlessness among Men and Women in Urban Areas in South West, Nigeria," *Journal of Social Sciences* 21, no. 3 (2009): 205.
20. E. J. Nwagwu, "Unemployment and Poverty in Nigeria: A Link to National Insecurity," *Global Journal of Politics and Law Research* 2, no. 1 (2014): 23.

his slaves, and therefore took her as one of his many wives. When other wives delivered their babies, they were usually treated with loving delicacies. But when this slave girl put to bed, she was not so treated. She was given a cooked lizard to eat. The slave woman therefore cursed the husband and the entire family saying that any child born in the family would die if the child's mother was not presented with a cooked lizard to eat, and that failure to do so would be punished with the death of the other children. It is reported that since that day, the curse became operational in the family even on the unborn children.[21]

In addition, one respondent I interviewed clearly illustrated this type of curse. According to this person, there was a family in one of the Yoruba ethnic groups in Africa, and the family had maltreated a slave girl in the olden days. The slave girl was impregnated by one of the sons of the family. The family rejected the pregnancy and forced the girl to remove the pregnancy. In the course of removing the pregnancy, the girl died. Shortly before she died and while in pain, she placed a curse on the entire family that any time any member of that family was pregnant, they would not give birth in a natural way but through pain, loss, surgical operations, and unusual ways. Since that time, every woman in that family has delivered through a surgical operation till this day.

Those who are under inherited curses are believed to be born already destined to face certain misfortunes and dominated by a force beyond human control. Such misfortunes are not acquired but are inborn. Only the victims suffer the consequences with little or no knowledge of the root of the curse.[22] The belief in generational or inherited curses is one of the major areas and the strongest curse aspect in Africa. This belief stems from the African view that no divisions exist between spirit and body, animate and inanimate, living and non-living, dead and living, and physical and metaphysical. Most Africans generally believe that humans are in constant relationship with one another and with the invisible world, and that they are in a state of strong dependence on nonphysical powers and beings.[23] As said earlier, in African cosmology the spiritual is not separated from the non-spiritual; therefore events or situations in economic, medical, and cultural spheres of reality are open to multiple interpretations.[24] For example, some tribes in Nigeria, Kenya, and Zimbabwe

---

21. J. Omosade Awolalu and P. Adelumo Dopamu, *West African Traditional Religion* (Lagos: Macmillan, 2005), 237.

22. J. Dupuis, *Christianity and the Religions: From Confrontation to Dialogue* (Maryknoll: Orbis, 2001), 20.

23. J. Cilleers, "Formations and Movements of Christian Spirituality in Urban African Context," *African Spirituality* 21 (2015): 10.

24. Owojaiye, "Problem of the False Prophets."

believe no family does not have an inherited curse. They believed that since the forefathers were not Christians, they must have sinned and committed their descendants to many dangerous covenantal stipulations.

Self-inflicted curses

The final type of curse is that placed by people upon themselves. For example, a situation is reported of a woman who was wayward and became pregnant very early in life. Therefore, it was difficult for her to give birth because she was too young. In the course of her painful delivery, she cursed herself that may she never give birth again in her life. It is said that through the remaining part of her life, she earnestly wanted to have children but she could not. This situation was interpreted as the result of the curse she placed on herself.

Who and What Can Be Cursed?
Individual humans

Africans widely believe that individuals can be cursed, and in fact that individuals are the principal and most susceptible objects of curses.[25] In other words, they believe that humans are the most prominent objects, targets, and causes of curses. Unlike in Western empiricism and epistemology, in African anthropological conceptions, humans are not viewed as purely material and mechanical objects but more as spiritual beings who can be affected by spiritual forces like curses. Africans believe that curses have the possibility of changing and altering a person's destiny. During oral interviews, Solomon Abogunrin, Oladele Balogun, and other respondents noted that in traditional African beliefs, one of the major purposes of curses is to destroy and reconfigure the destiny of victims.

Families, towns, communities, villages, ethnic groups, nations

In some cases, curses can be placed on individuals but also on their family, ethnic group, town, clan, dynasty, lineage, and even nation.[26] Africans believe that if an individual is cursed, that curse may be transmitted to the person's

---

25. Ayegboyin, "*Epe* (Oath of Cursing)," 198.
26. M. N. Muliro, T. M. Theuri, and R. M. Matheka, "Traditional Oath Administration and Cleansing in Africa: The Case of the Akamba Ethnic Group in Kenya," *The International Journal of Humanities and Social Sciences* 3, no. 6 (June 2015): 214.

family and unborn children. When this type of curse manifests in a family with blood links for up to two generations, it is referred to as a generational curse by the deliverance ministers in Africa.[27] Some Africans even believe that a whole continent can be cursed. For example, Soderton Hogskola said that the Blacks taught that they were a cursed people and that the punishment for their ancestors' acts was slavery.[28] In fact some Yoruba Christians of Nigeria believe that the Yoruba ethnic group was cursed by an ancient Yoruba king named Aole. His curse was that the Yoruba race would be poor, enslaved, wretched, and have ill luck in the Nigerian political leadership. So many Yoruba Christians believe that this curse is the reason why many Yoruba lose political elections even up till the present time. I have heard many Nigerians, even Christians, interpreting the political plight of the Yoruba extraction in the light of the historical curses of King Aole.

Traditional Africans also believe that human names can be cursed. Family names can be cursed. Family eulogy can also be cursed. The fear of curses is real in Africa.

Ghosts or spirits

Some Africans believe that not only can people or human-related entities be cursed, even a ghost or spirit can similarly be cursed. When a ghost haunts the living or roams about after burial rites have been performed, such a ghost is believed to be cursed.[29] Many Africans believe that it is possible for the spirit of the dead to roam around in this world for many identifiable reasons. In fact, some have mentioned instances in which they saw or noticed a spirit of the dead revisiting their family. This belief is the reason why some Pentecostal churches in Africa place curses on spirits and ghosts that are believed to be the main cause of the misfortunes of the living. Even before people are dead, Africans believe that the spirit of the living can be invoked and curses can be placed on those people even without their awareness. People whose spirit has been cursed would just notice some unfortunate occurrences in their life. This belief is part of the reason why Africans are so fearful of the power of curses.

---

27. Lekan Babatunde, *No More Curses* (Lagos: Grace House Media, 2010), 17–18.

28. Soderton Hogskola quoted in D. Friedrick, *My Bondage, My Freedom* (New York: Miller, Orton, 1857).

29. Kayode, *Understanding African Traditional Religion*, 44.

Possessions or properties

Africans believe that properties, assets, and personal belongings can be cursed. In fact, an individual's source of blessing, income, joy, and comfort can be cursed. A degree certificate can be cursed. Farm land can be cursed so that it will not yield the expected produce. An ongoing building project can be cursed so that the owner of the building will not be able to complete the project. This cursing of property is the reason why some African Pentecostals make sure they pray every time they are on their land for building projects, and on many occasions, Pentecostal pastors ask their members to bring their working cutlass, farming equipment, writing materials for students, and other occupational equipment for anointing services.[30] Many students believe their writing pen needs deliverance and anointing so they can pass. During an oral interview, a female respondent from Laughter Assembly Pentecostal Church in Nigeria narrated a situation about a man who started a building project, but he could not complete the project because the land on which he was building is cursed.

Marriages, occasions, and events

When a married couple is not able to produce children, or when divorce always threatens the stability of their marriage, Africans believe the marriage is cursed. This cursing is possible when a man and a woman get married without seeking and securing the proper consent of their parents. The belief that a marriage can be cursed is one of the reasons why in some churches in Africa, the would-be couple will go through deliverance services to ward off a curse before they are joined together in holy matrimony. Other occasions and events can also be cursed so that they will not bring the expected results.

Character and moral consciousness

Traditional Africans believe that the character and moral life of a person can be cursed. For instance, when someone steals some items and refuses to confess and return the items, the owner of the items and the elders of the community can place a curse on the offender. This type of curse usually includes that the offender would always be stealing other people's property. Specifically, that the person under this type of curse would always steal things that are not

---

30. Deji Aiyegboyin, "'But Deliver Us from Evil …': The Riposte of the MFM and Its Implications for the Reverse in Mission," *Orita: Ibadan Journal of Religious Studies* 37, no. 1–2 (June/December, 2005), 38.

important. This type of curse often puts its victims into public shame and negative labeling. In addition, if a woman is involved in extramarital affairs, her husband may place curses on her sexual moral life such that the woman would always be involved in sexual affairs that will put her into shame and damage her image. Also, families in some African villages are believed to have a curse on their character, such that any child born into such families would not have any option other than to exhibit a particular set of negative traits that have been spiritually associated with the family through the curse. The power of curses in Africa is dreadful!

The Causes of Curses

Africans do not believe in a causeless curse because for any curse to come to operation, there must be a definite, identifiable cause. The field research I conducted revealed that Africans believe that offenses to family or community gods and goddesses can result in curses on the offenders and their family or community. Also, breaking the stipulations of communal or societal taboos is a major cause of curses.[31] In African societies, many families and communities have taboos, that is, things that must not been seen, done, or permitted. Usual societal restrictions include rivers where women must not bathe or fetch water or forests where little children must not go. Other taboos are related to times or seasons, for example when women must not go out because of certain festivals that are ongoing. Others relate to animals that must not be eaten in certain clans and communities. More space is given to the relationship between curses and taboos below. If anybody dares break any of these prohibitions, curses are the major results on the offender. Apart from taboos, breaking covenant can also result in dangerous curses. The concept of covenant is very strong in the belief systems of Africans. People believe that covenants exist in families, between families, and between families and certain deities. Anytime any party to this covenant breaks the stipulations of the covenant, curses will result.

In addition, indecent behaviors and acts such as incest can lead to curses. Sex is more than physical intercourse in the African context; it is also a spiritual union. Sex between members of the same family is highly prohibited. If anyone

---

31. This finding is in line with Randee Ijatuyi-Morphe, *Africa's Social and Religious Quest* (Jos: Logos Quest House, 2011), 22–24; Odejobi Cecilia Omobola, "An Overview of Taboo and Superstition Among the Yoruba of South West Nigeria," *Mediterranean Journal of Social Sciences*, Sapienza University of Rome 4, no. 2 (2013): 221–28; O. O. Familusi, "The Threat to Taboo as a Means of Inculcating Ethics in Yoruba Society," *Orita: Ibadan Journal of Religious Studies* 41, no. 2 (2009): 102–11; and F. Steiner, *Taboo* (London: Routledge, 2004), 44.

is found doing such acts, curses can be placed on him or her. Disobedience to parents is also a major cause of curses in African traditional belief. Parents are feared and respected in Africa. If someone beats a father or a mother, Africans believe that person's children will also beat that person, and this behavior may result in generational curses.

However, there are some extreme cases where people may be cursed not because of their misdeeds or those of anyone related to them. Some wicked curses can also be placed on innocent people due to the wickedness of a curser who is overcome with envy, unhealthy rivalry, etc. Cursing the innocent is one of the thorny issues in the subject of curses in Africa!

The Cursing Process

There is no singular cursing process or way to curse in traditional African society. Sometimes cursing involves a mere utterance of negative words, and sometimes the words may not have to be uttered or pronounced. However, when the cursing process involves cursing professionals, some rituals may be involved. Africans believe that when a cursing priest or herbalist is involved, the curses are more powerful. Particular actions are also said to make the curse more powerful, sometimes the process involves placing a charm on the tongue or putting a prepared charm on a tiny gourd and kissing it before uttering the curse on someone.[32] Sometimes, the methods and cursing process may not involve ordinary words.

Some Africans believe that some curses do not need to be pronounced before they become operative and potent. For example, certain actions can constitute cursing. For instance, a mother exposing her nakedness to her grown son for something offensive he did constitutes a curse which would negatively affect the son.[33] Sometimes, a person can be placed under a curse without the curser uttering the curse. If a person breaks a serious taboo, or trespasses some covenanted agreement, Africans believe that person is under a curse as a result.

---

32. This finding on cursing processes agrees well with previous qualitative field research conducted by George Simpson on the traditional healing system in the Ibadan and Lalupon lands of Nigeria. See G. E. Simpson, *Yoruba Religion and Medicine in Ibadan* (Ibadan: Ibadan University Press, 1980), 82.

33. Wachege, "Curses and Cursing," 1–11.

The Symptoms of Curses

How do curses manifest in a person's life? Africans believe that curses are highly symptomatic. The effects are referred to as symptoms, and they can be disastrous. Symptoms are also used to diagnose the causal factors of life misfortunes in African society.[34] However, sometimes, curses may not be immediately symptomatic; they may delay in bringing forth signs. When this happens, Africans believe that the curse has been strategically planned for a future appearance. But when the symptoms show up, they serve as a pointer to the presence of a curse in a person's life. The following are some of the symptoms of curses.

1. **Stagnancy in a person's life.** When a person's progress becomes unusually stale in spite of much effort, sometimes people take it as a sign that the person is under a curse. For instance, if a married couple cannot have children when expected, people may believe that the couple is under a curse from either their family, their parents, a family god, or even from an ex-boyfriend or girlfriend.

2. **Regular occurrences of misfortune or a recurring negative pattern.** Africans believe that if misfortune or ill luck regularly happens in a person's life or in a family, the misfortune is a pointer to a particular curse in that family. For instances in some families, every male child dies at the age of forty. In others, every female child of a family cannot find suitable marriage suitors until they are more than thirty years of age.[35]

3. **Marital failures.** Instances of marital stagnancy, barrenness, marital instability, miscarriage, and stillbirths can be taken as signs of a curse in a person's life. In some families, female children do not live long in their husband's house; one or other reason always brings them back to their father's house. These problems are seen as symbols of a curse.

4. **Sudden decline in fortune.** A person who struggles to gather a lot in life and suddenly becomes poor and wretched through a series of negative occurrences can be said to be under a curse.

---

34. J. Kwabena Asamoah-Gyadu, "Broken Calabashes and Covenants of Fruitfulness: Cursing Barrenness in Contemporary African Christianity," *Journal of Religion in Africa*, 37 (2007): 441.

35. D. K. Olukoya, *How to Obtain Personal Deliverances* (Lagos: TBCCM, 1996), 30.

5. **Index of continuous disappointment.** If a person's life is perpetually disturbed with unfortunate circumstances whenever that person wants to move higher or do any great thing, this inability to achieve can be seen as a sign of a curse.

6. **Recurring sicknesses with unknown causes.** If a family or community experiences the challenges of recurring sicknesses like strokes or psychiatric disorders, people see these incidences as a sign of a curse. In some cases, when a person is sick and the medical doctors cannot find the cause of the illness, people believe the illness to be a sign of a curse in operation. Similarly when a person continually has bad dreams involving deaths and bad instances, the person is seen to be under a curse.

7. **Sudden, untimely death.** If a promising young person suddenly dies, people often believe the death to be an expression of a curse in operation in that person's life.

8. **Poverty and socioeconomic backwardness.** When people work hard but their handwork does not bringing any social or economic effects as expected, a curse may be diagnosed.

9. **Character disorders.** Curses can also affect the moral nature of a person. I heard instances in my field research of people who were well behaved and had with good moral standards suddenly becoming ill-behaved when a curse was placed on them. In some parts of Africa, vices such as drunkenness, adultery, giving birth to children out of wedlock, and chronic stealing are seen as signs that a person is under a curse.

10. **Almost succeeding but never succeed syndrome.** When a person under a curse tries what every other person tries and succeeds at, that person will fail at the very point of success. In most instances, there will not be any identifiable reason for the person's failure.

Taboos and Covenants in the Notion of Curses

The belief in taboos and covenants in African society deserves space in this work. An identifiable relationship can be seen between taboos, covenants and the potency of curses in African traditional understanding. When one enters into a covenant with a divinity, the covenant usually includes sanctions and taboos. One has to obey all of the covenantal regulations and taboos, otherwise a curse may be inflicted. Africans believe in the sacredness of covenantal relationships and the concept of taboos as cohesive forces that bind the community together. Both individuals and society are involved in each other, and the conduct of individual members of the society affects the entire society for good or for evil. The term "covenant" means an agreement between two people with the implication that the one who breaks the agreement will be penalized for doing so. In the African religio-cultural context, covenant has a deeper meaning and is a more binding force.[36] The concept of covenant in the African context has both vertical and horizontal dimensions. The vertical dimension is the type of covenant that exists between an individual, a community, and a divine being, while the horizontal dimension is the type of agreement that exists between two individuals. In the horizontal type of covenant, a divine being is usually invoked or invited to bear witness and to offer divine sanctioning. Now a lot of punishment stipulations are attached in the process of making a covenant, especially covering the event that any party to the covenant breaks or disobeys the terms and conditions, particularly in the horizontal dimension of a covenant.

The findings from my primary research show that one of the sources of curses in the African context is breaking covenants. In fact, breaking the stipulations of certain long-standing covenants is one of the chief causes of curses. Africans believe that in ancient times, some families and ethnic groups in their search for help in the many intertribal wars and crises secured this help from gods, goddesses, and other divine beings by entering into covenantal relationship. In some instances, the stipulations of these covenants included that if the covenant was broken, every male child of the family or the community would die untimely at a certain age, or that no male child of the community would ever succeed if they travel outside of that community. In this way, the covenant curses became transgenerational and resulted in the struggles in the family or in the community.

Along with the concept of covenant, the African notion of curses is related to the concept of taboos. Taboos are unwritten laws and societal codes of set don'ts and dos that are designed to restrain people from breaking social norms and to preserve the needed social harmony through good relationships between human beings.[37] Taboos are forbidden things and prohibited actions, and breaking them incurs supernatural punishment. Therefore, when a taboo is infringed, one of the resultant effects is a curse. Awolalu Omosade notes that –

---

36. Awolalu and Dopamu, *West African Traditional Religion*, 233.
37. Omobola, "Overview of Taboo," 221–28; Familusi, "Threat to Taboo."

In African communities, there are sanctions recognized and approved as social and religious conduct on the part of the individual in the society and of the community as a whole. A breach of, or failure to adhere to the sanctions is a sin, and this incurs the displeasure of Deity and His functionaries. Sin is therefore doing that which is contrary to the will and directions of Deity. It includes any immoral behavior, ritual mistakes, and any offenses against God or man, breach of covenant, breaking of taboos and doing anything regarded as abominable and polluting. We cannot speak of sin in isolation – it has to be related to God and to man. To disregard God, divinities and ancestral spirits is to commit a sin. Likewise, to disregard the norms and taboos of the society is to commit a sin.[38]

Solutions to Curses in Primal African Society

Interestingly, Africans have a lot of traditional methods which are usually prescribed to help and deliver the victims of curse. Three steps are usually taken to remove a curse: divination to discover the type and source of the curse, ritual activities, and sacrifices. The first step is for individuals or a community who knows they are under a curse to consult an oracle so as to know the cause and type of the curse and the situations that surrounded the beginning of the curse.[39] Most Africans believe that there cannot be any curse without a definite cause. Though its originating cause can be hidden from the victim, the oracle is capable of discovering and revealing it. After divination has been done to know the type and the cause of the curse, the oracle prescribes the appropriate steps to be taken to remove the curse. This second step may include appeasement and restitution to the person who placed the curse on the victim or to a god or goddess that is responsible for the operation of the curse. The third step is to offer a sacrifice which is usually part of the efforts to appease the powers behind the curse. The sacrifice may be offered at night, near streams, at a fork in a road, in thick groves of trees, or preferably at road junctions which are believed to be the rendezvous places of spirits at night.[40] The oracle through divination may even prescribe ritual washing of the head of the victim or

---

38. J. O. Awolalu, "Sin and Its Removal in African Traditional Religion," *Journal of the American Academy of Religion* 44, no. 2 (1 June 1976): 279.

39. Mbiti, *African Religion and Philosophy*, 170.

40. Ayegboyin, "*Epe* (Oath of Cursing)," 195.

killing an animal such as a goat or fowl and using the blood to replace that of the victim of the curse. Sometimes ritual marks and incisions will be made following the head washing and smearing or daubing the head or other parts of the body.

The above presentation is an objective description of what Africans believe on the concept of curses. It is clearly evident that the concept of curses is still largely strong in the contemporary African belief system in spite of the influx of Western education, technological advancement, civilization, and modern spirituality and religions. What are the implications of the African belief in the potency of curses for biblical Christianity, evangelical spirituality, Christian social morality, and Christian discipleship in Africa? Do contemporary African Christians believe that they can be affected by curses? What is the nature and relevance of the African church response to the dilemmas and fear of curses in the lived experience of Africans? How do African preachers and church leaders interpret the Bible in relation to the traditional theology of curses in Africa? The next section will answer these questions.

6

The Reality and Fear of Curses in African Christianity

The previous chapter presents the themes and issues included in the African traditional theology of curses. This chapter examines the concept of curses in contemporary African Christianity. Particularly, we look at the fear that African Christians have of curses and how that fear is expressed and treated. Two questions are asked and answered in this chapter: How do African Christians interpret their lived experiences in relation to curses, and how do they express their fear of curses in relation to their experiences? This chapter examines the real-life, empirical issues and phenomena of curses in the contemporary African Christian context.

The African church exists in a context which has a high level of fear, frustration, anxiety, and despair. Too many children die of hunger; too many persons suffer injustice against their human rights; too many are tortured unjustly. In fact, in too many eyes, the years of war have extinguished the fires of hope and joy, and too many bodies are bowed down by the weight of that particular repugnant death called fear and despair.[1] Of the many struggles a person may have, the fear of evil and the attack of unseen powers such as curses can be some of the more frightening. The horrible fear of curses and their dangers is one of the troubles in African Christianity. While fear of unseen forces such as curses is a major issue in African Christianity, the extent to which the fear is genuine is debatable. Therefore, any valid discussion on the expression of curses and fear of them in African Christianity must start with the genuineness of the experiences of the African Christian.

---

1. Akan Boesak, *If This Is a Treason, I Am Guilty* (Grand Rapids: Eerdmans, 1987), 28–29. See also Orobator Agbokhiamegbe, "The Idea of the Kingdom of God in African Theology," *Studie Missionalaia* 46 (1997): 327–57.

The Reality of Curses in the African Experience

Is the African fear of curses real? Do African Christians also fear curses? The fear of curses is real and strong in contemporary Africa. Typical Africans fear curses more than they admire blessings. Africans come to Christianity with many cultural beliefs, and one of the cruxes of these cultural beliefs is the fear of metaphysical powers. But is the fear of curses a reality or a mere emotion?

While hypersensitivity, overconsciousness, and syncretism may be related to the concept of curses in Africa, we must be empathetic and careful not to overunderestimate or be hypercritical in our understanding and assessment of the experiences of Africans in relation to curses. Many may be tempted to argue that the African concept of curses is entirely superstitious and emotional since cursing cannot be empirically proven. But while the African pragmatic approach to the existential questions of curses may be influenced by hypersensitivity, syncretism, and a close rapport with the African cultural matrix, their experience must be neutrally discussed, and these experiences must be factored into any valid pastoral care. In fact, before any valid theological reflection will be done on African Christians' fear of curses, their experiences must first be empathetically studied.

There are many important reasons why African experiences of curses must be empathetically examined. First, religious experience is very important in African religious understanding and has been the founding factor for many churches, especially AICs.[2] For example, the foundation of Joroho, People of the Spirit of Luo extraction of Kenya, is centered on the mystical traumatic experience of Alfayo Odongo Mango, and that of the Celestial Church of Christ is attached to the mystical experience of Oshoffa while marooned in the forest in search of timber. Virtually all of the church denominations and ministries associated with AICs trace their emergence to a traumatic religious experience of their charismatic founders that became a major turning point in their histories and form the major foundation bedrock for their festivals, liturgy, and theology. Second, religious experience is included in the recent paradigmatic shift in the phenomenological study of religions because it helps us to understand the varied fronts of impact that a religious concept has on practitioners. An objective evaluation of African religious experience will help us to arrive at an unbiased assessment of their theology. Lastly, the pragmatic approach to Christian life and existential issues adopted by most African Christians can only be understood in the context of their experiences. Many African writers and other writers on African Christianity have pointed

---

2. Adogame and Jafta, "Zionists, Aladura and Roho," 320.

out ways in which the Africa context influences African Christianity, but the particular impact of experiences as a theme in the African context has not been adequately assessed. The most important thing is not to have scientific proof for the Africans' experiences of curses that is in line with Western empiricism but to note that many Africans have complicated and mysterious lived experiences which we must pause to examine, and we must bring to the fore the theology expressed in their experiences.

For us to interrogate further, we have to understand various ways in which the fear of curses is expressed in contemporary African Christianity. Since we have seen that the experiences of Africans are real to them and that while Western empirical models may not capture African experiential categories, the Africans have contextual meanings for their experiences, we can move to the various means of expressing the fear of curses in the African context.

Contemporary Expressions of the Fear of Curses

While this list cannot be exhaustive, the following suffice for an adequate understanding of how the fear of curses is expressed in the African context.

Name changing phenomenon

Because many Africans believe that curses from their ancestors can be transmitted through names and family blood lines, many usually change their names, especially when they become a Christian. They change their surnames because they believe that the curses reside in the name and that these curses can be discontinued when the name is changed. The practice of changing names is common among members of African Pentecostal churches and AICs who believe that a Christian name is more powerful than their traditional names.[3] Names are powerful to the named and the one naming in African religious consciousness and are believed to carry deep intrinsic connections between the past and present and between the living and dead. Names are believed to carry African ontological and anthropological codes which include personality, destiny, status, wishes, blessings, curses, and the whole program of life.

A story is told of an African pastor who initially named his son "battle-ax" but had to change the name because the boy was very stubborn and rude. I

---

3. J. K. Ayantayo, "The Phenomenon of Change of Name and Identity in Yoruba Religious Community in the Light of Social Change," *Orita: Ibadan Journal of Religious Studies* 42, no. 1 (2010): 1–16.

know of some Christians who bear Yoruba surnames such as Awoyemi (which means "occultism has profited me"), Esudara ("Satan spares this one"), and Ogungbemi ("god of iron protects me") have changed and discontinued the surname so as to discontinue some negative family trends. Others have have changed their indigenous names such as Babatunde ("the late father has come back"), Esubiyi ("the devil has given birth to this"), Jekayinfa ("let us thank the oracle"), Awokoya ("occultism has relieved me of suffering"), Ifafoore ("the oracle spoke well"), Esugbami ("the devil rescued me"), and Arogundade ("someone who is happy for war") to Christian names such as Stephen, Moses, Prosper, Jesugbami ("Jesus has rescued me"), Gentle, Marvelous, Peace, Glory, Blessing, Precious, Abraham, Joseph, Godwin, etc. This name change phenomenon is not only present among the Yoruba; the same is practiced elsewhere such as among the Igbo of Nigeria. I was told of an elder in a church in Ebonyi state in Nigeria who changed his name from Dibiamaka, which is related to occultism, to Chukwuamaka, which means God is good. He changed his name because he noticed that some negative trends that had happened to his family were reoccurring in his own life. What is amazing is that this elder who changed his name has long been a Christian, and as a committed Christian, he still felt that changing his name would help to relieve him of some repeated life challenges.

Many scholars such as Igboin, Bujo, Ayantayo, and others have discovered that colonial, Western, modern factors are behind the current name changing phenomenon in Africa and have criticized the practice as an expression of mental slavery.[4] But based on my interactions with many Africans and hearing about their experiences, in most instances African Christians changed either their personal name or surname due to their fear that some curses may be transmitted from the past. Two things must be noted to forestall ambiguity. First, this practice does not mean that only the fear of curses causes many Africans to change their given names, surnames, or ancestral names. Many reasons apart from the fear of curses can be attributed to these name changes.

Second, it is surprising to note that some Africans who have more fearful ancestral names such as Ikusemran, meaning death has added to the calamity, do not change it because even though their family name is literally attached to evil, the family that bears the name has so attracted wealth, posterity, and

---

4. B. O. Igboin, "Names and the Reality of Life: An Inquiry into Inherent Power in Names among the Owan People of Nigeria," *Ado Journal of Religions* 2, no. 1 (July 2004): 9–26; L. Bujo, *African Christian Morality at the Age of Inculturation* (Nairobi: Paulines, 1990); and E. A. Ayandele, *The Missionary Impact on Modern Nigeria 1842–1914* (London: Longman, 1966).

success that every member of the family wants to identify with it. Therefore, although the meaning of the name may be bad, the members of the family choose not to change it because they want the advantages of being known with the family. However, this desire also shows that the name changing phenomenon in Africa is an expression of fear of some perceived negative patterns and trends in a family or in a life. Many Africans also confirmed to me that when they changed their names from some occultic-related name to a Christian-related name, they began to see differences in their life situations. These kinds of experiences must be taken into consideration in developing a uniquely African Christianity.

Low self-esteem

The fear of curses is also expressed in the low self-esteem of many African Christians. These Christians are affected in their self-evaluation and understanding of the power of Christ by their incessant fear of curses. Many still believe that they have to forcefully remove their curses through prayer, fasting, and deliverance. Some have allowed local prophets to tie them with ropes, beat them with a cane and wash them with "spiritually produced soap" so that they can be cured of their curses. Some have been stigmatized because people believe there are curses in their family lineage. J. K. Asamoah-Gyadu shows that in Ghana, many people are carrying the enslaving effects of their belief in curses and have been entangled in shrine slavery.[5]

Popular prayers and deliverance programs

Curses are one of the themes in the pragmatic approach to the existential questions of life among African Christians. Generally, Africans demonstrate a pragmatic approach to Christian life through prayers, songs, and hymns. Special effort is made on healing, deliverance, and exorcising curses to conquer the myriads of evil forces that are operating curses in their lives. Spiritual songs, hymns, and sacred languages are commonly used in many African indigenous churches to battle against curses. Invocations of psalms and prescriptions of fasting and prayer are common in these churches. For example, periodically the Mountain of Fire and Miracle Ministries (MFMM), one of the rapidly

---

5. J. K. Asamoah-Gyadu, "Mission to Set the Captive Free: Healing, Deliverance, and Generational Curses in Ghanaian Pentecostalism," *International Review of Mission* 93, no. 370–71 (2004): 389–406.

increasing neo-Pentecostal churches in Africa, publishes annual prayer manuals accompanied with seventy days fasting and prayers in an attempt to liberate their members from a myriad of evil attacks, in which curses rank as premium. A brief excerpt from the 2010 edition of their prayer guide shows that from prayer items 52 to 186, up to twenty deal with generational curses and bloodline evil.[6] In addition to these prayers, Dr. Daniel Olukoya, the founder of MFMM, gave seven deliverance prayer points during his sermon titled "Breaking Family Curses." Some of these points are the following: "Every curse in my family bloodline, die by the Blood of Jesus. Witchcraft curses in my family line, die in Jesus's Name. Ancestral Pharaohs in my family, die in Jesus's name. Any power that pursued my parents and is still pursuing me, die in Jesus's name. Collective captivity in my family, scatter in Jesus's name."[7]

Many devotional books on prayer produced by other African gospel preachers including Pastor W. F. Kumuyi, Pastor E. A. Adeboye, Bishop David Oyedepo, Evangelist Ojo Ade, and many others usually have numerous prayer items on curses and how to secure deliverance from curses.[8] In the next chapter we give close attention to selected sermons on curses from popular African preachers.

Apart from sermons and prayer content, I found out from attending church programs, deliverance, and revival services, or watching online through social media, that most of the program themes in contemporary African churches are largely centered on ways to confront the fear of curses. A few examples and some evidence will explain these programs more clearly.

---

6. Mountain of Fire and Miracles Ministries, *2010 Seventy Days Fasting and Prayers* (Yaba: MFM Press, 2010), 66–79.

7. Daniel Olukoya, "Breaking Family Curses," YouTube (2 October 2020).

8. W. F. Kumuyi, *Curses and Cures* (Lagos: Zoe, 1990); E. A. Adeboye, *Curses and Blessings* (Lagos: Christian Living Books, 2011); David Oyedepo, *Breaking the Curses of Life* (Ota: Dominion, 1997); and Ojo Ade, *Parents'-Caused Implications* (Lagos: Ojo Ade Press, n.d.).

The Reality and Fear of Curses in African Christianity   99

Figure 1: The word written in the caption above reads *Ori-Oke Pegunre* (translated: "A Prayer Mountain where Curses are Broken and Cured"). This church signpost in Osun state, Nigeria, shows that the church is a mountain of prayer where curses are cured. In fact, "curse" form the major part of the name of the inter-denominational prayer Centre.

Figure 2: A flyer designed to create awareness for when services concentrating on breaking generational curses will be held.

Figure 3: A program flyer creating awareness on prayer sessions that were held for the purpose of deliverance from generational debt.

In addition, Rev. Gordian Okezie, a deliverance minister with Evangelical Church Winning All (ECWA), relates an instance in which a pastor was attacked due to his ineffective prayer life and ran mad. He was taken to hospital, but Okezie and his team asked permission to take the pastor out of the hospital for deliverance prayer. And after the prayer, the man was cured. Okezie believes that curses are one of the causes of such attacks even on Christians.[9]

Communal activity abstinence and home visitation apathy

The fear of curses has also made many African Christians indifferent about living in or visiting their native village or town. Many fear that once they see their family household, the spirit of their inherited curses will enter their life and cause dangerous happenings. In fact, many African Christian youth have been told by their parents not to ever visit their hometowns. As a pastor in one of the villages in southwest Nigeria, I came across a family who refused to come home for many years. When I intervened, it was reported that the family sensed that a curse of sudden death was running in their family lineage and that the only way to avert the curse was to abstain from home and that their feet must not touch the land of their village.

Abandoning family possessions and apathy for generational inheritances

Many African Christians have left their family inheritance because of their fear that death may arise from the family curses. For example, a family in Ijesha land in southwest Nigeria believed that if any man should inherit or use the family property, he would die at the age of forty. The Mada tribe of Nassarawa in northcentral Nigeria believe that inherited curses have not allowed any person from their tribe to emerge as governor because any promising person who attempts to contest the gubernatorial seat begins to face life difficulties. In fact if anybody, either a Christian or a non-Christian, from that tribe tries to contest for the governorship in the state, he dies.

A story is told of a member of an evangelical church in Lagos, Nigeria, who went home with his new car, contrary to his pastor's counsel. When he came back from his native village, he fell sick and died. While in the village, he was said to have had an encounter with some traditional curses in his home. This incidence took place in May 2021. These are the real-life experiences that make African Christians fear the danger of curses.

---

9. G. Okezie, *Christians and the Challenge of Occultism* (Jos: Midland, 2001), 17–19.

While we may see some of these perceptions as superstitious, subjective, and unreliable, we must also be very careful not to overlook the general characteristics of religious experiences. What is basically important in religious experiences is not their scientific nature according to Western indices, but what they tell us about a phenomenon as perceived and interpreted by those who experienced it.

Mass migration to Pentecostal and Charismatic churches

Another expression of the fear of curses is the mass migration of Christians to African neo-Pentecostal churches and AICs that promise through their programs and prayer sessions, crusades and deliverance, divine calling and anointing to cure curses and other demonic manifestations. Ordinarily Africans seek to answer to their fear and existential questions, and since the Pentecostal churches seem to provide pragmatic answers, many Africans have moved either partially or totally into the new generation churches. Many Africans have created a trust in the efforts of these Pentecostal ministers in finding solutions to their spiritual problems. This experience of migration has been identified as one of the current trends in African Christianity. The migration is usually from historic mission churches to Pentecostal, charismatic, neo-Pentecostal, and African independent churches.[10] This migration is evident in Nigeria, Ghana, Kenya, South Africa, and many other parts of Africa. While this movement can be understood as a multifaceted religious phenomenon, it is a good angle from which to see the level of fear of curses among African Christians. Many testimonies are shared in these new generation churches of how people who have been bedeviled by family curses and witchcraft became victorious when they joined.

Media and popular Christian movies

As succinctly summarized by Bimbo Fafowora and Raha Nyaga, we may not be aware of it, but what we do and how we do it are influenced by media.[11] The multitude and popularity of video plays and movies produced by top Christian drama ministries in Africa also point to the reality of the experience

---

10. E. K. Sarbiah, C. Niemandt, and P. White, "Migration from Historic Mission Churches to Pentecostal and Charismatic Churches in Ghana," *Verbum Ecclesia* 4, no. 1 (2020): 5.

11. B. Fafowora and R. N. Nyaga, "The Media," in *African Public Theology*, ed. S. B. Agang (Carlisle: HippoBooks, 2020), 307.

of Africans related to curses and their expressions of fear. A few samples will be enough to make the point. Mr. Shola Mike Agbooola of EVOM drama ministry in Nigeria wrote a Christian movie titled "Unknown Curse."[12] Set in a local village in an ancient time, the story is about a controversy between the family of Oyemosu and another family of an herbalist, Ifajumo, over a piece of land. The controversy reached the king, and the king ruled in favor of Oyemosu. As a result, Ifajumo the herbalist, a callous man, placed a curse on the entire family of Oyemosu. In the composition of the curse, Ifajumo prayed to his family spirit and gods that whether Oyemosu was guilty or not, the family spirit should sanction the curse on them, male and female, old and young, born and unborn. The dictates of the curses included that no woman from Oyemosu's family would have a child, that those who managed to have a pregnancy would carry their pregnancy in deep sorrow, and that those who managed to give birth would not live long to enjoy the fruit of their labor on their children. The curse on the men of Oyemosu's family was that they would never make progress; they would work for success and see success but never achieve success in life; and sickness and sadness would be their portion forever.

In the movie, these curses became operative and effective as the calamities pronounced by Ifajumo began to hit the family of Oyemosu. Any woman from the family who got pregnant either lost the pregnancy or died in the course of delivery. The same went for the male children of the family; they were very brilliant and academically intelligent. But they either ran mad or were unemployed. Even those who became educated and went to churches in the city still had these curses tormenting them, until one of the male children got someone who prayed for him to secure deliverance from the power of the curse.

Many other Christian drama productions emphasize the African fear of curses.[13] What is common in these Christian movies is the activities of demonic spirits that kept the record of all the curses a person utters and ensures that they come to pass. Sometimes a film shows a secretary who meticulously keeps a record of negative words uttered against a person, and even when that person becomes a Christian and very prayerful, the spirit still ensures that the negative spell comes to pass in that person's life. Until the victim attends a serious deliverance prayer session, he or she live under the curse. While these movies are created to educate Christians on the dangers of uttering negative words or the dangers of cursing one's children, they also reveal how fearful

---

12. S. M. Agboola, "Unknown Curse," EVOM Christian Film, YouTube (5 June 2020).

13. See for example 'Shola Mike Agboola, "Akowe Oro," EVOM Films, YouTube (23 October 2020), https://youtu.be/mBamW-HvgBY.

curses are in the experience of African Christians. Many other popular films are produced in Africa by popular Christian drama ministries such as Mount Zion in Nigeria, Kollywood and African entertainment, J. B. Blessing and Mbugua in Kenya, Nankani Studios in Accra, Ghana, and others that deeply emphasize the dangers, effects and existential fear of curses in Africa. African Christian films use narrative and dramatized stories that show a variety of experiences as well as hopes, fears, and anxiety.[14]

These movies confirm the arguments of Asonzeh Ukah and Ihejirika that Pentecostals in the African setting seek to appropriate indigenous cultural beliefs in their media productions and to reveal a convergence of Pentecostal spiritual practices in their attempt to make sense out of African social, political, and religious experiences.[15] Ihejirika's analysis of this convergence hypothesis shows that the media is a central factor used to identify religious experiences, realities, and identity. Like Owojaiye concludes, the majority of religious media and movies produced in Africa are produced by Pentecostal missions and leadership and are expressions of their theology, and that those products dealing with the concept of curses are expressions of the fear Africans have of curses. Christian movies produced on the concept of curses do not only have influence on Christians in Africa; these movies also show their experiential reality. Therefore, while these Christian movies on curses represent the influences of African Pentecostal theology, they also serve as means of expressing the fear for unseen forces such as curses and spells among contemporary Christians in Africa.

Therapeutic use of concrete or anointed physical objects

The fear of some Africans on the dangers of curses is also expressed in their prodigious use of "special anointed objects" such as wrist bands, mantles, consecrated water, candles, anointed oil, crosses, sacred numerology, and hand bells. For example, a spear or staff is used by some members of AIC such as ama Zioni, Roho, Arathi, Cherubim and Seraphim, and Celestial Church of Christ to remove demons, spells, and unseen wicked forces. Specifically, sanctified water is important for therapeutic and prophylactic functions to wash away

---

14. B. Meyer, "Praise the Lord: Popular Cinema and Pentecostalite Style in Ghana's New Public Sphere," *American Ethnologist* 31, no. 1 (2004): 92–110.

15. Walter Ihejirika, "Research of Media and Culture in Africa: Current Trends and Dialogue," *African Journal of Communication Research* 2, no. 1 (2009): 1–60 cited in Owojaiye, *Evangelical Response*, 85–87.

curses and to invoke spiritual healing of various sicknesses caused by curses. In addition, many Africans believe that all their properties must be anointed so as to remove or prevent any curse that may want to come near them. A minister of God from an evangelical church in Lagos, Nigeria, explained that some of his members put twelve anointed stones under the foundations of their buildings when laying the foundations. In addition, the members always get anointed oil and anoint the grounds on which the foundations are to be laid. When interrogated further, he confessed that his members disclosed to him that one of the reasons for this practice is because the members want to be sure that the spirit of their inherited curses will not be able to afflict their properties.

When discussing the use of symbols and items for spiritual protection and healing in Africa, the *omi iye* (healing water) of Christ Apostolic Church (CAC) must be mentioned. CAC members believe that God commanded Ayo Babaloa, one of the heroes of African indigenous churches, to bless and sanctify water and river sources for healing curses and preventing diseases and sicknesses.[16] As a result, establishing anointed water centers is a major feature of African indigenous churches in Nigeria. For example, CAC has Agbala Itura (Comfort Center), Oyo state; CAC Automatic Ashi Ibadan, Oyo state; and CAC Miracle Center, Alekunwodo, Osun state in Nigeria, just to mention a few. These deliverance centers have never lacked participants and attendees since their establishment. To keep the healing water potent, some gender restrictions are usually put in place in these prayer centers. For example, women are not allowed to fetch water from these healing waters. This healing water is another area in which African traditional thought is strongly transferred and expressed into African Christianity.

Constructing sacred spaces and popular mountaineering exercises

The rate at which African Christians organize mountain prayers, river prayers, groove prayers, and prayers in other ordinary spaces that are transformed into sacred grounds points to their level of fear of curses and their interest in solving their existential problems spiritually. Usually, those spaces are filled with prophets and prophetesses who are ready to diagnose people's existential problems and give spiritually coded information on how to solve them. The research visits I made to popular prayer mountains and religious centers in Nigeria confirms this practice. There is a serious and growing interest in

---

16. S. O. Ajayi, "Sanctified Water and Healing Miracle: Impact on the Growth of CAC in Oyo State, Nigeria," *BAJOR* 3, no. 1 (September 2017): 35.

mountaineering activities in Africa because mountains are seen as very sacred places that people visit to seek the face of God to find solutions for their spiritual dilemmas and existential battles.[17] In Nigeria alone are countless prayer mountains: Ikoyi Prayer mountains, Osun state; Mercy Prayer Mountain, Erio Ekiti; Victory Prayer Mountain, Efon Alaye; Ori Oke Iyanu – Miracle Prayer Mountain, Ido Ile, Ekiti state; Oke Ajaye, Oyo state; Ajibode Prayer Mountain, Oyo state; CAC Prayer Mountain, Odo Owa, Kwara state; CAC Power House, Odo Owa, Eye bi Okin Prayer Mountain, Osun state; Ori Oke Akinkemi in Ibadan; Ori Oke Aluyo in Afijio, Oyo state; and numerous others. I visited many of these prayer mountains and studied their liturgy, deliverance sessions, and spiritual practices not for condemnation or criticism but for understanding and wisdom. What is most common in these prayers sessions is the teaching and prayers for deliverance from curses, especially inherited curses.

I also conducted focus group studies with many mountain prayer participants and the prophets who are usually called Baba Ori Oke, the minister in charge of the prayer mountain, to examine the frequency of the topic of curses in their prayers. The participants revealed that the concept of curses and related problems are why many people go for mountain prayer. One of the study participants noted that some life problems cannot be solved on level ground but must be taken to a prayer mountain, and curses are one such problem. While traditional understanding of prayer mountains implies an elevated, rocky plain, my visits to many of the emerging prayer mountains in Africa revealed that some are just plain ground without any rocks or elevation. This shift in understanding has enabled many lower level site to be easily turned into prayer mountains. What these sacred spaces and beliefs show to us is the fact that African Christians also fear curses like those in the traditional African societies.

Dietary prescriptions and prohibitions

Some curses are associated with certain diets. Africans believe that if some people eat certain foods, the curses in operation in their families become operational. Therefore, these people abstain from these foods to prevent the curses from victimizing them. For example during oral interviews, some

---

17. A. A. Akindolie, D. O. Oni, and F. B. Akintunde, "Social Change and Adura Ori Oke (Mountain Top Prayer): A Phenomenon in Africa Christianity in South Western Nigeria," in *African Christianity in Local and Global Contexts*, ed. S. A. Fatokun (Ibadan: Department of Religious Studies, University of Ibadan, Nigeria, 2019), 467.

Christians revealed that their family must not eat some meats because their forefathers carried away animals that were shot by other hunters in the bush. The hunter who originally shot the animal sought for it and could not find it, then he pronounced curses that no male child of the family of any man who carried his animal away must taste this animal again. Ever since, if any male child of this family ate that type of animal, they would die after seven days. Therefore, the new generation of that family is fearful of death if they should taste that animal. Even when they became Christians, they still nursed the fear of the curses that predated their Christian encounters.

Sayings and parables

The fear of curses is also expressed in popular sayings and wisdom sayings in contemporary African society. Parables and sayings are communicative devices that reflect the experiences of certain people. African proverbs are very much influenced by African social, religious, and spiritual experiences. African proverbs are indicative of African orientation and are expressions of their fears, worries, optimism, pessimism, expectations, norms, and belief systems. According to Akporobaro, the major functions of African proverbs are not only to teach morals; they are also structures for wider phenomena of life.[18] They reflect the joy and sorrow of the people and are expressions of lived experiences, fears, worries, anxiety, prohibitions, dos, and don'ts. For example, an Igbo (Nigerian) proverb states, "When a man says yes, his *Chi* will also say yes." This proverb is usually said to warn others of the dangers of their negative utterances. The Yoruba in Nigeria, Ghana, and the Benin Republic have an adage that states, "*Adura san ju epe lo, bi o bagba, bi ko gba, adura san ju epe lo*" which means "prayer is better than curses; even if the prayer will not be answered, it is still better than curses."

In fact, some indigenous churches include these words in the songs they sing during church services. Other popular sayings that show the reality and fear of curses among the Yoruba tribe are "*Araye nii sinii mu epe kii sin i ja*" – "It is human beings that mistakenly fight someone, but curses do not miss their targets/ victims" – and "*Ogun a ma sin i mu, epe kii sin i pa*" – "Someone maybe mistakenly killed in a war, but curse cannot miss its target." These sayings and others are used to warn people to be careful not to do what can cause curses. By conceptualizing varied experiences into picturesque epigrammatic expressions, some African proverbs and sayings provide indications of the fear of curses

---

18. F. B. O. Akporobaro, *Introduction to African Literature* (Lagos: Princeton, 2012), 84.

in Africa. What has been established here is the fact that Africans, even contemporary Christians, still have similar traditional conceptions of curses.

I include these real expressions to show through observable phenomenon in contemporary African Christian contexts that even with the coming of modernization, civilization, urbanization, and Christianity, the fear of curses is still huge in African societies. The questions that immediately come to my mind as I ruminate over these expressions of the fear of curses in African Christianity are how has the African Christian church responded to the fear and dilemmas of curses? How has the Bible been interpreted and applied to the belief in curses in Africa? What major biblical texts are used by African Christians in their theology of curses and practice of curse deliverance ministries? How have African preachers and writers treated the concept of curses in their sermons? These are major questions that must be answered. The next chapter answers these and other relevant questions.

7

The Treatment of Curses in Contemporary African Christianity

This chapter deals with coping strategies of African Christians for the dilemma and fear of curses with special attention to African Pentecostal, neo-Pentecostal, charismatic, and AICs, with a few references to some evangelical, historic mission churches. This focus is because while the concept of curses is ubiquitous in African Christianity, it takes up more space in the liturgy, homiletics, and theology of Pentecostal, charismatic, and African independent churches than the historic mission churches. While categorizations, taxonomies, and brandings of blocs in contemporary African Christianity have been made, this discussion merely uses the contemporary African church as a collective taxonomy to enhance simplicity of identity and presentation of issues. And because the concept of curses is usually present in almost all main Christian groups in Africa, dedicating huge space for clarification on taxonomy is unnecessary.

Here we examine the solutions that are usually provided to the dilemmas of curses in contemporary African Christianity through African Christian theology and practices of deliverance prayer, prophetic church rituals, Bible interpretation and application, sermons, publications, and social media. Popular and top Christian preachers and writers were selected from Kenya, Ghana, Nigeria, the Benin Republic, Cameroon, and other countries. Their sermons and publications were selected and analyzed to understand how the majority of African Christian leaders and preachers attempt to help their followers cope with the fear and confusion of curses.

However, it must be put on special record that I do not aim at criticizing these preachers nor other popular African preachers but strive for a purely objective analysis of their attempts at engaging the struggles of Africans with the existential problems of curses. The sermons selected for illustration are available on YouTube with no copyright restrictions. In fact, some of these sermons include notices telling the general public that they are available for research and devotional use.

Curses and Imprecatory Prayers: Cursing or Praying?

Imprecatory prayers are far more common in African settings than in any other context of Christianity. This type of prayer is seen as a tool of vengeance and destruction of enemies. "Spiritual enemy consciousness" is rife in the spiritual orientation of African Christians. When average African Christians pray against their enemy, they usually have a known person in mind as the enemy who is behind their curses and misfortunes. The use of imprecatory prayers is ubiquitous in African Christianity, but it is more pronounced in AICs and African Pentecostal denominations. Some who feel that they have been ill-treated by their enemies through curses and spells approach God to tell him what to do to their offenders. On most occasions, these prayers involve using curses to solve curses, or what is popularly called "back to sender" prayer bombs.

Common prayers in contemporary Christianity include for example, "In Jesus name I curse everyone born of a woman who is delaying my success." "In Jesus name I curse every enemy of my father's house, that they shall die, die, die by fire, now." "May every enemy of my father's household receive fire and burn to ashes." "May every gathering of evil people putting curses on my family, business, and career be paralyzed in Jesus's name." "Oh Lord, send your arrows to the foundation of my life and roast to ashes anyone behind my misfortunes." And "My father, return every curse to the curser and set me free." While prayers such as these look interesting to prayerful people, a deeper look at them shows that they are only prayers on one side but curses on the other side. These prayers are like using curses to heal curses, cursing in response to curses, and a reactionary religious practice. They are equal to doing the same thing that the "enemy" is accused of doing. These prayers look like changing the biblical model and purpose of prayer from noble and spiritual to selfishness and banality of existential considerations.[1]

In addition, these prayers reflect how African Christians understand and use the Bible in the warfare of life. One of the ways the Bible is appropriated in the struggle against curses in the African church is to harvest certain verses that are imprecatory in nature and to recite them to counter the power of curses. Many African Christians engage in an existential and reflective approach to the Bible. They see the Bible as not only an inspired text but also as a collection of oracles that can be pronounced when seeking protection, healing, and life successes and also to engage the devil and his manifestations such as curses.

In many African churches, the book of Psalms is selectively used for this purpose, which I call "Christian cursing." The book of Psalms is seen as a magical booklet. For example, some psalms are read either three or seven times after which the page or pages of the psalm are dipped into drinking and bathing water. Sometimes African Christians recite imprecatory psalms in the center of a circle of burning candles of different colors at a prescribed time, usually in the middle of the night. On some occasions, reading imprecatory psalms is accompanied with killing animals, or with placing materials like sugar cane or palm oil at a crossroad, market place, or sea bed. Psalms 35 or 109 are sometimes torn, folded, and wrapped with the skin of a particular animal and worn round the waist while traveling or hung on the door post for protection and to ward off any enemies and their manifestations such as curses.[2] Is this not very close to syncretism?

The situation becomes more disappointing when some Christians, even some church leaders, also visit local shrines to invoke curses, prevent curses, or cure curses.[3] In the Ashanti province of Ghana and in southwest Nigeria, the practice of invoking gods to curse offenders is rampant even among Christians and pastors. Many African Christians are driven by the fear of curses pronounced in the name of local deities. Therefore, when some are faced with

---

1. I. M. Oludele, "The Medicine as Poison, the Physician as the Killer: Modern Pentecostal Theology and Practices as Sources of Insecurity," in *Religion and Insecurity Issues*, ed. J. K. Ayantayo and S. A. Fatokun (Ibadan: University of Ibadan, Department of Religious Studies, 2015), 203.

2. S. O. Abogunrin, "Decolonizing New Testament Interpretation in Africa," in *Decolonization of Biblical Interpretation in Africa*, ed. S. O. Abogunrin, NABIS, series 4 (Ibadan: Alofe, 2005), 258.

3. T. A. Oduro, "Who Answers Prayers Quicker: Ancestral Deities of Africa or the God of Abraham: Exploring a Puzzle of African Christianity," in *African Christianity in Local and Global Context*, ed. S. A. Fatokun, University of Ibadan, Department of Religious Studies Series 7 (Ibadan: Baptist Press Nigeria, 2019), 148

dilemma of life, they visit local deities to invoke grievous imprecations. For example in the Ashanti region, the phone of a pastor, evangelist Kofi Adu, was stolen, and he went to the local shrine to invoke Antoa Nyamaa, a local deity, to curse the offender. He was fined by the local community leader and required to pay three sheep and drinks to elders of the Tepa traditional council for abuse of local deities.[4] Similarly two ministers, Rev. Ebenezer Adarkwa-Yiadom of Ebenezer Prayer Mission and Bishop Daniel Obinim of the International God's Way Church in Ghana, used Antoa Nyamaa to curse each other. Because of the abuse of shrine invocation, the local traditional leader, Osei Tutu II, the king of the Ashantis, banned shrine cursing and shrine invocation.[5] The African Christian conception of cures is largely traditional and does not reflect adequate biblical reflection. What could have caused this misconception? Is it not due to the interpretation of life and experiences?

Interpretation of Lived Experiences

Before we examine the African Christian hermeneutic of texts related to curses, it is profitable to say a word or two on the pattern of how African Christians interpret their life situations. Although I make allusion to this pattern in the introduction, a deeper discussion is needed here. Africans are more than hermeneutical. They not only interpret the Bible; they also interpret ordinary life occurrences and experiences. In fact, they interpret every instance and occurrence and seek to generate super-ordinary explanations. African Christians who are influenced by traditional mystical causality seek to identify causes beyond the natural for every occurrence, and it is this interpretation of life events that influences African interpretations of biblical texts related to curses. And they bring these cultural experiences to the Bible.

The analysis of Asamoah-Gyadu of two events in Ghana that were interpreted supernaturally by both Christians and non-Christians will make this point clear.[6] In June 2003, the now defunct Ghanaian Airways had a series

---

4. Asare Boadu, "Pastor Invokes Antoa Nyamaa over Stolen Mobile Phone," Asare Boadu's Stories blog (February 2000). https://asareboadu.blogspot.com/2008/02/pastor-invokes-antoa-nyamaa-over-stolen.html.

5. Joe Awuah, "NDC Goes Antoa with Schnapps," Daily Guide Ghana (2012).

6. J. K. Asamoah-Gyadu, "Conquering Satan, Demons, Principalities and Power: Ghanaian Traditional and Christian Perspective on Religion, Evil and Deliverance," in *Coping with Evil in Religion and Culture: Case Studies*, ed. N. Doom-Harder, vol. 35 (Leiden: Brill, 2008), 89; J. K. Asamoah-Gyadu, "Christ Is the Answer, What Is the Question? A Ghana Airways Prayer Vigil and Its Implication for Religion, Evil and Public Space," *Journal of Religion in Africa* 35, no. 1 (2005): 93–117.

of technical problems. The staff and leadership of the airline interpreted these problems as mysterious and believed that they must have been caused by something more than ordinary. Therefore, the corporation leaders organized a night vigil to spiritually solve the technical faults which had been interpreted to be supernatural. A charismatic deliverance minister was invited to lead the staff in declaring the deliverance of the airway. The pictures taken from the vigil show the staff members raising their hands while calling to God to fix the ailing airline.

The second event was in January 1981. A train disaster in the Juaben area of eastern Ghana claimed the lives of twenty-two passengers and left 133 seriously injured. People began to mourn and search for what could be responsible for this national calamity. In the end, the traditional worshippers were able to convince the nation that incident was due to the fact that one of the territorial goddess in charge of the spot where the train disaster occurred, Asuoyaa, was annoyed due to a lack consistent sacrifices and appeasement. In response, the nation's vice president, de Graft Johnson, led some people to the spot with some cows and a number of sheep that were killed to appease the offended goddess. The blood of these animals was sprinkled on the spot where the passengers had died. While the appeasement was ongoing, a twenty-four-year-old priestess named Adwoa Anan claimed in a spiritual ecstatic seizure that the spirit of the river, Asuoyaa, who had been giving the citizens of the entire region water to drink, was annoyed because the nation had not been appreciating her through consistent observance of sacrifices. The priestess said that because the goddess was not worshipped, she decided to drink the blood of humans and concluded that the nation must continually give to her what sacrifices were due.

This explanation was criticized by many citizens who argued that the reason for the incident was a sharp corner where train disasters had been occurring and that modern technological recommendations for the government to divert the railway had been made. But the government said there was no funding for this project, and later sought funding to purchase the cows and sheep for sacrifice at the insistence of those who supported the traditional mystical explanation and recommendations.[7] The voices of those who believed in the mystical interpretation of these occurrences overwhelmed a few "modern Christians" who believed the interpretation was superstitious. However, these stories illustrate how the majority of African Christians interpret

---

7. Asamoah-Gyadu, "Christ Is the Answer, What Is the Question?" 94. A. Tsolu, "Religious Hallucination among the black race," *Graphic Online*. (20/09/2017).

their personal life situations. Metaphysical interpretations are preferred to ordinary explanations. And this interpretive lens is brought to the Bible in African Christianity.

Similarly, people of the Yoruba ethnic extraction largely believe that one major reason why there is no unity and singularity of purpose among them is that a curse was placed on the entire ethnic group by one of the ancient kings called Aole. Historically, some traditions believe that King Aole placed a curse of disunity on the entire Yoruba society that their voices would never be united. Till this modern time, many social and political incidences that have not been favorable to the Yoruba people are said to have occurred as a result of this ancient curse. Even some Yoruba Christians believe in the effectiveness of this longtime curse.

What I intend to show here is that African Christians bring these lenses of interpretation to the Bible in their attempt to make it provide meaning for their varied life experiences. Let us now examine how African Christians including church leaders, preachers, and writers interpret and apply curse texts in the Bible. According to Elizabeth Mburu, for the Bible to be adequately interpreted and applied in Africa, two sets of cultures must be understood: the cultures of the Bible lands and those of the African context. The above analysis is on the nature of interpreting life occurrences in African culture and society. This cultural influence must be understood so as to avoid a "double gap" in the application of Bible in Africa.

Analysis of Curses in Popular African Sermons

Sermons preached by popular preachers in Ghana, Nigeria, Kenya, and Cameroon were selected and analyzed with a view to how these preachers tried to help their audiences solve their fear and break the bondage of curses. These selected sermons are only representative of many others. In these sermons, curses are grouped into categories: family curses, divine curses, self-inflicted curses, curses of a short life, and curses of moving close to success but never achieving it, among others.

The first sermon was by Dr. D. K. Olukoya, the founder and senior pastor of Mountain of Fire Ministries (MFMM) in Nigeria and many other African countries, who has preached enormously on the concept of curses. On 8 October 2020, he presented a sermon and deliverance service with the title "Breaking Family Curses"[8] which is available on the YouTube platform

---

8. Olukoya, "Breaking Family Curses."

of the church, and permission was given to use this sermon for research and teaching. Olukoya read and analyzed 1 Samuel 2:29–33 and defined curses as the opposite of blessings. He emphasized that curses are mandates given to Satan to harm people including their marriage, business, career, and body. Olukoya noted that curses are spoken words that the devil uses to create a fence to bind people and torment them. He emphasized that major symptoms of curses include working without success, hatred, incessant failure, and the near success but no success syndrome. After the general introduction, Olukoya focused on family curses which he defined as the collective calamity of a family, or punishment for the sins of past parents which runs down the bloodline of a family and is automatically transmitted to any member of that family. Olukoya noted that if a person is born out of wedlock, he or she may also have children out of wedlock. Family curses are powers that reduce the quality of life of a family through acquired bloodline surveillance. Olukoya concluded that evil behaviors like drug addiction and sexual immorality; chains of poverty, mental problems, insanity, and teenage pregnancy; and problems such as sudden and untimely death, irrational fear, and uncontrollable anger can be inherited.

According to Olukoya, the solution to break the bondage of family curses is a three-step deliverance session. First, victims of curses must give their lives to Christ if they have not done that before. Second, they must confess every known and unknown sin of their past family members. Third, they have to make some recklessly violent declarations to counter their family curses. These steps show that the preacher believes that curses can afflict even Christians, and until special prayers are conducted, curses do not respect even born-again Christians.

The second sermon was by Rev. Dr. Samuel Love Adebiyi, the senior pastor of ECWA Chapel Ilorin, Nigeria, who has preached several sermons on existential issues including curses and life negative patterns. For example, he has preached on fear and intimidation among Christians in Africa. The sermon under analysis was broadcast on October 2020 through Harmony FM Radio in Nigeria. Adebiyi defined fear as a phenomenon that results from unpleasant life experiences. He exposited Genesis 3 as the origin of fear and intimidation and stated that repeated negative patterns in the life of Christians is one of the causes of fear. According to Adebyi, unpleasant life challenges and misfortunes are among the experiences of Christians in Africa, and he concludes by showing that the devil uses these experiences to create fear and intimidate the Christians. Adebyi's engagement of repeated negative life occurrence shows that even among evangelical preachers, life occurrences are a subject matter, and repeated negative life patterns are a major theme in the African theology of curses.

Similarly, Pastor Enoch Adeboye, the general overseer of the Redeemed Christian Church of God (RCCG), also has preached extensively on the concept of curses and deliverance from curses. For example, on 10 May 2020 through the RCCG special online service, he preached a sermon titled "Redemption from Curses,"[9] which is available on the YouTube platform of the church and has no restrictions for use for research and teaching. Adeboye related the bondage of curses with the background of what Christ did at Calvary. He introduced his sermon by showing that opposites are always in the world, for example life and death, light and darkness, blessings and curses, and good and evil. Using Deuteronomy 28, he defined curses as the direct opposite of blessings and argued that curses are unseen forces that hinder human progress, or make efforts fail with the sole aim of destroying the victims. Like Olukoya, Adeboye showed that "near success but never succeeding syndrome" is a feature of curses. He noted that if people are victims of curses, what their mates are doing successfully will be difficult for them. Adeboye preached that curses can bind the hands, womb, brain, and mind of its victims. He showed that when a curse is broken, there is a sudden change of story from evil to good, from stagnancy to progress, etc. What is greatly novel in Adeboye's sermon is his introduction of what can be called a "cursing formula." He formulated that God has delegated authority to some people to curse, and when such people curse, the curse becomes effective. For example husbands can curse their wives, and wives can curse their husbands; parents can curse their children; a pastor can curse his members; and a general overseer can curse a pastor. If a member is cursed by a pastor, the general overseer can remove the curse, but if the general overseer curses a person, only God can be appealed to in order to remove the curse. However, if God curses a person, no appeal can be made to anyone. This hierarchical formula in cursing theology is novel and creative. Adeboye concluded by showing that Christ's work on Calvary was to bring blessings in place of curses. Although Adeboye did not clearly prove that curses cannot inflict Christians, his emphasis shows that he believes Christians need to be mindful of curses.

In addition, Bishop David Oyedepo, the presiding bishop of Living Faith Church, also known as Winners Chapel, has preached a series of sermons and conducted impartation services that were centered on curses. For example on

---

9. E. A. Adeboye, "Redeemed from the Curse," YouTube (10 May 2020).

22 April 2012, he preached a sermon titled "Breaking Generational Curses 2"[10] at Canaan Land, Ogun state, Nigeria. In this sample sermon, Oyedepo noted that Christians are Abraham's children, and all Abraham's children are supposed to be a global phenomena and to be envied. But curses are not allowing many Christians to enjoy the blessings of Abraham. Oyedepo maintained that there is a prophetic anointing that can counteract curses and provided that Christian spiritual forces are needed to destroy the power of curses. One of these forces is the light which gives revelation. Another force of deliverance is the truth which brings revelation that provokes reaction. Lastly, Oyedepo mentioned testimony as a force that carries anointing to cure curses and win spiritual battles. Out of many, the themes of prophetic anointing, an anointed mantle, provoking the Abrahamic covenant, and revelatory living faith are central to Oyedepo's theology of curses and were presented as solutions to receiving deliverance from curses. Obviously, Oyedepo believes that Christians also need to pray to break the bondage of curses, especially inherited curses.

In Cameroon, Apostle John Chi is popular for his deliverance and mass prayer sessions against the power of curses. On 30 January 2018, he preached a sermon titled "Breaking Every Curse Operating in the Name you Bear."[11] He used Jabez as his biblical case study to prove that in the mind of God, Christians are supposed to be blessed, rich, healthy, and successful, but it is the curses in people's names that bring failure, sickness, and stagnancy without success. Like Jabez, negative, evil forces operate in the names some Christians bear, and such names need to be sanctified and delivered. Chi argued that anyone named after an idol, occultism, or a witch doctor has a cursed name. He declared war on the curses in names using the name of Jesus in the deliverance session that he conducted after the sermon. Chi strongly believes that even Christians can be cursed, and until they are delivered, curses can ruin their lives.

In Kenya, six popular preachers are keen on deliverance from curses and their dangers. They are Rev. Teresia Wairimu, Rev. Allan and Kathy Kiuna of Jubilee Christian Church, Prophet David Awuor of Repentance and Holiness Ministries, Rev. Lucy Natasha, and Bishop Magret Wanjiru of Jesus Is Alive Ministries. To add gender balance to the sermon analysis, Rev. Lucy Natasha's sermon on curses was selected and analyzed. On 21 May 2019, she preached a sermon titled "Reversing the Curse" on her periodic Miracle Monday service

---

10. D. Oyedepo, "Breaking Generational Curses 2," YouTube (22 April 2012).

11. J. Chi, "Break Every Curse Operating in the Name You Bear (1 Chronicles 4:9)," YouTube (29 January 2018).

in Nairobi which was broadcast in Oracle TV.[12] She used 2 Kings 2:19–22 to show that when a curse is in a person's life, there will be delay, barrenness, and bondage. She used this text to prove that generational curses are real. In her analysis and deliverance sessions, she noted that some prophetic tools like salt, water, and oil are useful in reversing curses. She interpreted Elisha's request for a new bowl in 2 Kings 2 as a symbol of newness. Apart from prophetic tools, prophetic instructions are also very useful for reversing a curse. Natasha strongly believes that Christians can be afflicted with curses.

Lastly, Mensa Otabil and Eastwood Anaba of Ghana have shown interest in the topics of curses in their charismatic sermons. Eastwood Anaba has preached several sermons on the need to break family bondage. In one titled "Breaking the Yoke of Your Father's House," he interpreted the teaching of Jesus on marriage, "a man will leave his father and mother and be united to his wife" (Matt 19:5), as metaphorical and argued that leaving the family is necessary not only physically but even more spiritually.[13] Anaba used Yahweh's order to Abraham to leave his family as an example of a very necessary way to break free from his generational curses.

Mensa Otabil has also preached sermons centering on the relevance of the cross of Jesus to cure curses. For example in his sermon titled "The Power of the Cross" (preached in International Gospel Centre, Ghana on 31/08/2018), he showed from his readings of Deuteronomy 27 and 28 and Galatians 3:13–14 that the sins of past fathers can become curses.[14] Otabil noted that if there is idolatry in a family or stealing, these sins can cause generational curses. However, his interpretation of Galatians 3 led him to argue that the power of Christ's cross has abrogated the power of all curses. However, Otabil submits that ignorance can make curses torment Christians. In the end, his sermon shows that ignorance is a major issue related to African Christians' notion of curses.

The sermons are presented as preached with little or no comment. Comment and critical engagement with them is made later. However, one aspect that cannot go without immediate comment is the creative use of real-life experiences in these and many other sermons on curses in African Christianity.

---

12. L. Natasha, "Reversing the Curse," YouTube (21 May 2019).

13. E. Anaba, "Breaking the Yoke of Your Father's House," YouTube (30 August 2019).

14. M. Otabil, "The Power of the Cross," YouTube. Available at: https://youtu.be/JGrwHbeEPPI (preached on March 31, 2018, at International Gospel Centre, Ghana).

Popular Life Experiences in Sermons on Curses

The theology of curses in African Christianity becomes clearer by looking at how some life situations are dealt with in the popular sermons. Dr. Olukoya gave an illustration that is quite surprising. He recounted how a pastor of a church came to him for deliverance from a spirit of fornication. During the deliverance session, a demon spoke through the pastor saying that the bondage of fornication was a result of some curses and that the symbol of this curse was kept on the roof of the pastor's family house in their village. The pastor went to check the roof and found an old magazine with nude pictures of women that had been kept there by his forefathers. These events revealed that the pastor had inherited the bondage of fornication from his fathers. The pastor burned the magazine and was healed from the bondage of fornication. This account reveals that not only can African Christians have tendencies to be cursed, even their pastors can be cursed, and demons of curses can speak out through them.

Another illustration was given by Enoch Adeboye, and many other preachers have used this illustration which has become popular in deliverance ministries in Africa. A pastor noticed that he was not successful in his ministry. If he prayed for people and God answered and miracles happened, those he prayed for would go to another pastor for appreciation and thanksgiving. When the pastor noticed this negative pattern in his life, he went for a deliverance service. During this deliverance session, the Lord revealed that the pastor's calamity was due to a curse placed on his ancestors by a pastor a long time back in history. It was revealed that in that time past, a pastor had been taken to their village. All of the members of his church had agreed to buy a bicycle for him to make his ministry easier. But the suffering pastor's great grandfather had objected and disallowed the purchase of the bicycle. Annoyed by this development, the aggrieved pastor placed a curse on the family of the man who objected to his progress. Ever since this curse had been operating in that man's family till this modern time, and this curse was why the pastor who came from that cursed family could not enjoy his ministry. He was prayed for and was delivered. These illustrations are fantastic and show the deep place that curses occupy that influences how African Christians interpret and treat life issues. Major comments are made on these points later.

Interpretations of Biblical Cursing Texts

In the interpretation model of African Christianity, some texts are often used to prove points and educate the church on curses. Here we look at those texts and how they have been understood and applied in Africa. These texts are

Curses on Adam and Eve: Genesis 3:14–19

The punishment that God pronounced on Adam and Eve in the garden of Eden is significant to the African Christian theological understanding of curses. African preachers usually say that the curses pronounced on Adam and Eve are still effective today, even on Christians. African Christians trace curses of childbirth pain, failure in life efforts, struggling without success, and enmity between snakes and humans to this text. The punishments of painful childbirth and struggling for daily living are used to unlock any painful circumstances that surround childbirth in African women and difficulties in the lives of African men. While this understanding is true to some extent, it obviously does not comprehensively engage the texts concerned. A comprehensive look shows that the punishment God pronounced on Adam and Eve includes the first promise of redemption. Non-comprehensive engagement of the text in African Christian preaching usually leads to overexaggeration of the cursing part without looking at the positive side. As the chapter dealing with the biblical theology of curses reveals, curses and blessings always work and walk together in the Bible, especially in the Old Testament. What is needed is a round-table hermeneutical engagement that helps to totally unlock the theological and didactic import of biblical texts. Contrary to popular African preachers, Adam and Eve were not directly cursed by God, but the earth and child delivery were cursed on their account. Again, a reading of Genesis 3 that emphasizes curses alone is unfair, for the same text that details how God punished Adam and Eve also houses the first promise of redemption for all of mankind. Biblical curses are not blind! Note that some established authoritative Bible editions and versions do not list Adam and Eve among those God cursed in the Old Testament. For example, in the topical index of the *NIV Topical Study Bible*, the entry on "curse" and "cursing" does not include Adam and Eve in the lists of people cursed in the Old Testament.[15]

---

15. V. D. Verbugge, ed., *The Bible League NIV Topical Study Bible* (Grand Rapids: Zondervan, 1998), 36. The curse on the serpent and land are mentioned here but Adam and Eve are omitted from the list of curses in the Old Testament.

Curses of the patriarchs: Genesis to Deuteronomy

Another set of important biblical texts that are central to African Christian understanding of the theology of curses are in the patriarch corpus. The accounts of the patriarchs are not just lessons for contemporary Christians but have a wider transgenerational and transcultural reference.[16] For example many African Christians and preachers see the recurring negative patterns in the lives of Abraham, Isaac, Jacob, and Joseph as generational curses. The same patterns are also seen in the lives of Sarah and Rachel. The most pronounced negative patterns are the pattern of famine, the pattern of barrenness, and the pattern of deception. Popular African interpretation of the patriarch narratives notes that Abraham's experience of famine (Gen 12:10) is repeated in the life of Isaac (Gen 26:1). Also, Abraham's barrenness experience (Gen 15:2–3) is repeated in Isaac's life (Gen 25:21) and also partly in Jacob's life (Gen 30:1). A pattern of deception is also seen in Abraham's lineage. For example, Abraham is reported to have deceived Pharaoh about Sarah (Gen 12:10–20) as well as Abimelech (Gen 20:1–16), and this deceptive behavior is also seen in Isaac's deception about his wife, Rebecca (Gen 26:1–11). Jacob deceived his brother Esau (Gen 25:29–34), and Jacob's children deceived him about the death of Joseph (Gen 37:29–34). Besides, many African Christians also find a repetition of negative patterns in the lives of Sarah and Rachel in that the two matriarchs asked their husbands to attempt to have children for them with their maidservants because of their barrenness (Gen 16:1–4; 30:1–6). Finally, many African Christians believe that the death of Rachel during childbirth (Gen 35:16–19) was caused by a curse unknowingly placed on her by Jacob (Gen 31:30–32).

While these examples represent creative and intelligent interpretations of the Scriptures, they also show how many African Christians merely focus their biblical theology on a few selected biblical texts without adequately considering other texts. The patriarchs were the forefathers of Judeo-Christian traditions, but a whole theological system must not be built on them exclusively without considering other biblical texts. A little effort at intertextual engagement of these texts with other texts in the Bible would give a fresher and more robust understanding. Most importantly, one Old Testament principle that must not be overlooked as we engage the Bible is that God not only ruled in Israel's affairs but was also actively involved in happenings and situations. Sometimes

---

16. J. K. Asamoah-Gyadu, "Learning to Prosper by Wrestling and Negotiation: Jacob and Esau in Contemporary African Pentecostal Hermeneutics," *Journal of Pentecostal Theology* 21 (2012): 69.

God himself vowed to bring some situations to pass through his power and sovereignty.

The curse on Eli's family: 1 Samuel 2:30–36

The curse that the Lord placed on the priest Eli's family has also been significant in the development of the theology of curses in African Christianity. This text has been used to show how a family that had been in God's favor can be cursed, and that a curse can continue in a family lineage. In addition, this text has been used to prove that curses can reverse blessings and destroy destiny. What is missing in the interpretation of the narrative on Eli, however, is the recognition of the cause of the curse. The curse was justified by the waywardness of Eli's children, and the fault of Eli was that he never corrected his children. Also, the place of human moral responsibility in the biblical conceptualization of curses is largely ignored. This curse on Eli's family can be categorized as a conditional curse because it was due to the sins of Hophni and Phineas. It is not just a curse; it can also be seen as punishment for sins.

The Jabez narrative: 1 Chronicles 4:9–10

The naming of Jabez has been deeply significant to the African theology of curses and has been used again and again during deliverance and prayer sessions. The narrative has been used to show that while a God-given destiny may be good, some contextual existential problems can change it. As discussed in chapter 6, names are more important than just for ordinary social identity; a name also carries a spiritual code which can affect the life of the bearer. The situation of the one naming and the named are essential in the power of a name, and for the naming of Jabez, the situation was his mother's experience of the painful agony she went through in childbirth.[17] Many programs and sermons use the Jabez narrative to show that curses can reside in a name. Because they believe that names can be cursed, as noted in chapter 6, many African Christians have changed their names to redeem themselves from "name curses." But what should be the implication of the name of Jesus to any name that people may bear? Is Jesus's name not capable of rededicating any name to God?

---

17. E. O. Malomo, *Model Prayers for Contemporary Christians* (Ilorin: Amazing-Grace Print Media, 2020), 26.

The Jericho curses: Joshua 6:26; 1 Kings 16:34

After the fall of Jericho, Joshua pronounced a curse on anyone who would attempt to rebuild the city:

> At the cost of his firstborn son
> he will lay its foundations;
> at the cost of his youngest
> he will set up its gates. (Josh 6:26)

Joshua's curse came into effect when Hiel of Bethel rebuilt Jericho: "He laid its foundations at the cost of his firstborn son Abiram, and he set up its gates at the cost of his youngest son Segub, in accordance with the word of the LORD spoken by Joshua son of Nun" (1 Kgs 16:34). These texts have been variously used to show that a curse pronounced by a prophet will surely come to pass and cannot be changed in many instances except if God intervenes. While this interpretation is true to the text, it does not identify the reality of the experience of Joshua and the people of Israel in Jericho and the place of Jericho in the exodus. In other words, this interpretation ignores the historical context of the text. The fall of Jericho and the curse placed on the ruin by Joshua were expressions of Yahweh's divine project to wipe out idolatrous kings and cities that Israel encountered in their journey into the land of Canaan. The fulfillment of the curses on Hiel was because he rebuilt the city during the idolatrous reign of Ahab. The curse was not made just to discourage rebuilding the city; it was on what rebuilding the city represented: idolatry. This argument becomes more valid if we read the Bible further. It was not that the city was rebuilt that made the rebuilder to lose his children as pronounced by Joshua. It is that the rebuilding of the city represented a revival of idolatry under the reign of Ahab. The Bible shows in 1 Kings 16:29–34, that the city was rebuilt by Hiel during the time when the laws of the Lord were strongly despised by Ahab and his foreign wife, Jezebel. This shows that Joshua's curse was only an anti-idolatrous confrontation and prophecy designed to scare anyone who would attempt to rebuild the city against the will of God and for idolatrous purposes.

Jesus becoming a curse for us: Galatians 3:13–14

The most common New Testament text used in discourses on curses in African Christianity is Galatians 3. This text is used to show the importance of Jesus's redemption work in removing human curses. However, most preachers who use this text end up creating contradictions. While they often start their discussion on the fact that the atonement of Jesus at Calvary has the power to remove all curses, they usually end up giving their Christian members – who are supposed to be enjoying the work at Calvary – practical steps to secure deliverance from curses. Why would those who enjoy the atonement of the cross still need practical steps to be delivered from curses? Do Christians even have to pray against curses since they enjoy the work of atonement? The curse of the Lord in the context of this Galatians text is the covenant curse pronounced on law breakers in Deuteronomy 27:26 from which Christ has redeemed us by becoming a curse when he carried all of our sins to the cross. The law does not bring a curse, but since people have been breaking the law, the law has become a curse for them. Technically, if the rabbinical exegetical principle called *gezerah shawah* (equal category) is used to unlock this text, we will see that Jesus is described as the one who interchanged the curse meant for law breakers with his own sinless life.[18] The apostle Paul used this point to argue for the redemptive nature of Christ's death. His argument becomes clearer if we examine the context of Galatians 3. For example, in verse 19, Paul shows that the law, and its curses, was in force "until the Seed" had come. Therefore, what should be emphasized here is not the curses but the cross where the curses were exchanged for blessings.

Many other relevant texts are frequently used to prove points in the African theology of curses, but due to the economy of space, those discussed here are enough to make a valid assessment.

Critical Comments on African Interpretations of Cursing Texts

While the purpose of this discussion is not to blindly criticize African preachers, the integrity of biblical hermeneutics will be offended if we do not consider some critical issues. First, modern sermons tend to overemphasize the experiences of biblical characters but ignore the divine purpose and historical context of the texts. For example, the curses in the patriarchal texts are usually taken out of context and anachronistically interpreted through twenty-first century perspectives. By contrast the patriarchs should be examined within the scope of their dispensational differences to ours.

Second, in the sermons of popular African preachers illustrations of personal spiritual revelations are extensively used but are sometimes overgeneralized. Illustrations are a wonderful aspect of any good sermon, but illustrations should be ornaments, not key aspects of the sermon. The most important aspect of a sermon is that it engages the biblical text, not that it is

---

18. Bruce, *NIGTC: Galatians*, 165.

full of illustrations. Illustrations should be given in the light of biblical truth; they must not become opportunities to exaggerate or to take the freedom to formulate a personal theology that cannot be generalized. Personal religious experiences are good, but since they cannot be verified, care must be taken in generalizing them to others.

Third, many African preachers narrowly select the texts they use when preaching on curses. More often than not, they concentrate on using the Old Testament texts and make scanty allusions to the New Testament texts. Their homiletic attention tends to be on the patriarchs, David, Joshua, and the prophets without the expected attention to the wider context of the whole Bible, because the best interpreter of biblical texts is the Bible itself. In particular, the Old Testament is to be interpreted in the light of the New Testament. Adequate biblical theology cannot be established from narrowly selected texts of the Bible.

Another concept common in African Christian interpretations of cursing texts is "patternism." African preachers seek to interpret similar patterns and repeated occurrences in the Bible as expressions of curses. While similar patterns can sometimes be caused by curses, they should not be overgeneralized.

African Christian Literature on Curses

Apart from sermons and imprecatory prayers, African Christians have written enormously on the concept of curses. A few of these works are discussed here. For example, W. K. Ayitey has written a devotional text on curses and how Christians can obtain deliverance from their curses and dangerous demons.[19] Also a notable African preacher and evangelist and the founder of Light House Chapel International, Dag Heward-Mills is popularly known for his Healing Jesus Crusades all over Africa, and he has written on the subject of curses. For instance, in his book titled "How to Neutralize Curses," he shows that curses are everywhere and real in this world.[20] He argues that there are no curses in heaven, but in this world, no one can escape the danger of curses. Heward-Mills believes that there are cursed lands, cursed families, cursed professions, and cursed characters. He advances that Christians should have proper respect for curses, and any Christians who do not believe in curses are like people who play with snakes because curses are very powerful and their

---

19. W. K. Ayitey, *Broken Chains: Deliverance from Curses and Demons* (Accra: Mallsberg, 2001).

20. Dag Heward-Mills, *How to Neutralize Curses* (Ghana: Parchment House, 2017).

danger knows no boundary. No curse will go without coming to pass no matter how long it takes. Curses are specific and merciless. No matter their level of education and spirituality, no one is free from the blow of curses. Heward-Mills specifically shows that curses abound in every profession, be that profession managerial, medical, scientific, legal, educational, financial, administrative, or entrepreneurial, or unskilled labor or the military and even that of clergy and pastors. Although Heward-Mills concludes that curses can be broken, he also argues that no matter how much a Christian may have faith, faith does not go above curses.

Similarly, W. F. Kumuyi gives a spiritual perspective on the concept of curse and cursing from an African perspective.[21] Kumuyi opines that God's perfect will is that believers should enjoy perfect health, spiritual and material blessings, victory, promotion, peace, joy, and satisfaction throughout their sojourn on earth. The Bible contains thousands of promises that should make believers blessed all the days of their life. Kumuyi applies this teaching more to the area of health and healing. He underscores with great emphasis the activity of Satan through concepts such as curses that hinder prosperity, especially in the area of health, and the need to get rid of curses before true prosperity can be experienced. Where curses are perceived to be the problem, the power to effect a change in circumstances through casting out an evil spirit, according to Kumuyi's teaching, lies in the power of the individual's faith.[22] However the question that one immediately asks about his emphasis on poverty as the star evidence of a cursed life is "What about those who have wealth but face problems in their health and family including sudden death and hatred, or other ill-fated life situations?"

The hermeneutic engagement of Old Testament patriarchs is unique in the African Christian notion of generational curses. For example, Ghanaian preachers Mensa Otabil and Eastwood Anaba creatively argue that Jacob was not a cheater but a smart wrestler who wrestled with entities that were greater than himself using the wisdom of choices and the power of struggle.[23] These two popular African preachers believe and usually preach that life is all about wrestling, and destiny is made by choices and wrestling. They believe that the

---

21. Kumuyi, *Curses and Cures*.

22. Kumuyi, 28–30.

23. Mensa Otabil, *Buy the Future: Learning to Negotiate for a Better Future than Your Present* (Accra: Altar International, 2002); Eastwood Anaba, *The Quest for Supremacy* (Bolgatanga: Desert Leaf, 2004).

choices made by Esau and Jacob not only affected them but also affected their generations of descendants.

What is noticeable in all these examples is the fact that while many African writers and preachers seek to help African Christians to deal with their fears and dilemmas of curses, they unwittingly end up creating more confusion and fear.

Deliverance Programs and Spiritual Solutions

African Christians measure Christianity by its capacity to conquer evil forces and life misfortunes. One of the ways Christianity is used to solve human curses is through deliverance. Usually the deliverance sessions for curse victims include extensive recitation of psalms, songs, and prayers; clapping of hands; and some declarations to reverse the curse. Many specialized songs are considered spiritual and useful in deliverance sessions. In African Christianity songs are important, and they serve different purposes based on the context, situation, and denomination. But in almost all the deliverance sessions examined in this study, spiritual songs were used and were considered to be very important for spiritual warfare.[24] In fact, most deliverance sessions started with spiritual songs.

Deliverance sessions are moments in which the Holy Spirit and his anointing are used to conquer evil and curses. They are a solution mechanism that African Christians use to deal with their fear of hyperactive evil curses. Interdenominational programs with titles such as "Jericho Hour," "Hour of Deliverance," and "Jabez Hour" are frequently organized. Deliverance of curse victims is usually done in selected places such as mountains and groves.

On some occasions, the victims of curses who are under deliverance are chained for days and their movement restricted, especially when the effects of curses have become violent. Sometimes canes or brooms are used to beat the victim so as to disturb the spirit of curses to move out of them.[25] The deliverance involves intense prayers and prescribed fasting that ranges from marathon fasting to white fasting, depending on the nature of the curses to be cured. During the deliverance prayers, the victims may be sobbing, groaning, shouting, roaring, falling, or struggling on the ground. These signs are taken as indications of the success of the deliverance session. When the victims

---

24. Owojaiye, *Evangelical Response*, 107.
25. A. A. Adeniji, *Ethical Evaluation of Deliverance Practices in Pastoral Ministry* (Oyo: Ajibol Golden Links Ventures, 2013), 9.

eventually get up from the ground after the deliverance prayers, it is believed that they have been cured of the curses.

The actual deliverance sessions are usually preceded by a diagnosis which involves an oral examination or filling out a written deliverance questionnaire so that the deliverance ministers know the specific type of curses tormenting the victims and are able to determine the supernatural causes of their problems. Those who are looking for deliverance are then queued up to see the minister. Victims are usually asked to write down the names of their parents and family members, and later such lists are burned to break the chain of curses.

Deliverance is conducted for marriages, villages, firstborn children, heads, reproductive organs, farming equipment, writing equipment, offices and shops, clothes, etc. For example, the Power Must Change Hands programs of MFMM, an equivalent of RCCG's Holy Ghost Service, for March 2012 was on deliverance of "Firstborns."[26] Lastly, I have personally ministered in many wedding ceremonies in Nigeria in which the couple is asked to kneel and a prayer of deliverance from the power of curses is offered for each of them before they are joined together because it is believed that each of them might carry some inherited family curses that must not be allowed to follow them into marriage.

One interesting fact is the popularity of these deliverance programs and their locations. In fact, many non-Christians also attend some of these Christian programs. Charismatic prayer centers are obviously advertised everywhere with "high-visibility" stickers and banners promoting their televised all-night prayers, prayer mountains, and anointing services. In fact everywhere you turn in major African cities, you are aware of posters that advertise a range of forthcoming crusades, deliverance, and revival programs.[27] These developments have given birth to many apostles and prophets in African Christianity.

Spiritualizing Offers to Cure Curses

Giving a donation or paying some amount of money is part of the deliverance process in some African churches. Some church leaders emphasize giving, paying tithes, and financial generosity as ways of preventing or curing the effects of curses. For example, Rev. Natasha of Kenya believes that giving money to support God's work is an integral part of deliverance. This belief is why in some African churches, members are told to bring out their offerings and

---

26. Oludele, "Medicine as Poison," 202.
27. K. Ogbu, *African Pentecostalism: An Introduction*, 5–7.

tithes, hold them in their hands, and speak into the offering or tithe what they want and what they do not want. This theology of curses is foregrounded on the theology of sowing and reaping and usually preached that if a Christian sows a good seed to God and his servant, they will be blessed and can thereby escape curses.

However, the deliverance torture given to victims in some cases usually leads to some psychological condition that can worsen the conditions of some people. Instead of healing from curses, they are physically damaged with the curse unhealed. In addition, while curses are real in Africa, many negative life experiences that are interpreted to be caused by curses may not be related to curses at all. The question now is how do we identify real curses from mere general life experiences? What is the correct biblical interpretation of life experiences in the African setting, and how should the Bible be applied? These questions are discussed in later chapters.

Syncretism, Dialogue, or Contextualization?

While the efforts of African Christian leaders to provide a pastoral care and homiletical solutions to the dilemmas of curses are practical and commendable, a question that comes to a reflective mind is can we say that these responses represent a contextual approach, or are they merely syncretic? I see that while responses to curses are commendable and contextual, these responses have led to syncretism in African Christianity. The African Christian theology of curses is contextual because it is part of the effort to make Christianity relevant to the life experiences of Africans. However, it is alarmingly syncretic because it consciously and unconsciously adopts some elements of African culture and African traditional religions.

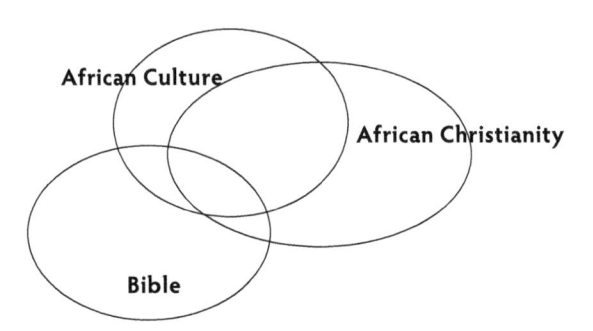

Figure 4: Model illustrating the interactions between African Christian beliefs in curses and the biblical theology of curses.

The figure above illustrates how contemporary African Christianity takes more from traditional African culture than from the Bible. The degree of the influence of African traditional cultural beliefs on African Christians is more than the degree of influence that the Bible has on Christians. African Christians' understanding of curses is predominantly an expression of influences from traditional cultural and religious beliefs. The Bible has not permeated African beliefs about curses.

Syncretism may not be entirely negative, and some scholars have argued that a positive definition is also possible.[28] However, as African Christians have encountered fear and confusion over curses, they have more often uncritically adopted beliefs and practices from their traditional culture than from the Bible. They have not allowed the Bible, especially the New Testament, to transform their traditional belief in curses.

Therefore, what I see as the greatest need in contemporary scholarship on the African Christian theology of curses is not unnecessary criticism but seeking methods through which African cultural beliefs can be transformed biblically. The question is how can effective biblical and theological interpretation be made to respond to the African dilemmas and fears of curses that will be truly biblical and contextual? The next chapter examines the African Christian theology of curses in the light of the Bible from an evangelical perspective.

---

28. Andre Droogers, "Syncretism: The Problem of Definition, the Definition of the Problem," in *Dialogue and Syncretism: An Interdisciplinary Approach*, ed. Jerald Gort, et. al. (Grand Rapids: Eerdmans, 1989), 7.

8

An Evangelical Solution to the African Dilemma and Fear of Curses

This chapter provides solutions to the dilemmas and theological confusion in African Christianity arising from curses. If rightly understood and examined, evangelical theological paradigms can be used to help Africans properly transact between their traditional beliefs on curses and biblical teachings. Here we interrogate African Christian experiences and beliefs in curses from an evangelical perspective and lay a solid foundation for practical guidelines that are both biblical and contextual to deal with curses. It must be noted that the meaning of the term "evangelical" as assumed and used in this book is largely different from the popular, political, and institutional understanding.

Some preliminary exposition on evangelicalism is needed to forestall ambiguity and a parochial misrepresentation because the term is understood differently in different contexts. In America for example, evangelicalism has been largely seen as a political as much as a religious group since the involvement of evangelicals in national politics beginning with the Democratic presidential candidate Jimmy Carter in 1976 and four years later with his Republican opponent Ronald Reagan.[1] Classically, evangelicalism is defined as a dynamic Christian tradition that started in Great Britain in the 1730s, moved to the United States in the nineteenth century, and later became a global phenomenon. Historically, evangelicalism is rooted in the theological emphases of the Reformers, but evangelical theological convictions did not

---

1. The Economist, "What Is an Evangelical Christian?" *The Economist* (1 March 2021).

become unique until 1730s when Jonathan Edwards, George Whitefield, and John Wesley developed a revivalist perspective on Reformation principles.[2] Doctrinally, evangelicalism is rooted in the authentic teaching committed to the saints; therefore it is neither a recent innovation nor a deviation from orthodox Christianity.[3] Evangelicalism can be understood in two basic ways.

First, evangelicalism can be seen as a movement of Christians who hold certain similar doctrinal tenets and emphases. These evangelicals are not restricted by denominations, either Pentecostal, neo-Pentecostal, charismatic, or African independent churches. What makes this category of Christians evangelical is not that they are found in historically pronounced, institutionally recognized evangelical churches but their fundamental belief system which closely follows evangelical teachings and beliefs. In this sense, some Christ Apostolic Church members and group churches in Africa which are institutionally categorized as AICs are evangelical since they believe in the cardinal tenets of evangelicalism, though they do not belonging to the World Evangelical Alliance (WEA) or the Association of Evangelicals in Africa (AEA). Also, some members of the Redeemed Christian Church of God in Africa are members of a Pentecostal movement by denominational grouping but are evangelical in their beliefs concerning the Bible, Christ, personal repentance, and other doctrinal concentrations. In fact, many Christians who have deep evangelical convictions do not use the term "evangelical" to refer to themselves.[4]

Second, evangelicalism can be seen as a group of institutionally recognized Christian denominations such as Evangelical Church Winning All (ECWA) and the Reformed Evangelical Church among others in Africa. These church denominations are members of larger evangelical bodies. This definition is restrictive because it only includes Christians who are members of denominations that have an institutional affiliation with an established evangelical institution.

The first view, the nonpolitical and noninstitutional understanding of evangelicalism, which sees evangelicals as transcending particular denominations, is adopted in this work. Therefore, this work is not limited in scope to African Christian denominations that are evangelical as a group of Christians who hold specific doctrines and religious practices. Instead the book encompasses African Christians who believe and teach certain

---

2. David Hilborn, "Evangelicalism: A Brief Definition," in *Evangelical Truth* (Leicester: Inter-Varsity Press 1999), 18.

3. John Stott, *Evangelical Truth* (Leicester: Inter-Varsity Press 1999), 16.

4. National Association of Evangelicals, *What Is an Evangelical?* NAE (n.d.).

tenets that give credence to the Bible and emphasize Jesus Christ, personal conversional encounters, and evangelism. These evangelicals can be found in almost all major Christian denominations in the world as well as in African indigenous churches and historic mission churches and in charismatic, Pentecostal, and neo-Pentecostal movements. Many other Christians such as Pentecostals, Catholics, Lutherans, and Presbyterians also share the basic beliefs of evangelicalism though they may not be members of an evangelical movement politically or institutionally. Therefore as evangelicals can be found in almost all denominations, this work deals with all African evangelical Christians, not just with Christians who belong to institutionally pronounced evangelical denominations.

The African context of evangelicalism is also adopted in this work. African contextual uniqueness has not been given due attention in the ongoing conversation on evangelicalism.[5] Unlike in the West, evangelicalism is understood in Africa by what evangelicals believe and do rather than their political or denominational groupings. Due to the nonfluid configuration of evangelicalism in Africa, the liturgical plurality and pragmatic expressions of many churches will not allow them to be easily classified as evangelical, but a thorough look at how they see the Bible and emphasize Jesus's cross, conversion, evangelism, and discipleship make them classifiable as evangelicals. Churches such as the African Inland Church, Baptists, Deeper Life Bible Church, Redeemed Christian Church of God, Four Square Gospel Church and Assemblies of God that have been categorized as evangelical in Western contexts are seen as nonevangelical by some in Africa.[6] For this reason, and to forestall a possible parochial application, the institutional classification of evangelicals in Africa is not adopted in this work.

The nonpolitical and nonfundamental expression of evangelicalism has four main theological tenets that are essential to the concept of curses in the African context. These tenets are the primacy of the Bible, the centrality of Jesus's cross, the necessity of a personal conversional encounter, and the needfulness for active mission and discipleship.[7]

---

5. A. O. Balcom, "Evangelicalism in Africa: What It Is and What It Does," *Missionalia* 44, no. 2 (2016): 117–28.

6. Owojaiye, *Evangelical Response*, 52.

7. Bebbington, *Evangelicalism in Modern Britain*, 20. See also D. W. Bebbington, *The Evangelical Quadrilateral, Characterizing the British Gospel Movement* (Waco, TX: Baylor University Press, 2021).

The Primacy of the Bible

2 Timothy 3:16 is central to the theological emphasis of evangelicalism: "All Scripture is God-breathed and is useful for teaching, rebuking, correcting, and training in righteousness." Similar is part of the Westminster Confession: "The Old Testament in Hebrew and New Testament in Greek, being immediately inspired of God and by his singular care and providence kept pure in all ages, are therefore authentical; so as in all controversies of religion, the church is finally to appeal unto them *as primary authority.*"[8]

The first major distinctiveness of evangelicalism is the high regard for and place of the Bible in Christian theology and Christian practice. Evangelicals stand on Luther's notion of *sola Scriptura* – by Scripture alone – which means that the Bible, Old Testament and New Testament, contain eternal truth as revealed by God which must take precedence over cultural beliefs, reason, personal existential experience, and ecclesiastical authority. The Bible is seen as the living and powerful word of God which serves as the "function of a judge; it condemns, acquits, judges sinners to death and gives new life through faith."[9] The role of the Bible in the theological process is not that of a witness to be cross examined for its veracity. Instead, it serves as the chief judge who passes the verdict. Like a judge in a court of law, the Bible pronounces the judgment of God. Evangelicals are convinced of the reliability, infallibility, inerrancy, and verbal-plenary inspiration of the sixty-six canonical books of the Bible in their original autographs. Evangelicals hold that while Christ is the primary focus of the divine self-disclosure, the Bible is the deposit of the divine revelation in history.[10] Moreover, evangelicals believe that what the dying world needs to survive is the word of God because the word of God is God himself speaking to humans that which is relevant for all ages.

This high view of Scripture is why evangelicals practice a devotional pattern of private and communal Bible study and why this practice is central to many evangelical Christians. This high view of Scripture is also why regular Bible reading and expository sermons are the highest points in any worship, whether private or communal. Their expectations for sermons are that they thoroughly expose biblical texts, loudly proclaim changed lives, and confront human thoughts. Specific texts or biblical themes are exposited with clarity

---

8. Westminster Catechism, quoted in Donald MacLeod, "The Bible and Textual Criticism," *Evangelical Presbyterian*, 37. Emphasis added.

9. S. Grindheim, "Biblical Authority: What Is It Good for? Why the Apostles Insisted on a High View of Scripture," *Journal of Evangelical Theological Society* 59, no. 4 (2016): 791.

10. S. J. Grenz, *Revisioning Evangelical Theology: A Fresh Agenda for the 21st Century* (Downers Grove: IVP Academic, 1993), 111.

and illumination for rightful application. Sunday school and Bible study classes are preeminent. This high view of Scripture is the rationale for emphasizing theological training and pastoral schools for church leaders. Memorization of biblical texts is advised for children and young adults, and translation of biblical texts into local dialects is also encouraged to make the Bible clear to human thought. Evangelicals see the Bible as authoritative, inspired, and sufficient. The Bible is unique in the sense that there is no other valid textual source of revelation of the one true God, and it possesses an exclusive level of authority as a judge of humanity. Rather than standing in judgment over the Bible and using it to judge human experience, which may allow rejecting some parts of it to make it in line with human sensibilities, the Bible is a judge on its own and not used to judge. While Christians who believe in the primacy of the Bible are found in many churches, the official statement of major evangelical bodies across nations and centuries such as the World Evangelical Alliance, The Evangelical Alliance, Evangelical Fellowship of India, Evangelical Association of Caribbean, and Association of Evangelicals in Africa have as the first point of their statement of faith the unique and primary authority of Scripture.

What are the implications of this high view of Scripture to African fears and dilemmas of curses? As can be easily discovered, this evangelical stand on biblical authority has strong implications for the fear of curses in African Christianity. More often than not, African Christians base their practice and theology on their existential experiences and interpret the Bible in the light of their experiences rather than interpret the experiences in the light of the Bible. In contemporary Africa, the voices of sound scriptural exegesis, exposition, and creative application are falling silent in the preaching and teaching of the African church. The evangelical position on the Bible is that the Bible should be taken as the judge of all human encounters and that human experiences should be interpreted biblically, not the Bible interpreted experientially. One cardinal point of evangelicalism which is very close to the Wesleyan quadrilateral is the primacy but not exclusive nature of Scripture, which means that while the Bible is not the only source for Christian theology, it is the primary and first source and should take preeminence in faith and practice.

How do African Christians interpret the cursing texts in the Bible? As we show in the previous chapter, most of the time African Christians adopt hermeneutical selectivity in their treatment of these texts. Many African Christians tend to concentrate their biblical engagement on selected Old Testament texts such as Genesis 3, Deuteronomy 28, 1 Samuel 2, Psalm 109 and many others and give scanty attention to New Testament texts that speak of salvation, reconciliation, new life, love, and forgiveness and forbid cursing.

In fact within the Old Testament, texts like Ezekiel 18 explaining that the children are not punished for the sins of their parents are totally neglected in contemporary African hermeneutics on curses. This selective practice is not in line with the evangelical stance that all sixty-six canonical books of Scripture are inspired and useful for doctrinal formation. And no particular text of the Bible is to be given primacy over others.

While Paul's argument in Galatians 3 is often cited by some African preachers talking on curses, they often commit an interpretive fallacy based on the argument that the same curse that Christ has removed can still influence Christians and that Christians still have to pray against curses.[11] Also, many African Christians often fail to take into account distinctions in the genre categories of texts in the Bible. They also use a metaphysical causation ideology in their interpretive process, the most obvious of which involves reading one's personal theology and experience into the biblical text. In other words, it is thinking that if event B happened after event A, then B happened because A caused it to happen.[12] African Christian experiences must be informed by scriptural truth and not vice versa.

Evangelical bibliology dictates expository engagement with a text in which the text is first understood in its original biblical context and then studied in the light of other Bible texts. This effort toward discovering the original intention of a text and the canonical implications of that text on the theology of the whole Bible tends to be omitted in the formulation of the theology of curses in the contemporary African Christianity. I hereby argue that an African Christian theology of curses can strongly benefit from an evangelical engagement and understanding the Bible. If the whole counsel of God as enshrined and a healthy biblical interpretation is declared, most of the fear and confusion on curses will lose their weight in African Christianity. The first solution to the fear and dilemmas of curses in contemporary African Christianity is adequate Bible interpretation. We return to this topic later to frame practical biblical guidelines for how African Christians can confront the concept of curses.

The Cruciality of the Cross of Jesus

First Corinthians 2:2 is fundamental to the evangelical thought: "For I resolved to know nothing while I was with you except Jesus Christ and him crucified." Here Paul shows that he is not a preacher of worldly wisdom and that if he does

---

11. D. A. Carson, *Exegetical Fallacy* (Grand Rapids: Baker, 1996), 118.
12. Carson, *Exegetical Fallacy*, 128.

not preach the crucified Christ, his preaching will lose its power.[13] While other Christological concepts such as the incarnation, preexistence, and humanity of Christ are honored, evangelicals see the atoning death of Christ on the cross as crucial for understanding the core purpose of Christ's ministry and the power behind the Christian life. Evangelicals stress the salvific death of Christ on the cross and its potency for redeeming humanity to God. The Son of God became an historical man, Jesus of Nazareth, who died on the cross not for his own sins but for the sins of the human race to make atonement for every person from every race, tribe, and tongue.[14] Dying on a cross carries a stigma, but God choose to save people from the calamity of sin through the cross experience. Paradoxically, it is through this stigma and suffering that sinners have their redemption. Because of the strong emphasis on the cross, Adonis Vidu refers to evangelicals as "evangelical *Christus* victor."[15]

Evangelicals believe that the only way to eternal life is belief in the atonement and lordship of Christ. Theologically loaded words such as "vicarious," "substitutionary," and "sacrifice" are used by evangelicals to describe the ministry of Christ and the centrality of his cross, suffering, and death for the salvation of mankind. They understand the blood of Christ to be potent enough to atone for any sin, past, present, or future. The death of Christ on the cross and the accompanying deep, unbearable suffering was a sacrifice and a dying in our place, paying the price of our sins and defeating all evil, and serves as the only way sufficient to reconcile people to God. Christ's work on the cross has made possible the only hope for mankind from eternal damnation occasioned by Adam's fall in the genesis of the human race. Christ's cross and suffering is then a major emphasis in the evangelical tradition. All people are under God's wrath – educated or uneducated, rich or poor – and all are in need of saving grace which is available through the Son of God's work on the cross where he died for sinners. Christ paid the ransom owed for all sins, for all curses (Mark 10:45).

However, the tempting idea that Christ paid the ransom to Satan must be forestalled. The atoning death of Christ on the cross does not imply that Christ pacifies the devil. Christ is at once the sacrifice, the "sacrifice," and the recipient of the sacrifice. The punishment of the sin of Adam and personal

---

13. F. Grosheide, *Commentary on the First Epistle to the Corinthians* (Grand Rapids: Eerdmans, 1953), 60.
14. Hilborn, "Evangelicalism."
15. A. Vidu, *Atonement, Law and Justice: The Cross in Historical and Cultural Contexts* (Grand Rapids: Baker, 2014), 184.

sins that people experience is only on a delegatory assignment. The sin of Adam was against God, not against the devil. But in the process of Christ's death on the cross, God reconciled the world to himself by himself.[16] It was a vicarious transaction made once and for all with Christ taking the place and stead of sinners.[17]

Christ did four main things on the cross.[18] First, he died as a substitution for the sins of mankind. Second, he paid the price of redemption and ransomed people from the bondage of sin and divine wrath. Third, he satisfied the judicial demands of God. Because of people's sin, divine righteousness has been violated, and it is only through the death of a sinless man that the sins of humans can be atoned for. Fourth, he reconciled the world to God. Therefore, all people need to do is redirect their trust from themselves to Christ. Sinners do not have any work to do to be saved by the atonement of Christ, only to believe and receive the benefit. The only base through which God saves is through the substitutionary atoning death of Christ.

One last thing to note is the potency of Christ's atoning death and suffering for forgiving all sins. When sinners are born again through repentance and the regenerating power of the Holy Spirit, their sins and the penalties for them are erased through the cleansing power of Jesus's blood shed on the cross. Christ has paid the full price for people's sins; their sins no longer condemn them because Jesus has borne the penalty for all sins. Even when believers commit sins during their Christian life, only additional, genuine confession of those sins is needed for forgiveness. All the sins of believing Christians, past, present, and future are atoned by Jesus's blood. Believers do not experience any punishment for sins, either big or small. The blood of Jesus has paid for all their sins. While there are many different human attempts to explain what happened at the cross (e.g. payment to Satan, recapitulation, moral influence, and many more),[19] at the heart of the evangelical view is the biblical presentation of Jesus's cross as the only means of salvation. Evangelicals consider the blood of Jesus that was shed in pain to be the only source of unspeakable joy for mankind.[20]

---

16. G. Aulen, *Christus Victor: An Historical Study of the Three Main Types of the Idea of the Atonement* (London: SPCK, 1983), 56.

17. R. P. Lightner, *Evangelical Theology, A Survey and Review* (Grand Rapids: Baker, 1986), 86.

18. Lightner, *Evangelical Theology*, 193–94.

19. Space will not allow a full exposition of these theories here. See John Walvoord, *Jesus Christ Our Lord* (Chicago: Moody, 1969), 154–57.

20. G. C. Berkouwer, *The Work of Christ* (Grand Rapids: Eerdmans, 1965), 151.

Then if people are redeemed through this cross of Christ, how can any curses in their family lineage have power over them?

Christ became the curse on the cross because he carried sins that were not his. What is the implication of this event to the current fear and dilemmas of curses in African Christianity? The first question is "what does Jesus as a Redeemer mean in the context of Africa?"[21] By the cross of Christ a person's sin has been expiated and forgiven. The guilt of both past and present sin has been removed. A person who has a sinful family background and idolatrous lineage is now justified. Christ has paid for the penalty of that person's sins. God has been propitiated and ransom has been paid. What the cross represents is a forensic effort that has redeemed people from the punishment of their sins, be they personal sins or inherited sins. Christ has died for sinners as a substitute for sinners who put their trust in him.[22]

The theology of the cross is surrounded by deeply significant soteriological terms that are enough to critique African Christians' fear of curses. For example, the Greek word *agorazo* (redemption, purchase) is used in the New Testament with the metaphor of market place to emphasize that Christ purchased sinful people through his death on the cross. All of the six times this word is used includes a reference to the death of Christ (Rom 5:8; 6:23; 1 Cor 15:3; 1 Cor 6:20; 7:23; 1 Pet 2:24; 3:18; 2 Pet 2:1; Rev 5:9; 14:3–4). Two other Greek words used in the Bible that bring to the fore the implications of Christ's cross for the concept of bondage of curses are *apokatallasso* (complete reconciliation), which is used by Paul in Ephesians 2:16 and Colossians 1:20–22 to express that Christ's reconciliatory mission is complete, and *hilaskoma* (propitiation) used in Hebrews 2:17.[23] If Christ has paid for the sin of a sinful person, has released that person from the bondage of sins, has reconciled that person to God, and has satisfied the requirement of God on that person's behalf, can curses still have power over such a Christian? Expectedly, the vertical reconciliation wrought by Christ will lead to baptism of the Spirit through which believers are united to the body of Christ and receive their new position in Christ. The Holy Spirit through regeneration breathes God's life into spiritually dead sinners; therefore, those sinners now enjoy the imputed righteousness of Christ which sanctifies them positionally and progressively.

---

21. S. O. Abogunrin, *In Search of Historical Jesus*, Inaugural Lecture, University of Ibadan, 1998 (Ibadan: Alofe, 2013), 44.

22. Walvoord, *Jesus Christ Our Lord*, 154–57.

23. Walvoord, 163–74.

It is theologically unfounded to overemphasize the fear of curses in the lives of genuine Christians as is done in contemporary African Christianity. According to the African perspective, the highest cause to occasion any curse is the shedding of human blood, and this type of curse is deemed unbreakable. However, the blood of Christ is the blood of a sinless man, the Son of God incarnated. Therefore, there is no curse, either empowered by human blood or animal blood or communal covenant that Christ has not atoned for.

In addition, the fact that Christ carried a painful and shameful cross to redeem mankind sends a signal that the Christian life involves carrying one's cross. Jesus himself admonished us: "Whoever wants to be my disciple must deny themselves and take up their cross and follow me" (Mark 8:34).

The Christian life is the life of the cross. This may not mean that all Christians will carry a physical cross like Jesus, but it implies going through some life challenges, pain, suffering, and persecution for Jesus's sake.[24] The apostle Paul writes, "You became imitators of us and of the Lord" (1 Thess 1:6) and "Follow my example, as I follow the example of Christ" (1 Cor 11:1). The Christian life may involve pain, delay, suffering, and disappointment. While I am not denying the veracity of curses in Africa, I believe that some of the life experiences that are interpreted as the results of generational curses are "cross experiences" that individual African Christians have to carry as part of their spiritual experience in Christ. Like Jesus's cross, the end of any cross that a Christian may carry is joy and reward. This joy and these rewards involve transformation and spiritual growth.

The campaign of health and wealth preachers in Africa for an exclusively joyous life does not fully consider the centrality of the cross.[25] The biblical definition of an abundant life of prosperity in Christ must be seen in the light of his cross. African Christians' fear of curses is shattered and unfounded on the ladder of Christ's cross. He became the curse himself for us all at once. When Christians go through difficult life situations, they are not necessarily experiencing the results of curses. Instead, they are usually experiencing part of God's plan to bring about a purpose in their life. When we suffer as Christians and by imitating the Lord, we remain calm in the face of these trials so the world is able to see Christ in us.[26]

---

24. F. F. Bruce, *The Hard Sayings of Jesus* (Downers Grove: IVP, 1983), 151.

25. Gordon Fee, *The Disease of the Health and Wealth Gospels* (Canada: Regent College Publishing, 2006), 13.

26. John Stott, *Life in Christ* (Eastbourne: Kingsway, 1991), 100.

The hermeneutical subjectivity of most African preachers allows them to interpret texts such as Deuteronomy 28 as saying that poverty and sickness are signs of curses in a Christian's life. God's promises of total healing and prosperity may not always be experienced immediately. For example, the apostle Paul noted that he knew hunger and satisfaction, lack and sufficiency, want and plenty (Phil 4:11–13). Do these verses mean that because Paul was in need at some point, he was under a generational curse?

Lastly, the overemphasis on "third-party agents," curse deliverance ministers, mediating deliverance from curses using some physical objects such as anointing oil, mantles, or consecrated water for head washing ignores the potency of Jesus's atoning death on the cross. The attempt to do deliverance for Christians who have genuinely confessed Christ as their Savior is contrary to the power of the cross. Must Christians who have dedicated their lives to Christ still be delivered? What then is the difference between believers and unbelievers? This is not to de-emphasize the relevance of deliverance and prophetic ministry for the African Church, but there must be a proper and biblical teaching to guide every deliverance minister.

The Centrality of Personal Conversion and Repentance

Evangelicals emphasize the good news of Christ's death and resurrection and stress that individuals must appropriate the work of the cross to themselves so that they can be saved. Being born again is the key to unlocking an eternal relationship with God through Christ and is a non-negotiable, non-inheritable, non-transferrable, and non-conferrable experience that every child of God must have. Without this conversion experience, salvation is not genuine.[27] Evangelicals believe that lives need to be transformed through conversion or a born-again experience which begins a life-long discipleship with Christ and through fellowshipping with other believers. The truth of Christ's death and resurrection transforms a life only through repentance which is meant to tune the mind of the sinner toward God. Salvation is free but it involves an intentional response and decision. While a community may genuinely decide for Christ, evangelicals emphasize personal conviction and repentance more than a collective decision. The salvation experience is a personal encounter which leads to a new beginning and transformation of life. Therefore, evangelicals expect the gospel to have a transformational impact on the individual's life and experience. The evangelical idea of salvation is the one that takes place between

---

27. Owojaiye, *Evangelical Response*, 61.

an individual and God through faith Jesus Christ and personal repentance from sins.

This idea of salvation formulated in terms of a rebirth experience is advanced by Paul in 2 Corinthians 5:17: "Therefore, if anyone is in Christ, the new creation has come: The old has gone, the new is here!" This verse shows that when people personally decide for Christ, they are transformed because the gospel of Jesus Christ has the capacity to change people, meet their deepest needs, and give them the ultimate answers to their questions of life. The new birth is the beginning of a new experience of new life in Christ. While this conversion experience is the beginning, progressive sanctification which deals with daily walking and maturing in Christ is emphasized. Thus, conversion is a process of encounter between the new life and the old life in which the new life transforms the old totally and the old gives way to the new. To receive Christ is therefore to bring the control of Christ over a life and to submit to his lordship, which must lead to the empowerment and liberation that a believer experiences in Christ. The born-again experience is a defining characteristic of evangelical teaching which sees all people as sinners, totally depraved, who become children of God only through the application of Christ's atonement via the regenerational ministry of the Holy Spirit through personal faith in Christ. The result of this personal encounter is a new nature (2 Cor 5:17), new righteousness (Rom 6:18), new life (Rom 6:4; Eph 4:22–24; 1 John 3:9; 4:7; 5:1), and eternal life (John 3:16; Phil 1:6).[28]

This new life in Christ involves a pilgrimage toward eternal life in Christ. Therefore, it requires diligence and commitment which is why evangelicals admonish each other to take charge of their lives and apply the word of God for their spiritual growth. This growth is ensured through discipleship, daily reading of the word of God, personal quiet time and devotion, fellowship with other believers, and a daily life of biblical integrity and spirituality.[29] No doubt this commitment involves self-denial in this world, but believers are assured of hope and peace in Jesus Christ. In addition, once believers are accepted into Christ's family, they become priests of God. They need no more intermediaries like the temple priest were in the dispensation of the law. While the church and communal fellowship is important, personal growth and maturity in the Lord is emphasized as a key.

One major fruit of the conversional encounter is that the believer becomes a new person. Repentance and conversion is a powerful experience. It is a new

---

28. Lightner, *Evangelical Theology*, 199.
29. Grenz, *Revisioning Evangelical Theology*, 49.

birth that enables sinners to overcome all of their previous guilt and suffering, which is a stark contradiction to the African Christian theology of curses. The interpretation of Galatians 3:13–14 to mean that Christ has become a curse for us has made many preachers see any negative events such as sickness to be expressions of curses in a Christian's life. But this view is not true to the integrity of proper biblical interpretation. In this Galatians text, Paul is not referring to curses as expressed in poverty or sickness, and he is not referring to the covenant curses in Deuteronomy 28.[30] Rather he is referring to redemption and comparing the two ways people thought they could receive it: through the law or through the saving grace of Christ who has become a curse for us in the process of removing the curse of the law. Many biblical heroes who have become examples for us now suffered some life difficulties that contemporary African preachers would tag as being the results of "curses." For example, Elisha suffered "from illness which he died" (2 Kgs 13:14). Paul had a thorn in his flesh which he prayed would be removed, but it was not (2 Cor 12:6–9). In fact, in Galatia, he preached as a result of his illness (Gal 4:12–15). Peter was delivered, but James was martyred (Acts 12:1–19). Was James under a curse that made God unable or unwilling to rescue him? Even though Peter was delivered, how did he eventually die? The Christian life is one of cross-carrying and cross-enduring!

Contrary to many African preachers, not all sufferings are caused by demons and curses. Biblically, some sufferings are a means to spiritual maturity. For example, in Deuteronomy 8, Moses shows that the suffering of the people in the wilderness was discipline to discover the content of their heart. Throughout the Bible we see God correcting, training, and instructing his children through discipline. Psalm 94:12 even declares, "Blessed is the one you discipline, LORD." All of the major prophets and apostles of God in the Bible went through experiences and lived in situations that they did not like. For example, the people threatened Moses with stoning when they run out of water (Exod 17:3–4). David, a man after God's own heart, was threatened by Saul with death (1 Sam 19:11, 15). Elijah was hunted by Jezebel and he ran (1 Kgs 19:1–3). The prophet Micaiah was imprisoned by King Ahab (1 Kgs 22:23–28). The king of Aram threatened Elisha with death (2 Kgs 6:8–16). Jeremiah suffered at the hands of government officials (Jer 37:15; 38:6). Shadrach, Meshach, and Abednego were cast in the fiery oven for righteousness (Dan 3:1–18). Job suffered intensely (Job 1–3). In fact, Psalm 44:22 states, "Yet for your sake

---

30. Fee, *Disease of the Health and Wealth Gospels*, 26.

we face death all day long; we are considered as sheep to be slaughtered." According to the Bible, tribulation develops endurance (2 Cor 1:6).[31]

Jesus clearly stated that the kingdom of darkness will be overthrown as a result of encounters with him (John 8:12; 12:46; see also John 3:18–21), but this reality has not been the experience of many African Christians. The reason is that while there are many crusades, many mountaineering prayers, many churches, and many pastors in Africa, many people have not had any personal conversional encounter with Christ.

Every genuine Christian is given authority in the name of Jesus through whom he or she was saved and joined to the family of God. Every believer becomes a God-sent minister with divine authority to overcome any manifestation of evil and any demonic force. Even when the answers to prayers are delayed or it seems that the same negative trends are occurring in a family of genuine children of God, Jesus promised "I have told you these things, so that in me you may have peace. In this world you will have trouble. But take heart! I have overcome the world" (John 16:33). In the Bible, God never disappointed any of his children. For example, he made Moses "like God to Pharaoh" (Exod 7:1), and no one was able to stand before Joshua (Josh 1:5). Today the Lord still proves himself. Christian faith and life include spiritual battles and warfare, but the Lord uses these struggles for his purposes.

The Necessity of Active Missions

John Stott notes that "we evangelicals are gospel people."[32] Evangelicals emphasize sharing the good news. Evangelicals and evangelism are not merely similar words; they indicate the priority in evangelical service. Evangelicals stress proclaiming the good news and gospel of Jesus and concentrate on giving invitations to whoever wants to believe and receive salvation through a personal encounter with God. This proclamation includes demonstrating the gospel through work in social reform and social responsibility. Gospel truth must be communicated in evangelism and soul winning, and strong emphasis is laid on the Great Commission mandate to reach the world and make disciples for Christ (Matt 28:18–20). The apostle Peter taught that when sinners are saved, they become priests (1 Pet 2:5). Their work as priests includes serving God in words and deeds and seeing others saved into the family of Christ.

---

31. Glenn M. Penner, *In the Shadow of the Cross: Biblical Theology of Persecution and Discipleship* (Bartlesville: Living Sacrifice Books, 2004).

32. John Stott, *What Is an Evangelical?* (London: Falcon, 1977), 10.

The call to witnessing and evangelizing others is a call to naturally express appreciation and gratitude for God's great salvation that one has received free of charge. Two major purposes of salvation are loving and serving God. "For we are God's handiwork, created in Christ Jesus to do good works, which God prepared in advance for us to do" (Eph 2:10).[33] Therefore, evangelicals have a sense of unconditional duty and mission to follow the selfless mission of Christ in preaching and discipling others which is seen as fulfilling God's mission on earth.

This mission effort also involves working to help the needy and less privileged. Involvement in social action is key to evangelicalism because the Scripture places social responsibility on God's people. Evangelicals believe that the word of God should be the basis for pursuing social action and righteousness. They see those who are not yet born again as lost (Luke 19:10), condemned (John 3:18), under God's wrath (John 3:36), dead in sin (Eph 2:1), and having no hope without the gospel (Eph 2:12).[34] While it is the grace of God that will save these sinners, personal decisions in response to active mission and evangelism are fundamental, which makes evangelism a key aspect of spiritual life.

What implications do the evangelical concepts of active mission, evangelism, and discipleship have on the dilemmas of curse and expressions of fear of curses in Africa? First, instead of cursing one's enemy in the church or using curses to counter curses, preaching the power of the gospel of Christ to those enemies will be more effective. The people or "cursers" who are seen as enemies should instead be seen as people in need of salvation and transformation by the gospel of Christ through evangelism.

Second, the practices of giving gifts to a prophet of deliverance or to appease the spirit of a curser who is dead are contrary to the holistic teaching of the Scriptures. In the Bible, giving is a part of mission, worship, and Christian living: giving is not a utilitarian business transaction as some African deliverance ministers say. This teaching is a tendency to make God serve human interest through some gift, and it is not biblical. Appeasing the spirit of a dead curser in order to cure a curse is also very unbiblical in the light of the power of the cross exposited above. The cross experience and salvation through the death and resurrection of Christ made the name of Christ to be above every other name (Phil 2:9-11) and to have power to cure every human problem. Christ

---

33. Lightner, *Evangelical Theology*, 214.

34. Philip Thomas, "Jesus and the Future: A study Guide from Rom. 8:18-25," *Evangelical Presbyterian Journal of the Westminster Fellowship* 23, no. 3 (2018): 32.

has appeased God who was wronged by human sin; but humans do not need to appease other humans to remove curses.

The best antidote to the hermeneutical anomalies and theological syncretism of curse preachers and teachers in Africa is to produce healthy doses of biblical theology based on excellent exposition of texts that are then applied properly to African lived reality in ways that are both biblical and contextual. This work is the goal of the next chapters.

How can African Christians explain some life incidences which defy conventional analysis and sound like mysteries? A relevant, comprehensive African theology of suffering must be framed that will engage some of these peculiarities. I say this because I am persuaded like Gustaf Aulen that no form of Christianity has any future without determining how to realistically and steadily offer a valid explanation for Christian experiences of evil.[35] How can we form practical guidelines that can help African Christians with their fear and dilemmas of curses from the above exposition?

---

35. Gustaf Aulen, *Christus Victor* (London: SPCK, 1983), 159.

9

Christian Moral Responsibility and the Dilemma of Curses

Before we lay out the necessary practical guidelines, we must look at the aspects of Christian morality that relate to curses in Africa. The confusion arising from curses is not a mental dilemma; it also involves theological confusion. One vital dimension of the concept of curses that emerges when the concept is critically examined is that curses constitute a form of evil. As a form of evil, curses are a problem of evil, like those discussed in theology courses, and raise questions that challenge orthodox Judea-Christian theism. Thus, apart from causing dilemmas for African Christians, curses also create a problem of evil that confronts the integrity of Christian definitions of God. African Christians who go through some experiences that they believe are the results of curses ask, "How could anyone believe in an omnibenevolent, omnipotent God when things like this happen?" Theologically, where do curses come from? Who created curses? Did God who is all loving, all knowing, and all powerful create curses?

One of the major puzzles that people have to grapple with is the logical incompatibility of the existence and realities of evil such as curses in a world created by the all good, all knowing, and all loving God. The popular understanding of God as omniscient, omnibenevolent, and omnipotent seems to contradict the reality and pain of curses as people perceive them to be.

This chapter briefly deals with this logical contradiction between people's understanding of God and their experiences of curses to bring out some salient points that will guide African Christians to understand the multidimensional nature of curses and obtain multidimensional solutions to their confusion about curses.

Curses as a Problem of Evil

Theists and atheists alike seem convinced that evil does indeed count against the existence of God or his attributes of goodness. While some evil might make sense in the light of the larger divine plan of God, how can we explain limitless suffering and evil occurrences such as curses bring?[1] The prophet Jeremiah says, "You are always righteous, LORD, when I bring a case before you. Yet I would speak with you about your justice: Why does the way of the wicked prosper? Why do all the faithless live at ease?" (Jer 12:1). Evil like the curses we see in this world does not fit our expectations of what the world should be like if it was created by God who is omnipotent, omnibenevolent, and omniscient. We expect that evil like curses would not exist in a world that God created out of love with his unlimited power and perfect knowledge of the past, present, and future. The thought that curses can be inflicted on humans who were created by God who is all loving is apparently incompatible with the attributes of God. This logical incompatibility is technically called the problem of evil.

Of all the objections to the Christian definition of God (theism), the most celebrated and oft-rehearsed by far is the problem of evil. The mental struggle of reconciling the existence of an infinitely good and omnipotent God with the strong reality of evil such as curses in the world creates psychological dissonance.[2] Curses are believed to be part of what people experience as reality in a way that is different from other human experiences.

While there are three expressions of the problem of evil, only one is our concern here. The three expressions are (1) the logical problem of evil for intellectuals and theologians; (2) the evidential problem of evil which deals with the variety and profusion of evil; and (3) the religious, emotional, or existential problem of evil which deals with approaching evil like curses in the life of believers in God whose faith is subjected to serious questioning because they believe that curses are operating in their life even while they have been following God. The major attention here is on the third: how to help believers in God who believe that their God is all powerful, all knowing, and all loving but whose life experiences of curses seem to contradict these attributes.

Looking at the causes of curses and the fact that people believe there cannot be a curse without a cause, I believe that curses constitute the religious problem of evil and that basically Christians who are attacked by curses need to be helped not by philosophical ruminations but by theologically grounded

---

1. Michael Murray and Michael Rea, *An Introduction to the Philosophy of Religion* (Cambridge: Cambridge University Press, 2008), 159.

2. A. Plantinga, *God, Freedom and Evil* (Grand Rapids: Eerdmans, 1977), 7.

pastoral care and counseling. Many Christians have attempted to explain why the existence of evil is compatible with the goodness, knowledge, and power of God. Theologians such as Augustine, Irenaeus, Alvin Plantinga, John Hick, and some African theologians have provided what is called "theodicy," justification of God, in response. What theodicy can we provide for the religious and existential problem of evil that the concept of curses generates?

Curses as a Form of Moral Evil

Obviously, curses inflict pain, suffering, and agony on victims. Curses like evil, are opposites of good and blessings.[3] The usual definitions of curses in Africa and elsewhere show that they are related to human misfortune, pain, and suffering. Curses are a form of injury, calamitous pain, and suffering that is inflicted on humans.[4] These definitions are the very same as those that describe evil in theological and religious discourse. Evil as a concept is a real human social and spiritual phenomenon in the world. Although no one seems to have a clear definition for evil, its experiential nature has made it a popular entity in human knowledge. There are three major types of evil in classical studies: moral evil, physical evil, and metaphysical evil.[5] To what category of evil do curses belong?

Almost every action related to the evil of curses is moral in nature. As the previous chapters establish, both in the Bible and as believed in African religious-cultural contexts, most curses are conditional curses that are put into effective when the cursed person has done some action that expresses a character disposition that is offensive to the curser. Therefore, the causes of curses are usually moral, and the pronouncements of curses are also moral. Curses are moral evil in their causes but may be metaphysical in their expressions. Because human misbehavior is usually the major cause of curses, once a curse becomes effective, it appears in painful events that are beyond the physical, are extraordinary, and are often inexplicable. The usual causes of curses are human moral ills. If there is no justifiable moral cause, a curse cannot be effective in a person's life. But once the curse becomes effective, it is metaphysical because it occurs in ways that may not be comprehended

---

3. G. A. Oshitelu, *Religion, God and Evil, Issues in Philosophy of Religion* (Ibadan: Hope, 2010), 50.

4. G. Adeboye, "Corruption as a Moral Evil: A Philosophical Analysis," in *Corruption: A New Thinking in the Reverse Order*, ed. B. Igboin (Oyo: Ajayi Crowther University Press, 2018), 107.

5. John Hick, *Evil and the God of Love*, 2nd ed. (New York: Palgrave Macmillan, 1977), 12.

with the ordinary lenses. In other words, the curse brings some misfortunes that the cursed may not be able to explain. Therefore I can say that curses are moral evil when defined in relation to possible causes of curses, but they are also metaphysical in the expressions of their effects.

The most common misconception of curses is the tendency to focus on the metaphysical expressions, the painful results, rather than the moral dimensions. If only the metaphysical aspects of curses are observed, then the question of why God allowed the curses will surface. But if the moral aspects of curses are examined, the moral misbehavior that caused curses will come into focus. For example, people who murder an innocent person have caused moral infringement and will incur curses on themselves. Therefore, this type of curses should not be seen as caused by God but by an act of one person or persons against their fellow human. This moral nature becomes very clear if we consider that the majority of curses pronounced by God in the Bible are conditional curses which only become effective if a person disobeys the precepts of God. Biblical curses are expressions of the justice and righteousness of God. Biblical curses are conditional curses that only affect people when they trespass a moral boundary.

The Moral Responsibilities of Christians

How can we help Christians who have experiences of evil that have been tagged as the results of curses? Three things must be emphasized as African pastors attempt to care for their members in the face of curses. First, a proper understanding of moral responsibility must be entrenchment in the moral consciousness of African Christians. They must be taught that their actions will have repercussions. We need to know that God has given us freewill for the purpose of making us morally responsible creatures who will use our freewill to choose between good and evil and face the effects of our choices. Rather than seeing curses as exclusively evil, we must see that evil also carries a notion of ethical development and personal character formation. Curses do not inflict innocent people.

Many have argued that human moral responsibility is incompatible with the divine sovereignty of God, but this is not an evangelical perspective. The correct and proper biblical teaching is that human moral responsibility and the divine sovereignty of God collaborate in the salvation of humankind. God created humans with a moral responsibility mechanism, and although God is sovereign, his absolute sovereignty does not diminish human responsibility and accountability. The Bible clearly shows that God is absolutely sovereign

(Isa 46:9–10; Dan 4:35; Prov 21:1; Rom 8:28–30) which means that all God has preordained will surely come to pass. But this doctrine does not necessarily contradict the validity of individual human moral responsibility. Human beings are fully accountable for the choices they make when exercising the freewill God gave them. Human beings are the causes or originators of their actions, and they are to receive blame or praise for the results of their actions. Curses were not part of what God created because all that God created was good and not evil (Gen 1:31). Curses and other forms of evil came because of the abuse of freewill by Adam and Eve. The Lord told Adam what the effects of his choices would be (Gen 2:16–17). The power of moral free choice includes the ability to do good or bad. The choice lies in the hand of each person, not God.[6]

The blame for the evil of curses rests with humans not God, for God does not tempt anyone with evil (Jas 1:13). In biblical Christianity, human actions are emphasized as the causes that determined the resulting effects of those actions. While God is not the author of curses, he foreknew in his eternal wisdom that humans would misuse their freewill to behave in immoral ways that result in curses. He willingly allowed the possibility to emphasize the importance of moral responsibility among mankind. As D. A Carson argues, "At no point whatsoever does the remarkable emphasis on the absoluteness of God's sovereignty mitigate the responsibility of human beings."[7]

Apart from Christian moral responsibility, the African traditional concept of communal salvation needs to be transformed by the New Testament individualistic notion of salvation by a personal conversional encounter with Christ. The New Testament shows clearly that while salvation is meant to create a community of called-out ones, the formation of this community starts with and depends on the genuineness of individual responses to the salvation call.[8] Africans have a collectivistic and interdependence philosophy that emphasizes the effect of one person's actions and inaction on other people in communal relationship. While this philosophy has been useful for fostering communal unity, it has been a major ideological source of extreme fear that the sins of parents and family members can affect people even when they have given their lives to Christ. What is needed is an effort to balance the African overt collectivist notion with the New Testament emphasis on

---

6. N. Geisler, *Chosen but Free: A Balanced View of God's Sovereignty and Freewill* (Minneapolis: Bethany House, 1999), 43.

7. D. A. Carson, *Divine Sovereignty and Human Responsibility: Biblical Perspectives in Tension* (Atlanta: John Knox, 1981), 2.

8. Isaac Boaheng, "Divine Sovereignty, Human Responsibility and God's Salvific Plan: An African Perspective," *ERATS Journal of Religious and Theological Studies* 1, no. 1 (2019): 89.

"whoever believes in him shall not perish but have eternal life" (John 3:16). This African traditional cultural emphasis is one area to which the Bible needs to be applied to transform.

Lastly, the perspective of curses in relation to morals and the problem of evil should basically include how best Christians should respond. African Christians should not only concentrate on the "why" of curses; they should first seek to understand what God wants to teach his children by allowing some experiences that are not expected. This understanding should be involved in practical guidelines for the Christians in Africa. The next chapter provides practical biblical guidelines for solving African Christians' dilemmas and fear of curses. Adequate background is given above; we now turn to giving Christians in Africa something they can follow in their struggle with the fear of curses.

10

A Contextual and Biblical Guideline for Responding to Curses

Based on the theological discussion of the evangelical perspective on the African Christian theology of curses in the previous two chapters, this chapter is an attempt to present feasible, practical recommendations for how Christians in Africa can be guided to biblically and contextually respond to curses. As you will soon see, the practical guidelines provided in this chapter are "African theology watered by native hands, pruned by a native hatchet, and tended with native earth."[1] While these guidelines can be useful for Christians elsewhere, they are basically presented here with the African context in mind.

Intercultural Hermeneutics and Application of Biblical Texts

A minister of God in Lagos, Nigeria, narrated to me how he creatively replaced a traditional structure with Christian methodology to satisfy the existential needs of his members. A man from Imo state Nigeria who was living in Lagos and attending his church told him what happens in his culture if a woman gives birth to a deformed child and the child dies. If they bury the deformed child without beating its dead body with a cane and a charmed razor, the next pregnancy of the woman may also be of a deformed child because the spirit of the first deformed child may return again to that family. Then the man told a story. A particular family gave birth to a deformed child, and after a few years

---

1. John S. Pobee, "Africa, Good News and Native Hands, Native Hatchet, Native Earth," in *African Christianity in Local and Global Context*, ed. S. A. Fatokun, University of Ibadan, Department of Religious Studies Series 7 (Ibadan: Baptist Press Nigeria, 2019), 27.

the child died. People instructed them to beat the child and to scorch his dead body with a charmed knife. But the family rejected this counsel arguing that they were now born-again Christians, and such traditional beliefs no longer hold true for them. They buried the child without beating and scorching his dead body with a charmed razor. However, their next pregnancy again resulted in a deformed child. After a few years this child also died, and they called the pastor to come and join them in beating his body and scorch it with knife. The pastor who understood their dilemma went and conducted a special prayer session and read the words of God in the house of the bereaved couple before he buried the dead child. The next time the couple became pregnant and gave birth, the baby was not deformed. Instead of criticizing their experience, the pastor had changed their method from traditional to biblical. This account is an example of an intercultural biblical engagement of traditional beliefs.

Biblical texts and theologies should be used to transform the cultural and traditional thinking of African Christians. Some syncretic traditional tools should be removed and replaced with Christian and biblical elements while still meeting the spiritual expectations and needs of African Christians. These Christians have a set of needs that they want Christianity to fulfill, and they sometimes resort to syncretic manners. But these syncretic elements should be replaced with biblical values.

Another important issue that must be dealt with in curbing the fear of curses in African Christianity is the treatment and application of biblical texts. Some texts such as Deuteronomy 28 and Genesis 3 that have been interpreted in ways that heighten fear of curses should be reinterpreted in the light of other relevant biblical texts to develop a holistic biblical understanding of curses. It should be noted that no one single portion of Scripture is enough to develop a coherent theology. Rather, every biblical text on curses should be interpreted in the light of other biblical texts. These biblical texts on curses should not be interpreted in isolation of the entire purpose of God as revealed in Scripture. The Bible is the best interpreter of itself!

Proper Use of So-called Imprecatory Psalms

I hereby provide an intercultural interpretation model on how imprecatory psalms should be interpreted and applied in relation to curses. In the African context, the book of Psalms is used for prayer to cure curses more than any other book of the Bible because the book speaks to almost all aspects of the people's life situations. Therefore, the book of Psalms has become a booklet for warfare and spiritual protection in contemporary African Christianity.

On many occasions, victims of curses are asked to recite imprecatory psalms three or seven times in the middle of the night. A short extract from one of the popular songs in the AICs in Nigeria proves that this practice of praying the Psalms is used:

> I will challenge all kind of spiritual attacks once I laid my hands on the Psalms.
> Praying with the Psalms is a sure source of victory;
> praying with the Psalms is a means of great protection;
> praying with the Psalms makes assurance for providence;
> praying with the Psalms is a virtue of healing;
> praying with the Psalms will bring joy and peace.[2]

While this song represents a good and novel mindset toward the use of the Bible in prayer which should be commended, the question is to what extent should African Christians use psalms for cursing their enemies? Are the curses found in the psalm totally useful for the Christian dispensation? How should African Christians interpret and apply imprecatory psalms? These questions are answered using a popular imprecatory psalm, Psalm 35.[3]

First, the imprecatory psalms must be studied in both their immediate and larger contexts. For example, Psalm 35 is connected to David and shows unity of authorship. It deals with David's life experiences as a king when his close, trusted associates who had been of help turned to be his enemies. Therefore Psalm 35 is a psalm of lament of an individual.[4] It describes his agony amidst several enmities in a cultural context of physical and intertribal warfare. If the Bible will speak to us, we must establish the similarities between the world of the authors and the world of Africans, which is the first leg of Mburu's four legs of intercultural dialogue discussed in chapter 3 on theological methods. Indeed, the cultural context of Psalm 35 and that of Africans are very similar. A difference is that the warfare in Psalm 35 was largely physical; while the warfare in the contemporary African cultural context is both physical and spiritual. The interpretation of Psalm 35 in Africa must be foregrounded on these contextual similarities and differences.

Second, the theological context of the psalm must be evaluated. African preachers must avoid reading the sentences of the psalms in isolation from

---

2. Participatory observation in some AICs, January to July 2021.

3. As noted earlier, the imprecatory psalms include Psalm 7; 58; 59; 69; 109, and others.

4. J. O. Adeogun, "Psalter: A Tool of Liberation in Aladura Churches," in S. O. Abogunrin (ed.), *Decolonization of Biblical Interpretation in Africa* (Nigerian Association for Biblical Studies: Ibadan, 2005), 184.

the theological context of the text. In the case of Psalm 35, the theological context is prayer that the judgment of God would come on the enemies of Israel, which lies in the larger context of the Abrahamic covenant promise God will punish the enemies of Israel (Gen 12:3). This theological context is the second leg of Mburu's intercultural hermeneutic. Note that Mburu does not argue for an interpretation of a text that conflicts with the integrity of the entire Bible. Instead, we must ask what does every other part of the Scripture say in relation to or on the topics of Psalm 35?

Third, the literary context of the psalm should be examined. Literary context is the third leg of Mburu's model of intercultural dialogue, and it involves the imagery, genre, language, and textual flows of the text. It must be emphasized that the book of Psalms is in the poetic category of biblical text, and the interpretation of such poetic literature must incorporate the parallelism, figures of speech, and other literary features in the text. For example, Psalm 35 includes imageries of innocence, invocation, imprecation, and thanksgiving. The setting of this poetic text indicates a trial in a law court in which David's enemies employed by Satan stand as defendants. The psalmist drags his enemies into the court of Yahweh for inflicting him unjustly (vv. 7–16). Obviously, the psalmist invites God to inflict these enemies with affliction (vv. 4–8, 26). But one thing the psalmist says is that he had spent time praying, fasting, and mourning, pleading for the healing of his enemies when they were sick (vv. 13–14), and he had sought for their welfare but they returned evil for good (vv. 11–12). Gunkel's category approach can also be used to identify the literary forms and nature of the psalm.[5] However in sum, the text is poetic in nature, and interpretation of it must take into account relevant interpretive skills needed for poetic literature. This literary context relates with the third leg of Mburu's intercultural model.

Fourth, the historical-cultural context of the psalm must be understood, which is the fourth leg of Mburu's intercultural model. The imprecatory psalms should be seen in the light of Old Testament ethics and the nature of Yahweh's holiness which is contextual and particular to the Old Testament. Seeing the imprecatory psalms in this context, we will discover that the writers primarily sought to rely on God who is holy and faithful to deliver them from their enemies. These psalms were prayers of trust in their context. In Old Testament ethics, curses can be conditional or unconditional, though unconditional curses are rare. Conditional curses are those which God pronounces on people who

---

5. This method is informed by the form-critical approach of Hermann Gunkel. See Gunkel, *Psalms*.

break his law and who have been forewarned about actions that will result in curses. The apparent curses pronounced on the enemies in Psalm 35 are in line with God's justice and covenant with Abraham, and they are conditional curses because they are punishment for sins. This historical-cultural context is the fourth leg of Mburu's intercultural hermeneutics. Therefore, Psalm 35 is not a psalm containing blind imprecations but a psalm that pronounces punishment on the enemies of God who have acted against the holiness of God. Rather than merely using this psalm in church for cursing one's enemies, African Christians can reflect on the theme of God's holiness that is imbedded in the psalm.

Fifth, African preachers can now apply the text of imprecatory psalms to the contemporary life situation of their audience, which is the "seat" of the stool in Mburu's model. African Christians must know that the spirit of imprecatory psalms is not totally Christian. Imprecatory psalms were written in the era before the experience of the cross of Christ. Unlike in the Old Testament, Christian warfare is not against known, human enemies but against spirits and principalities that do not respect human imprecations but only the name of Jesus. Using imprecatory psalms to curse one's enemies is to seek to pay back evil with evil. Instead, what is needful is praying to God for deliverance from the enemy. The New Testament concept of the enemy is spiritual and has to do with salvation. Thus imprecatory psalms should be Christianized in the context of the doctrine of reconciliation. However, proper prayer that is patterned after Jesus's model of prayer should be made to incapacitate enemies and their tactics.[6] Jesus taught us to pray, "And lead us not into temptation, but deliver us from the evil one" (Matt 6:13). This prayer model shows that Jesus has made provision for how Christians should respond to the activities of "the evil one."

When applying the imprecatory psalms, a question that must be asked is what is the need met by the imprecatory psalm in its original context? For example, Psalm 35 fulfills the purpose of showing that God will never leave his own children in the midst of provocation and suffering and that God will vindicate his children when they are cheated. Therefore, African preachers must determine the needs and allow how these needs are met to influence their application of the text. In other words, the text should be used to continue to meet the needs. Also, African Christians must allow the spirit of the gospel to override the spirit of teeth for teeth, hand for hand, eye for eye, foot for foot, burn for burn, wound for wound, bruise for bruise, and life for life that

---

6. Hughes and Laney, *Tyndale Concise Bible Commentary*, 213.

is apparently present in the Psalms (see Exod 21:24). They should allow the gospel theology of the cross and love of God to transform both the context of the imprecatory psalms and the context of the contemporary African readers for whom these texts are applied,[7] which will show both the rigor that is expected of sound biblical interpretation and the creativity expected of relevant contextual biblical application.

Steps for Determining If Someone Is Under a Curse

Not all life misfortunes are the result of curses. Some may be the result of curses; some are not. But how can we know if a life difficulty is the result of a curse or not? Are there other things we can inherit apart from curses? Or are some life difficulties that are not curses interpreted as curses?

While not all negative trends are the results of curses, some may be caused by curses in someone's life. What is needed is being able to know when a trend is a result of a curse or whether it is another form of life difficulty or something that God permissively allowed to prune his children for growth and maturity. Part of Christian life is the battle which is purely spiritual. These battles can be fearful and complicated experiences. Mankind is involved in one of the greatest wars of all time, a battle that involves every Christian. The real battle is against the devil and his principal angels. These battles or what some call "power encounters"[8] make the identification of curses more complex.

But some steps can be useful for identifying and ascertaining whether an experience is merely Christian warfare or specifically the result of a curse. The following guide can be of help. The first thing to ensure is the personal conversion of the person going through the agony. In other words, we must first ensure that the person who is in a dilemma that looks like the results of a curse is a born-again Christian. If the person is not born again, a pastor or a genuine born-again Christian should lead that person to Christ. If the person is born again, we should examine and ascertain if the person has unconfessed, secret sins. If there is one, the pastor or deliverance minister should ensure that the person confesses this sin and prays for repentance. If restitution is required, the person should be encouraged to do it. However, if the person is a genuine Christian and has no unconfessed, secret sins, then that Christian

---

7. Thomas Schreiner, *New Testament Theology: Magnifying God in Christ* (Grand Rapids: Baker, 2008), 266.

8. Mipo Dandang, *Exploring Power Encounter: A Biblical-Theological Perspective* (Jos: ACTS, 2016), 142.

is not likely under any curse because curses cannot penetrate the Holy Spirit's seal on Christians (Rom 8:11; 1 John 4:4). On many occasions, what African Christians interpret as curses or inherited curses in the life of a genuine believer may be one of the following. Also included are the ways African Christians can deal with curses practically not only through deliverance or noisy prayers but creative Christian engagement of issues:

1. **An inherited family behavioral pattern** which is not spiritual but entirely biological and can be broken by deliberate behavioral adjustments, not spiritual deliverance. For example, if a parent is fond of gossip with a tendency to tell lies, the children may be fond of gossip as well. This trait is not a curse if the children are genuinely born again. It only requires deliberate effort to change the unwanted behavior. If your father drinks alcohol or has a tendency for extreme anger, and you have now given your life to Christ, deliberately curtail your appetite and control your own tendency to anger. These are the tools of the devil. Those who have been genuinely regenerated can maintain their victory in Christ through daily devotion, self-discipline, consistent prayer life, and deliberate breaking and changing from bad family character traits.

2. **An inherited sickness or disease** which is purely hereditary and can be corrected through medical consultation, not deliverance. For example, some diseases like hypertension, diabetes, cancer, asthma, and obesity can be inherited.[9] These diseases are not inherited spiritually through curses but biologically through genes. When this trend occurs, it is not deliverance that is most necessary but medical attention. Therefore, if a mother has breast cancer and her daughters have the same cancer, this affliction may not be due to an inherited curse. Christians really need to discern and remember that not all life difficulties that repeat in patterns are curses. Some are purely biological.

3. **The consequences or punishment for unconfessed sin including lack of forgiveness**. Once people have a personal conversional encounter with the Lord, they cannot be cursed, and curses operating in their family lineage do not have any power over them except if they have secret or other sins they have not confessed. But once

---

9. Dr. Ogunkayode Tosin, MBBS, a family health expert, General Hospital, Ilorin, Nigeria. Oral interview, June 2021.

they confess and seek forgiveness, no curse is above the power of Christ. However, the Lord may use difficult experiences and trends to motivate his children to confess their sins and repent so they may grow in wisdom and maturity. It must be stated that breaking family curses also involves breaking family known sins and bad character traits that have been taken for granted by previous family members. Forgiving others for offenses done to you and recognizing negative thoughts are the starting points for being delivered from the manipulation of the devil. These steps should be followed by consistently reaffirm the lordship of Christ in you, resisting the devil through faith, and engaging in consistent fasting and prayer.

To summarize, the fear of curses among genuine Christians in Africa is biblically unfounded and is largely due to ignorance and lack of understanding of the complexity of the Christian life. Genuine Christians cannot inherit curses, but they can inherit some bad behaviors which can be corrected via deliberate effort. They can also inherit some diseases through blood and genes, but not curses. Deliverance and prayers are useful but they must be laced with adequate understanding and caution. If it is established that someone has genuinely gone through a conversional encounter, he or she may still go through some unwanted situations. But these unwanted situations are not inherited curses; they are part of the spiritual warfare that should be expected in any genuine Christian life.

Now if after a thorough assessment the persons we are diagnosing have not had a personal conversional encounter, then the misfortunes troubling them may be curses of their own causing or inherited. In fact, many are likely curses of God on those who deliberately choose to reject Christ's gospel, which are the very situations or experiences we can refer to without any mistake as curses. The best solution for this type of curse is to lead the people concerned to Christ. Once they have an encounter with Christ, they become a new creature. This transformation is the foundation on which deliverance prayers from curses can be made and is the real "deliverance" from curses.

Finally, it must be mentioned that some conditional curses can influence Christians. For example, if Christians do not humble themselves to serve God or pay their tithe, or they do not support the work of God with his material things, or they do not pray, then they can experience the repercussions of not worshipping God with what God has given. These repercussions are conditional curses. As a case study, the word of God shows that God is totally against the proud (Jas 4:6–10). Children of God are not expected to be proud, and if

Christians have an attitude of pride, then they experience some negative results. These are not the results of unconditional (inherited) curses but expressions and results of lack of giving attention and commitment to personal spiritual development and progressive sanctification.

Christologization of Deliverance Ministry on Curses

When we realize that the victims of curses are not born again upon counselling, listening, observation, and discussion, and when we understand from careful listening to the person that this is not some other kind of life difficulty, then we can consider that the problem may be due to a curse of some kind. Thus, first having a regeneration experience is essential for deliverance of victims. However, this deliverance process must be christological. How can a deliverance session be christological? By introducing the personhood, deity, birth, death, and resurrection of Christ to the victims. The people to be delivered should be made to know that they are not experiencing deliverance to pay a ransom for a debt in their lineage. They are experiencing to first encounter Christ, and Christ is enough to save them.

Again, the practice of appeasing wronged persons, for example that victims must go and present an appeasement gift to a stepmother or grandmother who has placed a curse on them, should be discouraged. Christ makes all the appeasement once the victim confesses him as Lord. No appeasement of a human person is needed. In some situations, restitution may be prescribed, but not appeasement. Confession of sins are needed, not payment of a ransom to a deliverance minister.

Also, the practice of commercializing deliverance from curses should be discouraged. The grace of faith to pray, what is needed to conduct deliverance, does not have a cost but is free of charge from God. African Christians and deliverance ministers should cease from collecting payment for deliverance because it is God who does deliverance, not humans. Deliverance is not a display of personal gifts but of God's grace.

Similarly, the messianic syndrome attached to the deliverance of curses in contemporary African Christianity must be discouraged. The emphasis on looking at a few selected people of God as the only ones who are qualified to conduct deliverance is not biblical. African deliverance ministers should approach deliverance services as servants of Christ, not as the "lords" of the victims to be delivered. Christ must be honored in and through every deliverance session. Deliverance and prayer sessions must not be filled with selfish requests and existential pragmatism. Christianity does not exist to fulfill the cravings and natural desires of followers. This is not to argue that Christians are meant to be poor or to be less-concerned about their material needs. But Christians are to be guided by Jesus's formula stated in Matthew 6:33. The yearning to seek the Kingdom of God must be prioritized. Other needs are secondary. Therefore, any Christian deliverance activity and all Christian deliverance ministers must be guided by this principle.

Active Mission and Strong Discipleship

The fact that the number of Christians is growing in Africa should not deceive us into believing that everyone found in the church or associated with Christian ministries or everyone who bears a Christian name has truly had a personal conversional experience. Some have emphasized that Christ does not call us to stay in the church but to do mission because "the fish are outside the church." But I argue that in the present, African Christians should make a deliberate effort to preach to church goers and confront them with questions of personal conversion and assurance of salvation. Unsaved, unconverted pastors and church members abound in African Christianity. They make religious noises, but they are not spiritually converted. They are the ones who make doctrinal confusion stronger in African Christianity. Such "unconverted Christians" do not want anything from Christ except money, wealth, breakthroughs, fame, healing, anointing, and other worldly achievements. To suffer for Christ or to endure hardship as God's children is strange to them. We need to make deliberate efforts to encourage these people to meet with Christ.

It is unfortunate that when many people give their lives to Christ in Africa, they are not adequately discipled. Efforts tend to focus on winning souls, but little attention is given to discipleship and spiritual growth. Many Christian converts from African traditional religions or African Islamic Sufism are left to grow on their own. These Christians deal with many dilemmas in their hearts on how to transition from their previous life reality to the Christian context. Many times, when other Christians do not labor to disciple them, they naively continue to carry their previous traditional and religious emphases and add these to their Christian beliefs and practices, thereby creating a Christianity that is not totally Christian nor biblical. These are the Christians who easily promote syncretism in the African context.

The mission given to the church to win the souls of sinners to Christ should not be taken in despair. Because the Holy Spirit is involved, it is a biblical task, a task of faith before becoming a human task.[10] The regenerated should seek to exhibit and spread the righteousness of the kingdom of God into which they have been introduced by their rebirth.[11] African pastors and preachers should develop a biblical vision of the gospel that prioritizes genuine individual conversion and adequate discipleship of new converts. Without serious attention given to preaching and teaching the importance of a personal Christian life, we cannot deal with the fear of curses. Service is an exceptionally central concept of the New Testament. Christians are called to serve, and the basis of this call to serve is a christological one; Christ himself came not to be served but to serve (Matt 20:28). Proceeding from the pattern of Jesus's ministry, service and evangelism should become characteristic of Christians. Discipleship and mission are both individual work and the collective work of the church.[12] The fear of curses in Africa is an indication that more effort is needed in active mission and discipleship. Evangelical preaching for conversion and discipleship after conversion are how every unbiblical orientation can be adequately brought under the lordship of Christ.

Strong and Intentional Pastoral Care and Counseling

African pastors and Christians tend to prefer deliverance and prayer to counseling. Every problem is taken for deliverance and exorcism. However, this practice has taken the attention of African Christians from some realities of life. If a life-altering incidence occurs, like someone suddenly losing a father or losing a child, after the time of mourning the bereaved is not given counseling. Once bereaved people stop crying, it is assumed that they have got over it. But this is not the case. African church leaders must realize the need for proper pastoral counseling for those who are going through life challenges so that these people will not misinterpret their experiences and develop unhealthy views about God, themselves, and other people around them. Perhaps more than other Christians, African Christians have several questions in their hearts for which they need answers. These answers cannot be adequately given when we exclusively concentrate on deliverance and exhibitionistic prayer sessions without accompanying these practices with diligent, phlegmatic, organized, and contextually relevant pastoral care and counseling.

---

10. George W. Peter, *A Biblical Theology of Mission* (Chicago: Moody Press, 1984), 164.

11. K. Bockmuehl, *Evangelicals and Social Ethics*, Outreach and Identity 4 – World Evangelical Fellowship Theological Commission (Exeter: InterVarsity Press 1979), 31.

12. Bockmuehl, *Evangelicals and Social Ethics*, 26.

Biblically Guided Prayer Sessions, Not Imprecation

There is nothing bad about praying against the power of curses. In fact, God commanded us to pray and wage war to restrict the devil. Christians who feel that they are tormented by curses can pray something like these prayers:

"I confront every manipulation of the devil appearing as curses and spells in the name of Jesus."

"I refuse and resist the devil and all the manifestation of his attacks and tricks in Jesus's name."

Jesus has given authority to Christians to order any ungodly spirits in his name. Luke 10 records how Jesus sent his disciples out to preach, and that the authority he gave them included overcoming spiritual enemies. Jesus's name is very powerful (see Phil 2:9–11; Acts 3:6–7, 16; 16:18). Therefore, Christians do not have to live in fear (see Ps 27).[13] After sincere prayers have been made in his name, African Christians need not fear curses again. Curses are not more powerful than Jesus.

In addition, African Christians need to know that the use of psalms requires a lot of hermeneutical caution. The historical context in which curses are pronounced as prayers in Psalms should be understood and contrasted with the new dispensational paradigm of New Testament era and theology. Psalms do not apply directly to this era because while for example David and Moses were fighting physical enemies, Christians are fighting spiritual, non-human enemies. As the apostle Paul notes, "For our struggle is not against flesh and blood, but against the rulers, against the authorities, against the powers of this dark world and against the spiritual forces of evil in the heavenly realms" (Eph 6:12).

A Hermeneutic of Resurrection for African Self-esteem

We need a biblical interpretation that will break the silence and build boldness, that will build courage not fear in African Christians. Life realities such as curses, fear, and misfortunes have reduced and silenced the self-esteem of many Africans and some communities, creating the need for psychological rehabilitation. Biblical interpretation and sermons that inflame fear and exaggerate the power of demons, witches, and wizards should be reversed to interpretation and applications that give assurance of God's presence, God's power, and God's love. Many Africans have been terribly terrified, and many have been through a lot of difficult situations that have caused them to develop

---

13. O'Donovan, *Biblical Christianity in Africa Perspective*, 315.

low self-esteem. They have lost hope in God and in themselves. They have been living at the mercy of self-adulated prophets who have a "messianic syndrome." Because their self-esteem has been shattered, many Africans have been unable to appreciate the role of their "self" in making decisions, deliberate actions, and choices in their life journey. African Christians must confront this low self-esteem through deliberate emphasis of the image of God in all people, including Africans, so that their esteem will resurrect in the Lord. While the fall recorded in Genesis has affected the image of God in humans, the hope of the risen Christ renews the image.

Personal Moral Responsibility and Progressive Sanctification

Could not the repeated failures and negative trends in someone's life be the result of personal recklessness and an unwillingness to take moral responsibility? Could not the emphasis on curses and demons causing failure and poverty in life be a way to passively throw personal responsibility on metaphysical entities? According to Kenneth Hagin's experiences in over fifty-five years of ministry, he never saw even a single Christian who was under a curse and only a few who were demonically influenced but not possessed. He concludes that the popularity of deliverance ministry is due to the fact people want to avoid personal responsibility.[14] Curses are overemphasized in Africa by some because claiming to be cursed has become an easy way out for personal misbehavior. For example, when people do what is very immoral and are challenged, the simple answer they give is that their bad behaviors are due to an inherited curse in their family.

Apart from these excuses, it should be emphasized that Satan thrives when Christians fail to progressively mature, and he cheats Christians out of growth with a lot of manipulative elements such as curses. Christians should be encouraged that while their salvation is entirely free, they have been called to live a life of continuous commitment and deliberate effort to become mature in Christ. This commitment and growth involve confession of sin, repentance, and abstinence from sinful behavior. Sanctification implies that Christians have positive moral and spiritual change in their lives. God has declared them to be holy, but they must make this declaration true in their daily living through the help of the Holy Spirit and their determination and deliberate readiness (see Rom 12; Heb 12). This effort will involve a battle between the new nature

---

14. Kenneth Hagin, *The Triumphant Church: Dominion Over All Powers of Darkness* (Tulsa: Rhema Bible Church, 2001), 251.

and old nature, but through the power of the Holy Spirit within, Christians can have victory over the flesh and be progressively changed into the likeness of Christ.[15]

Contextual Theological Training and Research

Many churches are planted in Africa, and many African Christians are discipled by church leaders who lack relevant pastoral training or theological maturity. This situation has resulted in what Idowu calls "theological poverty" in African Christianity.[16] What David Oyedepo meant when he said that "we have passed the era of doctrines and we are now in the era of mystery"[17] may not be totally relevant to African Christians because African Christianity needs to be built to cure it from its theological poverty. While there are over five thousand Bible colleges, seminaries, faculties of theology, and departments of religious studies in Africa, only a few can be said to be teaching vibrant contextual theological education because a majority of the teaching in these schools is fashioned using Western theological concepts which may not be applicable to Africans. In my own theological scholarship at a major evangelical theological institution in Africa, I found that some of the issues raised in the curricula were not relevant to Africa. For example, the course on Christian apologetics was largely filled with debates and arguments on proofs of God's existence, the veracity of miracles, etc. These are Western theological debates that nobody needs in Africa because Africans believe that God exists, though their belief about God is transactional and utilitarian. These courses should be revised to confront African theological realities, not Western issues. As a result, some contextual issues such as curses will be studied and theologized. Theological education and training should also be encouraged for all Christian preachers, deliverance ministers, and church leaders in Africa.

Apart from this contextualizing, the extreme departmentalization of fields of study in theological studies in Africa should be reconsidered. Many seminarians after graduation complain that they see little or no relationship between their theological education and the practical pastoral issues they

---

15. Fleming, *Bridgeway Bible Dictionary*, 392.

16. M. O. Idowu, "The Medicine as Poison, the Physician as the Killer: Modern Pentecostal Theology and Practices as Sources of Insecurity," in *Religion and Insecurity Issues*, ed. J. K. Ayantayo and S. A. Fatokun (Ibadan: University of Ibadan, Department of Religious Studies, 2015), 193.

17. David Oyedepo, *The Communion* (Lagos: Dominion Publishing House, 1994), cited in Idowu, "Medicine as Poison," 194.

are facing. Therefore, they throw away their years of theological training after the graduation. It must be realized that theology taught as a merely intellectual, academic discipline will soon drop out of the life of a pastor who is facing diverse practical spiritual issues. In addition, I observe that in many theological institutions in Africa, attention is given to general introductions of theological issues without going deeper into specific training on the practices of interpretation, exegesis, and communication. African pastors must be trained not just to have a general awareness and understanding but to be able to communicate their understanding to others.[18] Theological institutions in Africa should move from "introductory" to actually "doing" theology so that the students will be adequately grounded.

One final issue that must be mentioned is the wide gap between the intellectual vision and spiritual mandate of theological studies in Africa. Many theological institutions major on the intellectual academic mandate and forsake the primary need for spiritual formation in their pastoral training process. Contrarily, many other theological institutions major on the spiritual and create a loathsome hatred for thorough intellectual aspects in their pastoral training. Either of these two extremes will not benefit the African church. To produce vibrant pastors and church leaders, theological scholarship and spiritual formation must be seen as two sides of the same endeavor. Then I believe we will see an emergence of African pastors who are able to effectively handle the word of God to confront life issues, including curses.

I hope these reflections will be useful for handling the fear and dilemmas of curses among African Christians and that this chapter is useful for creating discipleship, Bible study, and course materials for Christians in Africa. Some extra spiritual issues also have remote roles in why Africans overemphasize spiritual misfortunes such as curses. These issues are what I call "The Real African Curses." The next section gives a very brief excursion on these issues as a way of concluding our discussion.

---

18. James Smart, *The Strange Silence of the Bible in the Church: A Study in Hermeneutics* (Philadelphia: Westminster, 1971), 167.

11

The Real African Curses

One final word is in order. While demons and spiritual problems like curses and witchcraft are real and faced by some people in Africa, they are not the only real problems. Besides presenting unbiblical theology of curses in African pulpits, Christian literature, Christian media, and Christian prayer in Africa, a set of real problems that are even more dangerous than the popular curses are presently waging war against the holistic development of African society that should be addressed in the content and direction of African Christianity. How can the church in Africa make a spiritual impact that will birth a holistic transformation of Africans?

To be contextually relevant to the life realities of modern African society, the curse of resource mismanagement, the curse of the paradox of plenty, the curse of corruption, the curse of poor interpersonal relationships, the curse of moral flaws such as laziness and bribery, the curse of negative ethnicity, the curse of disobedience to God, the curse of unhealthy politics, and the curses of incessant and blood-sucking insecurity, banditry, kidnapping, and rape must be the focus for African Christians in proclaiming the gospel. These are more dangerous and more difficult curses. These curses require more than deliverance and prayer; they required the deliberate attention of African Christians to embark on what I call "the evangelization of orientation and worldviews" of Africans.

Escapist, Ritualistic, and Pietistic Christianity and a Real Problem

One major reason why these problems have persisted is the type of Christian spirituality that dominates the African continent. This type majors on personal deliverance services, make-money-quick sermons, and extensively emotional, ritualistic liturgies that have no relevance to the burning issues in Africa.[1] As Stuart Fowler notes, the most dangerous weaknesses of Christianity in Africa are the secularization of public life and the parallel privatization of religious and spiritual piety. African Christianity has not exercised a transformational role beyond helping Africans fight personal spiritual enemies like witchcraft, demons, and inherited curses. Any moves by a few to relate biblical truth to the realm beyond private, personal spirituality and life challenges is tagged as having "heaven-less motivation." This dualization of African Christian values and public issues has narrowed the relevance of African Christianity to a mere pitiful, spirit-bombing mechanism. Much time and attention are given to ritual, but little time and attention are given to teaching and proclaiming the truth to confront African comprehensive problems. This focus has produced ritualistic but untruthful Christians in Africa. Personal responsibility, moral and character formation, and capacity building have been sacrificed on the altar of clapping, jumping, singing, and shouting in the church or on prayer mountains. More painfully, many African Christians use spirituality to explain away and provide excuses for their passivity and unhealthy, unengaging attitudes. Let us mention in briefest terms some results of this behavior.

First, African Christians are facing the curse of poverty which the church must address when proclaiming the gospel. Many African children live with daily hunger, malnutrition, lack of access to healthy water and good health facilities, no opportunity to go to school, child abuse, and forced marriage. The expressions of high poverty include high child mortality and exposure to malaria. The many international efforts and foreign-initiated funds will only scratch the surface if Africans themselves do not get involved in the transformation process. African churches also need to rise to these challenges through their proclamation of the gospel and by providing Christian education that will produce good citizens who can help build African society. The problem of poverty in Africa is not just the problem of NGOs or governments or families. Most African poor people are Christian children and youth, and therefore the churches must be involved in providing the solution. However instead of engaging this problem, many church leaders demand monetary gain from their poverty-stricken followers. They use big cars and other expensive equipment, but their followers are poor.[2] This behavior is a curse!

---

1. Turnbull, "Discipling Africa," 17.
2. Godwin Adeboye and Daniel Ajayi, "Despite the Increasingly Loud Religious Noise in Nigeria, Is There Any Change Potency in Nigerian Religion?" *JASSOSER* 1, no. 1 (2018): 23–36.

Second, African Christianity is suffering from the curses of nepotism, leadership problems, followership problems, and negative ethnicity. In a research I published through the faculty of Arts, University of Ibadan in 2017, I found that despite the fact that many African nations have leadership machinery, the challenges related to bad leadership, political instability, socioeconomic instability and inequality, and negative ethnicity have created anarchy and social disorder in Africa.[3] How can the churches in Africa be more holistic in handling the spiritual problems of their members and equally respond to these contextual challenges? Presently in Nigeria, multiple moves and campaigns for political separation have led to several societal, economic, and security problems that are claiming lives and destroying properties. Is the African church prepared to handle problems like these? While the church is a spiritual body, some extra spiritual matters must form part of our focus.

Third, the African church is faced with the problems of laziness and unhealthy campaigns promoting materialism. In 2017, I conducted research and found that the base of corruption in Nigeria (and even Africa) is simply the people's understanding of money and lack of work ethic. I found through field research that African Christians remain largely unconcerned about some vital social issues that are key to African social development and integrity.[4] Although a few efforts have been made to theologically interrogate African social issues, the majority of these efforts have been only at introductory levels; specific key issues and themes have been largely ignored. Again, even these few efforts have only been at academic levels. The majority of African preachers are only interested in taking their followers to heaven and helping them to conquer their curses and demonic attacks here on earth and do not include Christian social responsibility in their concerns. Although poor social-ethical orientation is becoming like an inherited curse in African society, members of the church feel unconcerned.

Fourth, the African church is faced with the challenge of Islamic radicalism leading to insecurity. At present, Africa is bedeviled with insecurity resulting in bloodshed, kidnapping, banditry, and fear. Oil-rich Muslim countries have

---

3. Godwin Adeboye, "Hobbesian State of Nature and the Quest for Social Order in Nigeria," in *Polity Debacle and the Burden of Being in Africa*, ed. A. B. Ekanola. Proceedings of the Third Biennial International Conference of the Faculty of Arts, University of Ibadan, (Ibadan: Faculty of Arts, University of Ibadan, 2017).

4. G. Adeboye, "Small Work, Big Money: The Implication of Nigerians' Philosophy of Money to the Ongoing Anti-Corruption Campaign in Nigeria," *Akungba Journal of Religion and African Culture*, Department of Religion and African Culture, Ondo State University 6, no. 2 (2018): 54–69.

been pouring massive amounts of money into sub-Saharan Africa sponsoring radical groups such as Boko Haram, Al-Shabab, and al-Qaeda who are bent on using Sharia law to revolutionize the continent by force and sword. These efforts have led to killing uncountable lives in Africa. The whole world now looks at Africa with surprise at what may come out of this interreligious struggle. Should not African Christians be actively and proactively up and doing to find a way for the future of African Christianity? Many times, when the issues of insecurity are raised in African Christian gatherings, the excuse for inactivity that is usually given is that people should pray about the problem, and some examples of biblical wars that were fought only through prayer are quoted. Rather than providing a holistic Christian approach to the security challenges, many call for fasting and prayers, and many people gather to pray and shout on mountains. These practices are good and commended. But they are not holistic engagement with the curses of insecurity in Africa. The church must devise a holistic approach including prayer, orientation, deliberate involvement in the military, teaching, and series of seminars on insecurity. The problem of insecurity in Africa is complicated; any relevant solutions must also be complicated!

Lastly is the resource curse and paradox of plenty in Africa. Africans are blessed people and blessed with natural resources. But what can be called the curse of mismanagement has bedeviled Africans and has caused their living experiences to be the opposite of blessing. Africans have great natural resources such as oil, diamonds, gold, and other minerals, but African countries have less economic and infrastructural development than countries that do not have these resources. For example, the Republic of Congo has one of the world's greatest deposits of copper which is an essential raw material, particularly for producing cell phones.[5] But the Congolese still largely import cell phones from China. The situation regarding petroleum is similar in Nigeria. These problems exist in Africa, and the best thing to do about them is not to keep quiet thinking that Jesus will soon come back and take us home. But as we earnestly expect the coming of Christ our Lord, we African Christians must see ourselves as among the solution finders to the African resource curse and rise through corporate social responsibility and the content of our gospel preaching and teaching to educate the African populace on the way out. These activities are part of the prophetic role of the church. Now, what can be a starting point for doing all these things?

---

5. David Taylor, "Africa in Crisis: Finding Hope in the Midst of Tragedy," *Mission Frontiers* published by U. S. Center for World Mission, Pasadena (2011): 6.

Evangelization of Orientation and Mindset

One way the church in Africa can be involved in solving these problems is to evangelize the mind, heart, and hands of Africans. The African mindset must be a subject matter when proclaiming the gospel. Evangelism and preaching in Africa must not be overly simplistic. Becoming born again and being baptized is not enough for Africans Christians, but character reformation and attitudinal transformation must be their goals. Many Christians live in Africa. Data shows that in 2000, there were nearly 350 million Christians in Africa, and the number is estimated to grow to 760 million by 2025, contrary to an earlier estimate of 700 million.[6] This makes African Christianity the fastest growing Christianity in the world. Many people have celebrated this growth, but I have a different perspective and a fear. The fear is that despite the many data analyses and reports that use physical programs and social media presence to measure the growth of African Christianity, African Christianity has not transformed many African Christians. I believe Africa needs a second missionary movement, not to make people into Christians but to make disciples out of the Christians in Africa. This effort may not involve holding crusades or hosting gigantic physical religious programs but having indoor, systematic discipleship efforts because through this discipleship process, negative worldviews and unbiblical cultural expectations can be confronted and transformed.

Many discipleship programs are ongoing in Africa, but many of these programs do not have the deliberate intention of transforming the orientations of Africans. In many of these discipleship programs, activities like clapping, dancing, shouting and singing, music concerts, and fundraising fill the space without giving time for confronting minds with the truth of the gospel. This type of discipleship has produced a Christianity of rituality and practice but without the accompanying and expected character development, orientation transformation, and truthfulness. This book is a call for African church leaders to review their discipleship efforts.

No doubt the challenges facing the African church are more than those discussed here, but these suffice to show that African Christians have a lot to do. Therefore, African preachers, teachers, and theologians should be more creative and holistic in their efforts to make Christianity contextual for Africans. There are many challenges in Africa. Curses and spiritual entities are only a few of these challenges. Can Jesus be relevant in all of these problems? Is the gospel of Christ capable of addressing all of these problems, such as curses, inherited curses, resource curses, bad leadership, poverty, insecurity etc.? The answers to these questions are obvious, and they are answered in the concluding chapter.

---

6. M. M. Canaris, "The Rapid Growth of Christianity in Africa," *Catholic Star Herald* (2018).

12

God Is Sovereign and Christ Is Lord Over All Curses

Finally, above all, God is sovereign. Although he allows some unexpected life occurrences to happen to his children, he only allows them for a limited time and for his ultimate glory and purposes. God is caring and wants a loving relationship with all of his creatures, especially human beings who he created in his image and likeness.

God and African Peculiar Experience

We started this book with a brief discussion on the peculiarity of African experiences in which the unique characteristic features of African Christians' experiences are clearly enumerated. All of the pages of this book have also attested to the fact that Africans have unique experiences that people of other climes may not have. But God is not racial or partial. The experiences of Africans may be different and unique, but God is sovereign and rules over the entire universe, even though local experiences can be different. God understands the peculiarity of human contextual experiences. But he is the same God who rules everywhere, and he wants to have the same loving relationship with his children everywhere irrespective of tribe, nationality, and contexts. God created us all, and he knows that our experiences will be different and unique. To some extent, the uniqueness of our experiences is part of his wisdom and glory. The peculiarity of African challenges including curses are not beyond the power of God.

Christ Above All Curses

Let us reflect on Paul's prayer in Ephesians 1:18–23:

> I pray that the eyes of your heart may be enlightened in order that you may know the hope to which he has called you, the riches of his glorious inheritance in his holy people, and his incomparably great power for us who believe. That power is the same as the mighty strength he exerted when he raised Christ from the dead and seated him at his right hand in the heavenly realms, far above all rule and authority, power and dominion, and every name that is invoked, not only in the present age but also in the one to come. And God placed all things under his feet and appointed him to be head over everything for the church, which is his body, the fullness of him who fills everything in every way.

This prayer states that the church is the body of Christ, and that body is filled with the power and authority that Christ invested in it through his death and resurrection. Paul's prayer explains that the power of Christ is working in the church. Paul also reminds us that the rule of Christ is above all rulers, authority and dominion because God has placed all things under his feet and made him the head of everything.

This prayer implies that Jesus Christ is above every situation and crisis. His lordship is unlimited. He is the Lord over every power both on earth and in heaven. He has power to conquer curses, poverty, witchcraft, resource curses, and any other contextual problem. The power in the resurrection of Christ has great implications for our Christian life. Christ is alive forever, and he is concerned about the life of every Christian. He is seated at the right hand of God the Father advocating for us. Our power for waging spiritual battle lies not in us but in Christ. Our fear is gone when we reflect on his power and lordship (Luke 10:19; Acts 10:38; 2 Cor 12:9; Eph 1:21; Col 2:6–10; 2 Tim 1:7).

This book deals with both theological and pastoral approaches to the dilemmas of curses in Africa and has situated the concept of curses in theological, spiritual, and academic contexts. I hope it is a useful guide for Christians, pastors and preachers, theologians, seminary students, seminary lecturers, and church leaders in Africa. I have tried to use simple language. But no doubt occasionally I have been led by theological and research technicalities because for us to arrive at useful practical and pastoral solutions to the African dilemmas and fear of curses, our approach must be foregrounded on theology and research. What therefore follows will be another effort to produce purely counseling and discipleship material that will serve as a manual for helping

African Christians who believe they are being attacked or have gone through an attack of curses, or similar existential life problems, live through the trauma and post trauma of those experiences.

PRAISE THE RISEN CHRIST, WHO BORE OUR CURSES.

Bibliography

Aalders, G. *The Students' Bible Commentary*, vol. 1. Grand Rapids: Zondervan, 1981.

Abogunrin, S. O. "Decolonizing New Testament Interpretation in Africa." In *Decolonization of Biblical Interpretation in Africa*, edited by S. O. Abogunrin, 248–79. NABIS, series 4. Ibadan: Alofe, 2005.

———. *In Search of Historical Jesus*. Inaugural Lecture, University of Ibadan, 1998. Ibadan: Alofe, 2013.

Acolaste, E. E. *Powers, Principalities and the Spirit: Biblical Realism in Africa*. Grand Rapids: Eerdmans, 2018.

Adamo, D. T. "Decolonizing African Biblical Studies." 7th Inaugural Lecture, Delta State University, Abraka, Nigeria, 2004.

———. "What Is African Biblical Hermeneutics?" *Black Theology* 13, no. 1 (2015): 59–72.

Ade, O. *Parents'-Caused Implications*. Lagos: Ojo Ade Press, n.d.

Adebo, A. O. *Freedom from Bondage: Expository Sermons on Romans Chapter 8*. Lagos: ADMED Nigeria, 2015.

Adeboye, G. "Corruption as a Moral Evil: A Philosophical Analysis." In *Corruption: A New Thinking in the Reverse Order*, edited by B. Igboin, 105–19. Oyo: Ajayi Crowther University Press, 2018.

———. "Hobbesian State of Nature and the Quest for Social Order in Nigeria." In *Polity Debacle and the Burden of Being in Africa*, edited by A. B. Ekanola, 683–709. Proceedings of the Third Biennial International Conference of the Faculty of Arts, University of Ibadan, Ibadan: Faculty of Arts, University of Ibadan, 2017.

———. "The Relevance of Pauline Theology of *Charismata* and *Sumpheron* in 1 Corinthians 12:1–7 to Christian Ecumenism in Nigeria." *American Journal of Biblical Theology* 16, no. 18 (2015): 11–27.

———. "Situating the Yoruba Concept of '*Ori*' within the Soft-Deterministic Frame Work." *International Research on Humanities and Social Sciences* 6, no. 7 (2016): 10–23.

———. "Small Work, Big Money: The Implication of Nigerians' Philosophy of Money to the Ongoing Anti-Corruption Campaign in Nigeria." *Akungba Journal of Religion and African Culture*, Department of Religion and African Culture, Ondo State University, 6, no. 2 (2018): 54–69.

Adeboye, G., and D. Ajayi. "Despite the Increasingly Loud Religious Noise in Nigeria, Is There Any Change Potency in Nigerian Religion?" *Journal of African Society for the Study of Sociology and Ethics of Religions*, no. 1 (2018): 23–36.

Adeniji, A. A. *Ethical Evaluation of Deliverance Practices in Pastoral Ministry*. Oyo: Ajibola Golden Links Ventures, 2013.

Adeniyi, S. F. *Moving from Curses to Blessings*. San Francisco, CA: CCC, 2000.

Adeogun, J. O. "Psalter: A Tool of Liberation in Aladura Churches." Nigerian Association for Biblical Studies, Ibadan (2005): 175–190.

Adogame, A., and L. Jafta. "Zionists, Aladura and Roho: African Instituted Churches." In *African Christianity: An African Story, Perspective in Christianity*, 309–29. Pretoria, SA: University of Pretoria, 2005.

Agbokhiamegbe, O. "The Idea of the Kingdom of God in African Theology." *Studie Missionalaia* 46 (1997): 327–57.

Aitken, J. L. *The Semantics of Blessings and Curses in Ancient Hebrew*. Ancient Near Eastern Studies 23. Leuven: Peters, 2007.

Aiyegboyin, Deji. "'But Deliver Us from Evil …': The Riposte of the MFM and Its Implications for the Reverse in Mission." *Orita: Ibadan Journal of Religious Studies* 37, Issue 1–2 (June/December, 2005): 33–64.

Ajayi, S. O. "Sanctified Water and Healing Miracle: Impact on the Growth of CAC in Oyo State, Nigeria." *Babajide Journal of Religion* 3, no. 1 (September 2017): 33–44.

Akindolie, A. A., D. O. Oni, and F. B. Akintunde. "Social Change and Adura Ori Oke (Mountain Top Prayer): A Phenomenon in Africa Christianity in South Western Nigeria." In *African Christianity in Local and Global Contexts*, edited by S. A. Fatokun, 43–56. Ibadan: Department of Religious Studies, University of Ibadan, Nigeria, 2019.

Akporobaro, F. B. O. *Introduction to African Literature*. Lagos: Princeton, 2012.

Anaba, E. *The Quest for Supremacy*. Bolgatanga: Desert Leaf, 2004.

Apostolides, A., and Y. Dreyer. "The Greek Evil Eye: African Witchcraft and Western Ethnocentrism." *Historical Theological Studies* 64, no. 3 (2008): 1021–42.

Asaju, D. "Afro-centric Biblical Studies: Another Colonization?" In *Decolonization of Biblical Interpretation in Africa*, vol. 4: *National Association of Biblical Studies*, edited by S. O. Abogunrin, 121–29. Nigeria: Alofe Enterprises, 2005.

Asamoah-Gyadu, J. K. "Broken Calabashes and Covenants of Fruitfulness: Cursing Barrenness in Contemporary African Christianity." *Journal of Religion in Africa* 37 (2007): 437–60.

———. "Conquering Satan, Demons, Principalities and Powers: Ghanaian Traditional and Christian Perspective on Religion, Evil and Deliverance." In *Coping with Evil in Religion and Culture: Case Studies*, edited by N. Doom-Harder, 85–103, vol. 35. Leiden: Brill, 2008.

———. "Christ Is the Answer, What Is the Question? A Ghana Airways Prayer Vigil and Its Implication for Religion, Evil and Public Space." *Journal of Religion in Africa* 35, no. 1 (2005): 93–117.

———. "Learning to Prosper by Wrestling and Negotiation: Jacob and Esau in Contemporary African Pentecostal Hermeneutics." *Journal of Pentecostal Theology* 21 (2012): 64–86.

———. "Mission to Set the Captive Free: Healing, Deliverance, and Generational Curses in Ghanaian Pentecostalism." *International Review of Mission* 93, no. 370-371 (2004): 389-406.

———. "Spiritual Warfare in the African Context: Perspectives on a Global Phenomenon." *Lausanne Global Analysis* 9, no. 1 (January 2020). https://www.lausanne.org/content/lga/2020-01/spiritual-warfare-african-context.

Aulen, G. *Christus Victor.* London: SPCK, 1983.

Aust, H., and D. Muller. "Curse, Insult, Fool." In the *New International Dictionary of New Testament Theology*, edited by C. Brown, vol. 1. Grand Rapids: Zondervan, 1975.

Awolalu, J. O. "Sin and Its Removal in African Traditional Religion." *Journal of the American Academy of Religion* 44, no. 2 (June 1976): 275-87.

Awolalu, O., and A. Dopamu. *West African Traditional Religion.* Lagos: Macmillan, 2005.

Awuah, J. "NDC Goes Antoa with Schnapps." Daily Guide Ghana (June 2019). http://ww.dailyguideghana.com/?p=69181. Accessed March 2019.

Ayandele, E. A. *The Missionary Impact on Modern Nigeria 1842-1914.* London: Longman, 1966.

Ayantayo, J. K. "The Phenomenon of Change of Name and Identity in Yoruba Religious Community in the Light of Social Change." *Orita: Ibadan Journal of Religious Studies* 42, no. 1 (2010): 1-16.

Ayegboyin, D. "'But Deliver Us from Evil. . .' The Riposte of the MFMM and Its Implications for the Reverse in Mission." *Orita: Ibadan Journal of Religious Studies* 37, no. 1-2 (June/December, 2005): 35-48.

———. "*Epe* (Oath of Cursing), *Egun* (generational Curse) *ati* (And) *Itusile* (deliverance) *Ni Oruko Re* (in His name)." In *Under the Shelter of Olodunmare*, edited by S. O. Abogunrin, 187-200. Ibadan: John Archers, 2014.

Babatunde, L. *No More Curses.* Lagos: Grace House Media, 2010.

Balcom, A. O. "Evangelicalism in Africa: What It Is and What It Does." *Missionalia* 44, no. 2 (2016): 117-28.

Bebbington, D. W. *Evangelicalism in Modern Britain: A History from the 1730s to the 1980s.* Oxfordshire: Rutledge, 1989.

———. *The Evangelical Quadrilateral: Characterizing the British Gospel Movement.* Waco: Baylor University Press, 2021.

Berkouwer, G. C. *The Work of Christ.* Grand Rapids: Eerdmans, 1965.

Bernard, G. N., and N. K. Dickson. "The Impact of Magic and Witchcraft in the Social, Economic, Political and Spiritual Life of African Communities." *International Journal of Humanities, Social Sciences and Education (IJHSSE)* 1, no. 5 (2014): 9-18.

Boadu, Asare. "Pastor Invokes Antoa Nyamaa over Stolen Mobile Phone." Asare Boadu's Stories blog (February 2000). http://asareboadu.blogspot.com/2000/02/pastor-invokes-antoa-nyamaa-over-stolen.html. Accessed August 2013.

Boaheng, I. "Divine Sovereignty, Human Responsibility and God's Salvific Plan: An African Perspective." *ERATS Journal of Religious and Theological Studies* 1, no. 1 (2019): 82–99.

Bockmuehl, K. *Evangelicals and Social Ethics*. Outreach and Identity 4 – World Evangelical Fellowship Theological Commission. Exeter: InterVarsity Press, 1979.

Boesak, A. *If This Is a Treason, I Am Guilty*. Grand Rapids: Eerdmans, 1987.

Brichto, H. C. *The Problem of Curse in the Hebrew Bible*. Journal of Biblical Literature Monograph Series 13. Philadelphia: SBL, 1963.

Britt, B. M. "Curses in the Hebrew Bible." Bible Odyssey (16 August 2022). https://www.bibleodyssey.org/en/people/related-articles/curses-in-the-hebrew-bible.

Bruce, F. F. *The Hard Sayings of Jesus*. Downers Grove: InterVarsity Press, 1983.

———. *The Epistle to the Galatians*. The New International Greek Testament Commentary (NIGTC). Grand Rapids: Eerdmans, 1982.

Bujo, L. *African Christian Morality at the Age of Inculturation*. Nairobi: Paulines, 1990.

Bullinger, E. W. *Figures of Speech Used in the Bible Expanded and Illustrated*. 1898. Reprint Grand Rapids: Baker, 2011.

Buttrick, G. A., ed. *The Interpreter's Dictionary of the Bible: An Illustrated Encyclopedia*, vol. 1. Nashville: Abingdon, 1983.

Canaris, M. M. "The Rapid Growth of Christianity in Africa." *Catholic Star Herald* (2018) https://catholicstarherald.org/the-rapid-growth-of-christianity-in-africa/, retrieved 1 July 2021.

Carson, D. A. *Divine Sovereignty and Human Responsibility: Biblical Perspectives in Tension*. Atlanta: John Knox, 1981.

———. *Exegetical Fallacies*. Grand Rapids: Baker, 1996.

Cilliers, J. "Formations and Movements of Christian Spirituality in Urban African Context." *African Spirituality* 21 (2015): 51–67.

Dandang, M. *Exploring Power Encounter: A Biblical-Theological Perspective*. Jos: ACTS, 2016.

Dillard, R. B. *An Introduction to the Old Testament*. London: Longman, 1994.

Dopamu, P. A. *Esu: The Invisible Foe of Man*. Ijebu-Ode: Sebiotimo Publications, 2000.

Driver, S. R., A. Plumber, and C. A. Briggs, eds. *A Critical and Exegetical Commentary on Numbers*. Edinburgh: T&T Clark, 1986.

Droogers, A. "Syncretism: The Problem of Definition, the Definition of the Problem." In *Dialogue and Syncretism: An Interdisciplinary Approach*, edited by Jerald Gort, et. al., 7–25. Grand Rapids: Eerdmans, 1989.

Dupuis, J. *Christianity and the Religions: From Confrontation to Dialogue*. Maryknoll: Orbis 2001.

The Economist. "What Is an Evangelical Christian?" *The Economist* (1 March 2021). https://www.economist.com/the-economist-explains/2021/03/01/what-is-an-evangelical-christian.

Eidinow, E. "Curses, Greece and Rome." In *The Encyclopedia of Ancient History*, edited by R. S. Bagnall, K. Brodersen, C. B. Champion, A. Erskine, and S. R. Huebner, 537–38. Oxford: Wiley-Blackwell, 2012. doi:10.1002/9781444338386.wbeah17108.
Elwell, W. A., ed. *Evangelical Dictionary of Theology*, 2nd ed. Grand Rapids: Baker, 2001.
Enns, P. *The Moody Handbook of Theology*. Chicago: Moody, 1989.
Fafowora, B., and R. N. Nyaga. "The Media." In *African Public Theology*, edited by S. B. Agang, 307–24. Carlisle: HippoBooks, 2020.
Familusi, O. O. "The Threat to Taboo as a Means of Inculcating Ethics in Yoruba Society." *Orita: Ibadan Journal of Religious Studies* 41, no. 2 (2009): 102–11.
Fee, G. *The Disease of the Health and Wealth Gospels*. Canada: Regent College Publishing, 2006.
Feinberg, C. L. "Curses." In *Evangelical Dictionary of Theology*, edited by Walter A. Elwell, 314. 2nd ed. Grand Rapids: Baker, 2001.
Fensham, F. C. "Common Trends in Curses of the Near Eastern Treaties and *Kudurru* Inscriptions Compared with Maledictions of Amos and Isaiah." *Zeitschrift für die alttestamentliche Wissenschaft* 75 (1963): 155–75.
Fleming, D. *Bridgeway Bible Dictionary*. Brisbane, Australia: Bridgeway, 2009.
Friedrick, D. *My Bondage, My Freedom*. New York: Miller, Orton, 1857.
Gager, J. G. *Curse Tablets and Binding Spells from the Ancient World*. Oxford: Oxford University Press, 1992.
Geisler, N. *Chosen but Free: A Balanced View of God's Sovereignty and Freewill*. Minneapolis: Bethany House, 2010.
Gelb, I. J., P. Steinkeller, and R. M. Whiting, Jr. *Earliest Land Tenure Systems in the Near East*, vol. 2, *Ancient Kudurrus*. Chicago: Oriental Institute of the University of Chicago, 1989.
Geller, M. J. *Forerunners to Udug-Ḫul: Sumerian Exorcistic Incantations*. Freiburger altorientalische Studien 12. Stuttgart: Steiner, 1985.
Gentry, P. J. "The Relationship of Deuteronomy to the Covenant at Sinai," *SBJT* 18, no. 3 (2014): 35–57.
George, A. R. "Forerunnners to Udug-Hul: Sumerian Exorcistic Incantations." DM 56. *Journal of the Royal Asiatic Society of Great Britain & Ireland* 118, no. 2 (1986): 260–63.
Gifford, P. *Christianity, Development and Modernity in Africa*. London: Hurst, 2015.
Gordon, C. *Ugaritic Literature*. Rome: Pontificium Institutum Bistirum, 1949.
Grenz, S. J. *Revisioning Evangelical Theology: A Fresh Agenda for the 21st Century*. Downers Grove: IVP Academic, 1993.
Grindheim, S. "Biblical Authority: What Is It Good for? Why the Apostles Insisted on a High View of Scripture." *Journal of Evangelical Theological Society* 59, no. 4 (2016): 791–807.
Grosheide, F. *Commentary on the First Epistle to the Corinthians*. Grand Rapids: Eerdmans, 1953.

Gunkel, H. *Psalm: A Form-Critical Introduction*. Biblical Series 9. Philadelphia: Fortress, 1967.

Guthrie, D. *New Testament Introduction*. London: Tyndale, 1970.

Hachalinga, P. "How Curses Impact People and Biblical Responses." *Journal of Adventist Mission Studies* 13, no. 1 (2017): 55–63.

Hagin, K. *The Triumphant Church: Dominion Over All Powers of Darkness*. Tulsa: Rhema Bible Church, 2001.

Harrisville, R. A., and W. Sundberg. *The Bible in Modern Culture: Theology and Historical-Critical Method from Spinoza to Kasemann*. Grand Rapids: Eerdmans, 1995.

Hartley, J. E. *Genesis*. Understanding the Bible Commentary Series. Grand Rapids: Baker, 2000.

Henry, M. *Commentary on the Whole Bible*. Edited by Leslie Church. Grand Rapids: Zondervan, 1960.

Heward-Mills, D. *How to Neutralize Curses*. Ghana: Parchment House, 2017.

Hick, J. *Evil and the God of Love*. 2nd ed. New York: Palgrave Macmillan, 1977.

Hilborn, D. "Evangelicalism: A Brief Definition." In *Evangelical Truth*, 16–17. Leicester: Inter-Varsity Press, 1999.

Holter, K. "The 'Poor' in Ancient Israel – and in Contemporary African Biblical Studies." *Mission Studies* 33 (2016): 209–21.

Hughes, R. B., and J. C. Laney. *Tyndale Concise Bible Commentary*. Carol Stream, IL: Tyndale, 1990.

Idowu, B. Olodumare. *God in Yoruba Belief*. Lagos: Longman, 1996.

Idowu, M. O. "The Medicine as Poison, the Physician as the Killer: Modern Pentecostal Theology and Practices as Sources of Insecurity." In *Religion and Insecurity Issues*, edited by J. K. Ayantayo and S. A. Fatokun, 186–213. Ibadan: University of Ibadan, Department of Religious Studies, 2015.

Igboin, B. O. "Names and the Reality of Life: An Inquiry into Inherent Power in Names among the Owan People of Nigeria." *Ado Journal of Religions* 2, no. 1 (July 2004): 9–26.

Ihejirika, W. "Research of Media and Culture in Africa: Current Trends and Dialogue." *African Journal of Communication Research* 2, no. 1 (2009): 1–60.

Ijatuyi-Morphe, R. *Africa's Social and Religious Quest: A Comprehensive Survey and Analysis of African Situation*. Jos: Logos Quest House, 2011.

Kasomo, D. "An Investigation of Sin and Evil in African Cosmology." *International Journal of Sociology and Anthropology* 1, no. 8 (2009): 147–59.

Kayode, J. O. *Understanding African Traditional Religion*. Ile-Ife: University of Ife Press, 1984.

Kittel, G., ed. *Theological Dictionary of the New Testament*. Grand Rapids: Eerdmans, 1972.

Kitz, A. M. *Are You Cursed?: The Phenomenology of Cursing in Cuneiform and Hebrew Texts*. Pretoria, SA: University of Pretoria, 2013.

Kombo, K. "Witchcraft: A Living Vice in Africa." *Africa Journal of Evangelical Theology*, 22, no. 1 (2013): 73–86.

Korošec, V. *Hethitische Staatsverträge: Ein Beitrag zu ihrer juristischen Wertung*. Leipziger rechtswissenschaftliche Studien 60. Leipzig: Weicher, 1931.

Kumuyi, W. F. *Curses and Cures*. Lagos: Zoe, 1990.

Kunhiyop, S. W. *African Christian Theology*. Grand Rapids: Zondervan Academic, 2012.

Larsen, T. "Defining and Locating Evangelicalism." In *Cambridge Companion to Evangelical Theology*, edited by T. Larsen and D. Trier, 1–14. Cambridge: Cambridge University Press, 2007.

Lightner, R. P. *Evangelical Theology: A Survey and Review*. Grand Rapids: Baker, 1987.

Luther, M. *A Commentary on St Paul's Epistle to the Galatians*. Corrected and revised by Erasmus Middleton. London: I. J. Chidley, 1844.

Malomo, E. O. *Model Prayers for Contemporary Christians*. Ilorin: Amazing-Grace Print Media, 2020.

Manus, U. C. "Decolonizing New Testament Interpretation in Nigeria." In *Decolonization of Biblical Interpretation in Africa*, vol. 4: *National Association of Biblical Studies*, edited by S. O. Abogunrin, 280–97. Ibadan, Nigeria: Alofe Enterprises, 2005.

Masenya, M. "Ruminating on Justin S. Ukpong's Inculturation Hermeneutic and Its Implication for the Study of African Biblical Hermeneutics Today." *Historical Theological Studies* 72, no. 2 (2016): 1–6.

Mbiti, J. S. *African Religion and Philosophy*. Nairobi: East African Educational Publishers; London: Heinemann Educational Books, 1969.

Mburu, E. *African Hermeneutics*. Carlisle: HippoBooks, 2019.

Mbuvi, A. "African Biblical Stories: An Introduction to an Emerging Discipline." *Currents in Biblical Research* 15, no. 2 (2017): 149–78.

McConville, Gordon. "Deuteronomy" in *New Bible Commentary* edited by D. A. Carson, R. T. France, J. A. Motyer, and G. J. Wenham. Downers Grove: InterVarsity Press, 1994.

McDill, W. *12 Essential Skills for Great Preaching*. Nashville: B&H, 2018.

McKenzie, J. L. "A Note on Psalm 73(74):13–15", *Theological Studies* 11 (1950): 275–82.

Mellor, G. H. "The Wesleyan Quadrilateral." *MET – Methodists Evangelicals Together* (2003). https://www.methodistevangelicals.org.uk/Articles/523338/The_Wesleyan_Quadrilateral.aspx. Accessed 4 May 2020.

Mendenhall, G. "Covenant Forms in Israelite Tradition." *The Biblical Archaeologist* 17 (1954): 50–76.

Mercer, S. A. *The Oath in Babylonian and Assyrian Literature*. Paris: Geuthener, 1912.

Meyer, B. "Praise the Lord: Popular Cinema and Pentecostalite Style in Ghana's New Public Sphere." *American Ethnologist* 31, no. 1 (2004): 92–110.

Mills, W. E., ed. *Mercer Dictionary of the Bible*. Macon, GA: Mercer University Press, 1990.

Modupe Oduyoye, M. "Potent Speech." In *Traditional Religion in West Africa*, edited by E. A. Adegbola, 218–39. Ibadan: Sefer, 1998.

Monisola, T. "The Socio-Cultural Perception and Implication of Childlessness among Men and Women in Urban Areas, South West, Nigeria." *Journal of Social Sciences* 21, no. 3 (2009): 205–9.
Mosala, I. *Biblical Hermeneutics and Black Theology in South Africa*. Grand Rapids: Eerdmans, 1989.
Motyer, J. A. "The Psalms" in *New Bible Commentary* edited by D. A. Carson, R. T. France, J. A. Motyer, and G. J. Wenham. Downers Grove: InterVarsity Press, 1994.
———. "Curse." In *New Bible Dictionary*, 3rd ed., edited by I. Howard Marshall, A. R. Millard, J. I. Packer, and D. J. Wiseman, 248–49. Downers Grove: InterVarsity Press, 1996.
Mountain of Fire and Miracles Ministries. *2010 Seventy Days Fasting and Prayers*. Yaba: MFM Press, 2010.
Mugambi, J. N. K. *From Liberation to Reconstruction*. Nairobi: East African Educational Publisher, 1995.
———. *Religion and Social Construction of Reality*. Nairobi: East African Educational Publisher, 1996.
Muliro, M. N., T. M. Theuri, and R. M. Matheka. "Traditional Oath Administration and Cleansing in Africa: The Case of the Akamba Ethnic Group in Kenya." *The International Journal of Humanities and Social Sciences* 3, no. 6 (June 2015): 211–18.
Murray, M., and M. Rea. *An Introduction to the Philosophy of Religion*. Cambridge: Cambridge University Press, 2008.
Muzorewa, G. "A Definition of a Future African Theology." *African Theological Journal* 2 (1990): 168–79.
Mwakana, H. A. *Crises of Life in African Religion and Christianity*. Geneva: Lutheran World Federation, 2002.
National Association of Evangelicals. *What Is an Evangelical?* NAE (n.d.). https://www.nae.org/what-is-an-evangelical/.
Naylor, Peter. "Numbers" in *New Bible Commentary* edited by D. A. Carson, R. T. France, J. A. Motyer, and G. J. Wenham. Downers Grove: InterVarsity Press, 1994.
Nihinlola, E. E. "Human Being, Being Human: Theological Anthropology in the African Context." First Inaugural Lecture, The Nigerian Baptist Theological Seminary, Ogbomosho, Nigeria. Ogbomosho: The Publishing Unit, Nigerian Baptist Theological Seminary, 2018.
Nwagwu, E. J. "Unemployment and Poverty in Nigeria: A Link to National Insecurity." *Global Journal of Politics and Law Research* 2, no. 1 (2014): 19–35.
O'Donovan, W. *Biblical Christianity in African Perspective*. Chicago: Oasis International, 1997.
Oduro, T. A. "Who Answers Prayers Quicker: Ancestral Deities of Africa or the God of Abraham: Exploring a Puzzle of African Christianity." In *African Christianity in Local and Global Context*, edited by S. A. Fatokun, 140–53. University of Ibadan, Department of Religious Studies Series 7. Ibadan: Baptist Press Nigeria, 2019.

Okezie, G. *Christians and the Challenge of Occultism.* Jos: Midland Press, 2001.

Oludele, I. M. "The Medicine as Poison, the Physician as the Killer: Modern Pentecostal Theology and Practices as Sources of Insecurity." In *Religion and Insecurity Issues,* edited by J. K. Ayantayo and S. A. Fatokun, 192–213. Ibadan: University of Ibadan, Department of Religious Studies, 2015.

Olukoya, D. K. "Breaking Family Curses." YouTube (2 October 2020). http://youtu.be/D037CyxWg7E.

———. *How to Obtain Personal Deliverances.* Lagos: TBCCM, 1996.

Omobola, O. C. "An Overview of Taboo and Superstition among the Yoruba of South West Nigeria." *Mediterranean Journal of Social Sciences,* Sapienza University of Rome, 4, no. 2 (2013): 221–28.

Orangu, A. *Destiny: The Manifested Being.* Ibadan: African Odyssey, 1998.

Oshitelu, G. *Religion, God and Evil: Issues in Philosophy of Religion.* Ibadan: Hope, 2010.

Otabil, M. *Buy the Future: Learning to Negotiate for a Better Future than Your Present.* Accra: Altar International, 2002.

Outler, A. "The Wesleyan Quadrilateral – in John Wesley." In *Doctrine and Theology in the United Methodist Church,* edited by T. Langford, 7–20. Nashville: Abingdon, 1991.

Owojaiye, B. M. *Evangelical Response to the Coronavirus Lockdown: Insights from the Evangelical Church Winning All.* Nashville: West Bow, 2020.

———. "The Problem of False Prophets in Africa: Strengthening the Church in the Light of a Troublesome Trend." *Lausanne Global Analysis* 8, no. 6 (November 2019). https://www.lausanne.org/content/lga/2019-11/problem-false-prophets-africa.

Oyedepo, D. *Breaking the Curses of Life.* Ota: Dominion, 1997.

Ozumba, G. O. "African Traditional Metaphysics." *Quodilbert: Journal of Christian Theology and Philosophy* 6, no. 1 (January-March, 2004): 8–19.

Parpola, S., and K. Watanabe. *Neo-Assyrian Treaties and Loyalty Oaths.* Helsinki: Helsinki University Press, 1988.

Penner, G. M. *In the Shadow of the Cross: Biblical Theology of Persecution and Discipleship.* Bartlesville: Living Sacrifice Books, 2004.

Peters, G. W. *A Biblical Theology of Mission.* Chicago: Moody Press, 1984.

Plantinga, A. *God, Freedom and Evil.* Grand Rapids: Eerdmans, 1977.

Pobee, J. S. "Africa, Good News and Native Hands, Native Hatchet, Native Earth." In *African Christianity in Local and Global Context,* edited by S. A. Fatokun, 27–35. University of Ibadan, Department of Religious Studies Series 7. Ibadan: Baptist Press Nigeria, 2019.

Reiner, E. *Surpu: A Collection of Sumerian and Akkadian Incantations.* Osnabruck: Biblio Verlag, 1970.

Salvo, I. "Experiencing Curses: Neurobehavioral Traits of Ritual in Spatiality in Roman Empire." *De Gruyter* (2020): 159–75. https://www.degruyter.com/document/doi/10.1515/9783110557596-009/html.

Sarbiah, E. K., C. Niemandt, and P. White. "Migration from Historic Mission Churches to Pentecostal and Charismatic Churches in Ghana." *Verbum Ecclesia* 4, no. 1 (2020): 1–10.

Sarr, L. "The Christian Experience in Africa Is a Very Specific Experience." *Religion*, LACROIX International (2018). Available at: https://international.la-croix.com/news/%20religion/the-christian-experience-in-africa-is-a-very-specific-experience/7613.

Scharbert, J. "'Fluchen' und 'Segnen' im Alten Testament." *Biblical* 39 (1958): 1–29.

Schreiner, T. *New Testament Theology: Magnifying God in Christ*. Grand Rapids: Baker Academic, 2008.

Silliman, D., and G. P. Jackson. "Ghana Pentecostals Come to the Defense of Accused Witches." *Christianity Today* (23 November 2020). https://www.christianitytoday.com/ct/2020/december/ghana-pentecostals-come-to-defense-of-accused-witches.html.

Simpson, G. E. *Yoruba Religion and Medicine in Ibadan*. Ibadan: Ibadan University Press, 1980.

Smart, J. *The Strange Silence of the Bible in the Church: A Study in Hermeneutics*. Philadelphia: Westminster, 1971.

Sofola, J. A. *African Culture and the Personality: What Makes an African Person African*. Ibadan: African Resources, 1978.

Steiner, F. *Taboo*. London: Routledge, 2004.

Stinton, D. B., ed. *African Theology on the Way: Current Conversation*. London: SPCK, 2010.

Stott, J. *Evangelical Truth*. Leicester: Inter-Varsity Press, 1999.

———. *Life in Christ*. Eastbourne: Kingsway, 1991.

———. *What Is an Evangelical?* London: Falcon, 1977.

Taylor, D. "Africa in Crisis: Finding Hope in the Midst of Tragedy." *Mission Frontiers* published by U. S. Center for World Mission, Pasadena, 2011: 6–10.

Tenney, M. C. *Galatians: The Charter of Christian Liberty*, rev. ed. Grand Rapids: Eerdmans, 1950.

———. *New Testament Survey*. Grand Rapids: Eerdmans, 1961.

———. *The Zondervan Pictorial Bible Dictionary*. Grand Rapids: Zondervan, 1970.

Thiselton, A. C. "The Supposed Power of Words in the Biblical Writings." *Journal of Theological Society* 25 (1974): 283–99.

Tsolu, A. "Religious Hallucination among the black race," *Graphic Online*. https://www.graphic.com.gh/features/opinion/religious-hallucination-and-phantasm-among-the-black-race.html (accessed 20/09/2017).

Turaki, Y. "African Traditional Religious System as Basis of Understanding Christian Warfare." *Lausanne Content Library* (22 August 2000). https://lausanne.org/content/west-african-case-study. Accessed January 2021.

Turnbull, K. "Discipling Africa through Higher Education: A Proposal for African Christian University." *Mission Frontiers* 33, no. 6, published by *The Bulletin of U.S. Center for World Mission* (November-December 2011): 16–18.

Ukpong, J. S. "Natural Hermeneutics: An African Approach to Biblical Interpretation." In *The Bible in a World Context: An Experiment in Contextual Hermeneutics*, edited by D. Walter and L. Urich, 17–32. Grand Rapids: Eerdmans, 2002.

———. "Reading the Bible with African Eyes: Inculturation and Hermeneutics." *Journal of Theology for Southern Africa* 91 (1995): 3–14.

Van Eck, E. "The Word is Life: African Theology as Biblical and Contextual Theology." *Historical Theological Studies* 62, no. 2 (2006): 679–701.

Verbugge, V. D., ed. *The Bible League NIV Topical Study Bible*. Grand Rapids: Zondervan, 1998.

Vidu, A. *Atonement, Law and Justice: The Cross in Historical and Cultural Contexts*. Grand Rapids: Baker, 2014.

Wachege, P. N. "Curses and Cursing among the Agikuyu: Social-Cultural Benefits." *Journal of Philosophy and Religious Studies*, University of Nairobi, Kenya, 12, no. 6 (2014): 1–11.

Walvoord, J. *Jesus Christ Our Lord*. Chicago: Moody, 1969.

Wenham, Gordon. "Genesis" in *New Bible Commentary* edited by D. A. Carson, R. T. France, J. A. Motyer, and G. J. Wenham. Downers Grove: InterVarsity Press, 1994.

Wesley, J. *John Wesley's Forty-Four Sermons*. Peterborough: Epworth, 1944.

West, G. "Interpreting the Comparative Paradigm in African Biblical Scholarship." In *African and European Reading of the Bible in Dialogue: A Quest for Meaning*, edited by G. West and H. de Wet, 35–48. Leiden: Brill Academic, 2008.

West, G. O. "African Biblical Scholarship as Post-colonial, Tri-polar and Site-of-Struggle." In *Present and Future of Biblical Studies*, edited by T. B. Liew, 240–73. Leiden: Brill, 2018.

West, G. and M. Dube (eds.). *The Bible in Africa: Transactions, Trajectories and Trends*. The Netherlands: Brill, 2001, 1–11.

Westermann, C. *Elements of Old Testament Theology*, translated by D. W. Stott. Atlanta: John Knox, 1982.

Wood, R. "Africa: Hope in the Midst of Darkness." *Mission Frontiers* 33, no. 6 (November-December 2011): 4–5.

Sermon Sources

Adeboye, E. A. "Redeemed from the Curse." YouTube (10 May 2020). https://youtu.be/eK5ao_GjVmM.

Agboola, S. M. "Unknown Curse." EVOM Christian Film. YouTube (5 June 2020). https://youtu.be/WVpbMPyIJuA.

Anaba, E. "Breaking the Yoke of Your Father's House." YouTube (30 August 2019). https://youtu.be/H5nYlHsw7LA.

Chi, J. "Break Every Curse Operating in the Name You Bear (1 Chronicles 4:9)." YouTube (29 January 2018). https://youtu.be/gYGe0uDpT9M.

Natasha, L. L. "Reversing the Curse." YouTube (21 May 2019). https://youtu.be/XTCPToxlmbY. (Accessed 5 December 2022)

Olukoya, D. K. "Breaking Family Curses." YouTube (2 October 2020). http://youtu.be/D037CyxWg7E.

Otabil, M. "The Power of the Cross." YouTube (31 March 31 2018). https://youtu.be/JGrwHbeEPPI, 1 December 2022.

Oyedepo, D. "Breaking Generational Curses 2." YouTube (22 April 2012). https://youtu.be/RQYxhyeX8g8.

Subject Index

A
Abogunrin, Samuel O. 23
Abrahamic covenant. *See* covenant
active mission 133
Adamo, Tuesday D. 24
Adebiyi, Samuel Love 115
Adeboye, Enoch A. 116
Adogame, Afe 26
African Christian 110
African Christian experience 8
African Christian films 103
African Christianity 1, 5–7, 9, 11, 15, 63, 93, 95, 101, 104, 109, 114, 119
African Christians 1–2, 4–7, 11, 13, 73, 93–94, 96–97, 100–101, 104, 109, 120, 122, 169
African church(es) 9, 13, 73, 93, 98, 111, 128
African contextual themes 15–16
African Indigenous Churches 19
African nations 75
African ontological 95
African Pentecostal 109
African Pentecostal churches 5
African Pentecostalism 5
African Pentecostals 95. *See* African Pentecostal churches
African preachers 49, 92, 120, 124, 126, 157
African proverbs 106
Africans' conception 4
African theology of curses 116
African traditional cosmology 8
African unique Christianity 97
Agboola, Mike Shola 102
AIC(s). *See* African Indigenous Churches
Akkadian 38, 40–41, 43

Aladura churches 5
Almost succeeding but never succeed syndrome 89
Anaba, Eastwood 118
anathema 37
ancient culture 42
ancient texts 38
ANE 43.
Anointed Physical objects 103
anthropological codes 95
Aole 114
Asaju, Dapo 23–24
Asamoah-Gyadu, J.K. 97
ase 77
Association of Evangelicals in Africa 19.
Asuoyaa 113
Awolalu, Omosade 81
Ayantayo, Jacob 96

B
Babaloa, Ayo 104
Balak-Balam narratives 50
Balak curses 43
beatitudes 66
Bebbington, David 18
Bebbington quadrilateral 19
Benin Republic 106, 109
biblical conceptualization of curses 122
biblical curses 44, 49–50
biblical theology 58
biblical theology of curses 52
blessing 95

C
Cameroun 109, 114, 117
Carson, D. A. 151
Carter, Jimmy 131
causality 78
causeless curse 86

centrality of Jesus's cross 133
character disorder 89
Christian cursing 111
Christologization of Deliverance
    ministry 161
church in Africa 1
church in the West 1
code of Hammurabi 43
collective calamity 115
collective taxonomy 109
communal curses. *See* forms of curses
communal salvation 151
conditional curse 122
conditional curses 39
convergence hypothesis 103
conversional encounter 142
coping strategies 109
covenant 39, 45, 86, 89
covenant and conditional curses 63
cross 118, 124, 137–139, 157
curse
  New Testament 36
  Old Testament 32, 34-35, 45
  of nepotism 171
  of poverty 170
  on the serpent 55
curses and blessings 50
curse texts 48
cursing process 87
cursing sanctuaries 45
cursing texts 120

D
Davidic dynasty 63
deliverance centers 104
deliverance ministers 141
destiny 95
development of African Christian
    theology 15
Dibiamaka 96
Dickson, Kwesi 23
dispensational differences 124
dispensational paradigm 164
divine curse(s) 49, 56
Dopamu, Adelumo 81

dual dynamic of curses 51
Dube, Musa 23, 26

E
"eat the curse" 42
Edwards, Jonathan 132
Egun 75
epistemological privilege 25
epistemology 83
evangelicalism 18–19, 131, 133
evangelical perspective 131
evangelicals 20
evangelical themes 19
Evangelization of Orientation 173
EVOM 102
exegetical fallacy 53
existential needs 12
experience(s) 2, 5–7, 14, 16, 19–20, 22,
    66, 93–94, 96, 103, 106, 135, 161

F
family blood lineage 95
family curses 100, 115. *See* Forms of
    Curses
fear 9, 11, 13–14, 45. *See* fear of curses
fear of curse(s) 100, 139–140. *See* fear
feminine power 80
forms of curses 78
four-legged interpretive hypothesis 27

G
General overseer 116
generational curses 11, 14–15, 76, 98–
    99, 121, 126, 140. *See* inherited
    curses
gezerah shawah 124
Ghana 101, 106, 109, 112, 114
Ghanaian Christians 3
Gifford, Paul 1
Gilgamesh epic 43
Global South 1
God of Africans 6
Goliath curses 43
Greco-Roman culture 47
Greco-Roman curses 46

Gunkel, Herman 33

H
Henry, Mathew 68
hermeneutical subjectivity 141
Hick, John 149
historic mission churches 101, 109
Hitite vassal treaty 42
holiness of God 48
holy matrimony 85
human curses 62
hunaire 75
hypercritical 94

I
Ifajumo 102
Igboin, Benson 96
Iguno 75
imprecation 70, 76
imprecatory 111, 155
inculturation hermeneutics 25
index of continuous disappointment 89
inherited curses 81–82, 105, 117. *See* generational curses
inherited family behavioral pattern 159
institutional classification 19
interactionism 78
intercultural hermeneutic 27
interpret 7
interpretation 3
interpretation model 119, 154
Interpretation of Lived Experiences 112
interpretive fallacy 136
invocation 39
Islamic radicalism 171
Islamic Sufism 162

J
Jackson, Griffin 3

K
karet curse 45
Kenya 101, 103, 109, 114, 117

Kirumi 75
Kollywood 103
Kumuyi, William 98, 126
Kunhiyop, Samuel W. 23
kutukwa 75
Kwabena, J. 3

L
Labeodan, Helen 26
Lausanne Movement 19
lens 114
lenses 14
logical incompatibility 148
low self-esteem 97
Luther, Martin 72

M
magical booklet 111
marshal-follower relationship 56
materialism 171
Mbiti, John 4, 23, 77
Mburu, Elizabeth 21, 23, 27, 29, 114, 156
McDill, Wayne 52
media 101, 103
Merril, Tenney 72
meshal 56
Mesopotamia 38
messianic redemption 58
messianic syndrome 161
metaphysical causality 77
Metaphysical interpretation 114
metaphysical powers 94
MFMM. *See* Mountain of Fire and Miracle Ministry
misfortune 3, 88
moral responsibility 77, 122, 150
Mosala, Itumelenge 23
mother's curse. *See* feminine power
Mount Ebal 66
Mount Gerizim 66
Mount Zion 103
Mountain of Fire and Miracle Ministry 97
Mugambi, Jesse 23, 26

mystical causality 112

N
name(s) 95, 122
negative patterns 97
negative prayer 76
negative trends 96, 158
neo-Pentecostal 109
neo-Pentecostal churches 98, 101
Nigeria 101, 103–104, 109, 114
Nihinlola, Emiola 20
non-Yahwistic component 123
nthembo 75
Nyamiti, Charles 23

O
oaths 47
O'Donovan, Wilbur 16, 21
Oduyoye, Mercy M. 26
Okure, Teresa 25–26
Olajubu, Ronke 26
Olukoya, Daniel 98
Omi Iye 104
Otabil, Mensa 118
overexaggeration 120
overgeneralization 21
Owojaiye, Babatomiwa M. 5, 103
Oyedepo, David 98
Oyedepo's theology of curses 117
Oyemosu 102
Ozumba, G.O. 78

P
Parables and sayings 106
paradox of plenty 172
pastoral care 94
Patriarch corpus 121
patternism 125
peculiarity of biblical curses 49
personal conversion 158
personal responsibility. *See* moral responsibility
phenomena 93
phenomenon 96, 101, 107
Plantinaga, Alvin 149

Poll, Evert van der 12
prayer mountains. *See* sacred space
preachers. *See* African preachers
primacy of the Bible 133
privatization 170
problem of evil 148
professional curser 40, 62, 69
prohibited actions 90
proto-evangelion 55

R
reactionary religious practice 110
recurring negative pattern 88, 121
Regan, Ronald 131
Repeated negative life patterns 116
resource curse 172
retributive justice 76
round table hermeneutic engagement 120

S
sacred space 104
secularization 170
Self-Inflicted Curses 83
serpent 55
shrine invocation 112
shrine slavery 97
Silliman, Daniel 3
social justice and retribution 40
social morality 77
sola scriptural 134
Solution to Curse 91
soteriological references 37
South Africa 101
South west Nigeria 100
spiritual enemy consciousness 110
spiritualization of gifts 145
spoken words 12
symptoms 88
syncretism 6, 8, 28, 94, 111, 130, 146

T
taboo(s) 86–87, 89
theme(s) 31, 95
themes of oppression 5

theological confusion 131
theological implications 15
theological inference 63, 66, 73
theological institutions 8, 167
theological maturity 166
theological method 19, 23–26
theology of curses 92
Torah 49, 121
transcultural reference 121
transdenominational definition 19
transformational role 170
transgenerational 121
treaty curses 42
Tumbuka tribe 80
types of evil 149

U
Ukpong, Justin 25
unconditional curses 47
unknown curse 102

V
vassal treaty 44
verbal-plenary inspiration 134

W
warfare 6
WCC. *See* World Council of Churches
Wesleyan quadrilateral 19, 135
Wesley, John 19, 132
West 1
West Africa 5
western empirical model 95
Whitefiel, George 132
witchcraft 3, 16, 77, 101, 169
World Council of Churches 1
World Evangelical Alliance 19.
	See WEA

Y
Yahweh. *See* YHWH
Yahweh Curses 51
Yahweh's blessings 63
YHWH 39, 51.
YHWH curses. *See* Yahweh Curses

Yoruba 2, 84, 106
Yoruba Christians 114
Yoruba ethnic extraction. *See* Yoruba

Z
Zimbabwe 82
Zionist churches 5
Zvomunodinta, J. W. 23

Scripture Index

OLD TESTAMENT

Genesis
1:1–11:26 54
1:31 151
2:16–17 151
2:17 58
3 .... 32–33, 57, 135, 154
3:8–13 55
3:13 51
3:13–18 35
3:14–15 .... 48, 55
3:14–19 .... 53, 55, 120
3:14–20 35
3:15 55–56
3:16 56
3:17 .... 43, 48
3:17–19 57
4:9–12 .... 32, 51
4:9–16 34
5:29 48
12:1–3 70
12:3 .... 63, 156
12:10 121
12:10–20 121
15 44
15:2–3 121
15:7–21 39
15:16 33
16:1–4 121
20:1–16 121
25:21 121
25:29–34 121
26:1 121
26:1–11 121
30:1 121
30:1–6 121
35:16–19 121
35:19 121
37:29–34 121

Exodus
7:1 144
8:23 50
9:4 50
11:7 50
17:3–4 143
20:7 49
21:17 49–50
21:24 158
22:28 50
34:7 70

Leviticus
19:14 49–50
24:10 50
24:10–16 .... 43, 49
27:28–29 33
27:29 33

Numbers
5:11–31 44
5:19–22 49
5:23 51
12:10–16 44
22:1–35 62
22:2–20 60
22:12 62
22:20 62
22:22–23 62
22–23 48
22–24 .... 32–33, 50, 59
22:36–24:25 62
22:37–38 60
23 .... 35, 43
23:5–13 61
23:7–10 61
23:8 63
23:18–24 61
24:3–9 61

24:8 63
24:9 63
24:15–19 61
24:17 63
24:17–19 63

Deuteronomy
5:9 70
11:28 33
21:22–23 72
23:21–23 33
26:10–30:20 64
27 .... 48, 118
27:15–26 49
27:26 .... 72, 124
27–28 49
28 .... 32, 118, 135,
141, 143, 154
28:1 65
28:1–4 65
28:1–14 66
28:2 51
28:15 .... 51, 65
28:15–20 65
28:15–44 64
28:15–68 .... 63–64, 66
28:45–68 64
29:19–20 51

Joshua
1:5 144
2:10 33
6:17 33
6:26 123
6:26–27 123
7:1–26 33
9:22–23 35

Judges
17:2 33
19–21 48

1 Samuel
2 135
2:29–33 115
2:30–36 122
11:6–7 42
14 48
17:42–44 43
19:11 143
19:15 143
20:17 70

2 Samuel
16:5–12 43
16:5–14 35

1 Kings
10:9 70
16:29–34 123
16:34 123
19:1–3 143
21:10 34
22:23–28 143

2 Kings
2:19–22 118
2:23–24 52
6:8–16 143
13:14 143

1 Chronicles
4:9–10 122

Nehemiah
5:13 39

Job
1–3 143
1:5 34
2:5 33–34
2:9 .... 33–34, 41, 43, 49
2:10 35
3:1–10 35
31:7 49

31:10 49
32:16–22 49

Psalms
1 32
27 164
35 155–157
35:4–8 156
35:7–16 156
35:10 69
35:11–12 156
35:13–14 156
35:26 156
37:14–15 69
41 32
41:1–2 69
44:22 143
72:9 55
94:12 143
109 .... 44, 66, 68
109:1 70
109:1–5 69
109:2–3 69
109:5 70
109:6–19 69
109:17 69
109:17–19 70
109:18 69
109:21–27 69
137:5–6 49

Proverbs
3:33 35
17:13 69
18:22–23 69
19:17 69
20:20 49
21:1 151
22:14 48
22:16 69
28:7 69

Isaiah
8:21–22 49
24:3–6 33
24:6 51
46:9–10 151

49:23 55
65:15 33

Jeremiah
12:3 148
17:5–6 51
24:9 35
29:18 51
37:15 143
38:6 143

Lamentations
3:29 55

Ezekiel
18 136

Daniel
3:1–18 143
4:35 151

Micah
7:17 55

Zechariah
5:1–3 32–33
5:1–4 35

Malachi
1:14 33
2:1–2 50–51
2:2 .... 32, 48
4:6 48

NEW TESTAMENT

Matthew
6:13 157
6:33 162
12:36 37
15:4 49
15:10–11 37
19:5 118
20:28 163
25:41–46 32
27:25 47
28:18–20 144

Mark
8:34 140
10:42–45 57
10:45 137

Luke
6:45 37
10 164
10:19 176
19:10 145
21:5 36

John
1:29 42
3:9 142
3:16 .... 142, 152
3:18 145
3:18–21 144
3:36 145
4:7 142
5:1 142
8:12 144
12:46 144
16:33 144

Acts
3:6–7 164
3:16 164
10:38 176
12:1–19 143
16:18 164

Romans
2:14–16 73
3:23 72
5:8 139
6:4 142
6:18 142
6:23 139
8:11 159
8:28–30 151
12 165
16:20 56

1 Corinthians
2:2 136
6:20 139
7:23 139
15:3 139

2 Corinthians
1:6 144
5:17 142
10:10 143
11:1 140
12:9 176
12:17 143

Galatians
3:1–9 71
3:10 36
3:10–12 72
3:10–13 36–37
3:10–14 71
3:13 .... 33, 36
3:13–14 .... 118, 123, 143
3:14 72
4:12–15 143

Ephesians
1:18–23 176
1:21 176
2:1 145
2:10 145
2:12 145
2:16 139
4:22–24 142

6:12 164

Philippians
1:6 142
2:9–11 .... 145, 164
4:10–3 141

Colossians
1:13 176
1:20–21 139
2:6–10 176

2 Thessalonians
1:6 140

2 Timothy
1:7 176
3:16 134

Hebrews
2:17 139
6:8 36
12 165

James
1:13 151
4:6–10 160
5:11–12 33

1 Peter
2:5 144
2:24 139
3:18 139

2 Peter
2:1 139
2:14 37
2:15–16 62

1 John
4:4 159

Revelation
5:9 139
14:3–4 139